HARVARD-YENCHING INSTITUTE

MONOGRAPH SERIES

XIV

Tanuma Okitsugu

FORERUNNER OF MODERN JAPAN

Tanuma Okitsugu, 1719–1788

FORERUNNER OF MODERN JAPAN

JOHN WHITNEY HALL

CAMBRIDGE, MASSACHUSETTS

HARVARD UNIVERSITY PRESS

1955

TO MY MOTHER

Marjorie Whitney Hall

Preface

Western historians describing Japan's spectacular rise as a world power have generally begun their narrative with the arrival of the Perry expedition to Japan and the consequent termination after 1854 of the country's long period of voluntary isolation. Unquestionably this event marks one of the crucial turning points in Japanese history. The Western world by forcing Japan's long-shut doors hastened the reform which in a few decades was to convert a feudal people into a modern nation state. But to overemphasize the role of the West is to neglect the dynamic forces of change already operating within Japanese society. The West might add stimulus, but it could not supply the energy or control the direction of Japan's modern revolution, the origins of which go back many decades before Perry's arrival.

How far back must we look to discern the first stirrings of this revolutionary urge? The Tanuma age (1760–1786) coming nearly a century before Japan's final emergence from seclusion appears as such a starting point. During this period of approximately a quarter of a century, the nation first turned from subservience to her feudal past towards a realization that her future lay ahead of her. In Tanuma Okitsugu (1719–1788), the chief shogunal minister of the day, Japan found a man, albeit ambitious and perhaps corrupt, who was not afraid to look ahead and to contemplate a break with political and economic traditionalism.

Tanuma's age foresaw the two dangers which were ultimately to wreck the feudal regime in Japan: the economic inconsistency inherent in an expanding society which had chosen to isolate itself from the outside world, and the menace of the Russians who appeared to Japan's north as vanguards of Western expansion. Tanuma's encouragement of foreign trade and his attempt to circumvent the sacred laws of seclusion stemmed from a realization that it was futile to continue the rule of the past. It matters little that the weight of reaction was against him and that his policies failed. Japan had been given a vision of the future. The ferment of change had begun to take effect.

Despite the historical importance of the seventeenth and eighteenth centuries to the later development of Japan, Western scholars have as yet given them but inadequate consideration. It was with this need in mind that the present study of Tanuma Okitsugu, his life and policies, was undertaken. Materials for the study were collected during the immediate postwar years, when contact with Japan was still difficult and when the libraries in this country had been unable to acquire the latest materials from Japan. For this reason the available sources were largely confined to those already existing in this country before the war, a limitation which was unavoidable at the time.

In preparing the present work every attempt has been made to keep the main body of the book free from technical terminology. Thus English translations of official titles have been used whenever possible. Those who wish to refer to the original Japanese terms will find them in the table of officials included in Chapter II and in the Index, where they are bracketed with the English translation. The character equivalents of Japanese words and phrases romanized in the text and notes will be found in the Character List. Characters for bibliographical citations are given in the Bibliographical List.

The author would like to take this opportunity of expressing his gratitude to several institutions and individuals which have made this study possible. He is indebted to the Rockefeller Foundation and the Harvard-Yenching Institute for encouragement and support during the period of preparation and writing. He is especially grateful for the kind interest and guidance of Professor Serge Elisséeff, who originally suggested this subject, and to Professor Edwin O. Reischauer for his painstaking reading of the original draft and for many suggestions which have been incorporated into the final work. The author also wishes to express his appreciation for the helpful comments and assistance given him by Dr. Donald H. Shively, Dr. Robert E. Ward, Professor Mischa Titiev, and his father Dr. M.

Ernest Hall. Finally his deepest gratitude goes to his wife, who has been a constant and patient help throughout the preparation of this work.

Ann Arbor, Michigan
August 1951   J. W. H.

Contents

Contents

Tanuma Okitsugu

FORERUNNER OF MODERN JAPAN

CHAPTER I

Introduction

Japan's sudden emergence from an obscure and decaying feudal society into a major world power is one of the dramatic episodes of recent history. It is an event made all the more spectacular by contrast to the experiences of other Far Eastern nations whose struggle for adjustment to the challenge of modern times has been so prolonged and fraught with conflict. Japan led the Orient in the process of Westernization. The forces of nationalism and industrialization, the revolutionary concepts of the rights of the common man, which today are shaking Asiatic societies, made their first imprint and achieved their initial successes in the Japanese islands. Japan alone of the nations of Eastern Asia managed to take the impact of Western civilization in stride and to absorb efficiently and rapidly the new institutions and ideas which burst in upon her after the opening of her doors in 1854. In slightly over half a century she succeeded in overcoming the threat of Western political domination and commercial exploitation to emerge a leading figure among the nations of the world.

In attempting to explain this modern transformation of Japanese society, Western observers have, with good reason, emphasized the part played by outside pressures in forcing through changes in Japan's political, social, and economic structure. The opening of Japan in the nineteenth century was not an isolated episode but part of a world-wide process in which an expanding Occident forced itself upon a sleeping Orient. There is no question but that the arrival of Perry's Black Ships in Japanese waters created a crisis which was to shake the very foundations of Japanese society. And yet the speed of Japan's reaction to this crisis, and the remarkable adaptability which she demonstrated, cannot be understood by an analysis merely of the events which surrounded the final breakdown of her long seclusion. The fact is that the revolutionary changes ushered in after

1854 were as much dictated by internal necessity as compelled by the pressure of external events. And though these changes were unquestionably stimulated by the impact of Western civilization, Japan's capability to renew herself came in large measure from within and was a product of her own historical development.

The impression is often given that, in the two centuries and a half prior to Perry's arrival, Japan not only remained in a vacuum with respect to the rest of the world but also static in her domestic development. The factors of isolation and stagnation, however, are greatly overemphasized. The harsh, inflexible regime maintained by the powerful Tokugawa house from 1600 to 1868, though nearly impregnable to direct assault, was nevertheless vulnerable to the softening process of internal decay. By the middle of the nineteenth century only the outward symbols of its former strength remained. Institutions of political control had weakened to a point where collapse was imminent, while dissentient forces within Japanese society had begun to gather sufficient strength to burst the bonds of tradition and to carry the country forward along new paths which in many ways anticipated the direction of reform eventually forced upon Japan by the impact of Western civilization. The history of the Tokugawa era is thus an indispensable prelude to an understanding of Japan's recent development as a modern state.

The social order under which the Japanese lived from the beginning of the seventeenth century is generally referred to as a form of late, or centralized, feudalism. The Tokugawa regime represented a final, vigorous phase of rule by the feudal aristocracy. Throughout its long duration, Japan continued to be dominated by a self-conscious military caste, extremely jealous of its special privileges. The methods by which this class administered the country, though they became less feudalistic as time went on, remained fundamentally militaristic in nature and were characterized by the use of repressive laws and an extreme insistence upon military discipline and social regimentation.

The establishment of this regime which so restricted the free development of Japanese society has generally been accredited to the inventiveness of the early Tokugawa leaders, especially the great Ieyasu (1542–1616). But the Tokugawa house could scarcely have succeeded in fossilizing Japanese society so completely had not the trend of the times played into its hands. The Tokugawa unification of Japan was accomplished after a century or more of incessant feudal warfare. By 1600 the dominant desire of the country was for peace and stability. It was the genius of Tokugawa Ieyasu that he was able to harness this urge for security, combine it with his own consuming desire to insure the perpetuation of his power, and thereby contrive a political, social, and economic order which was to endure for over two hundred years.

The system which resulted was eminently conservative in its conception and far-reaching in its application. At its apex stood the Tokugawa house, occupying a position which in large degree was based on the preëminence of its economic and military power. The Tokugawa family, with its collaterals and retainers, controlled over one-quarter of the productive capacity of the Japanese islands, and its military resources were so well distributed strategically that the Tokugawa rulers were able to clamp a nearly absolute political dictatorship over the other feudal houses as well as to relegate the Emperor and his court to obscurity in his ancient capital of Kyoto.

Beneath this massive superstructure of political control, Tokugawa society was squeezed into a rigid hierarchical mold and regimented both by edict and by the watchful activities of the ever-present secret police. The classes were deliberately frozen in place, and movement between them strictly interdicted. Status and occupation became hereditary, and precedent took on the force of law. As an ideological foundation for their system, the Tokugawa brought forward the stabilizing precepts of Confucianism, which, with its emphasis on class division and the virtues of social harmony, became the philosophical basis of a static society and the chief rationale of the feudal *status quo*. Not content to secure themselves internally from the danger of dissension or change, the Tokugawa put the final touches to their system by sealing off their country from the outside world, thus eliminating the danger of political or intellectual influence from the West and forestalling the growth of hostile native factions which might be encouraged by overseas trade or by contact with Christian missionaries.

But despite the rigidity with which the Tokugawa built, despite the attempt to maintain without change the framework of stability as it took final shape in the early seventeenth century, the effects of decay and evolution could not be staved off indefinitely. No regime is impervious to the ravages of time, and the Tokugawa system had its share of internal weaknesses and hidden inconsistencies which in the end were to bring the structure to the ground. In fact, looked at from our later vantage point in history, it seems a miracle that any ruling group was able to maintain for such a length of time a political and social order so essentially anachronistic. Despite the seeming logic behind everything the Tokugawa did, their system, in reality, attempted to reconcile two fundamentally contradictory social conditions — feudalism and political centralization.[1] Tokugawa society was from the start a hybrid organism, one arrested midway in its evolution from feudal decentralization to national centralization.

Japan of the sixteenth century had given many indications that it was ready to break out of the feudal mold. A trend towards national unification, the development of free cities, the blurring of the distinction between the warrior and non-warrior classes, a foreign trade of great volume, and an increasing interest in colonial ventures gave to Japan an aspect in many ways similar to that of her European contemporaries. But the establishment of political stability after 1600 failed to bring these anti-feudal tendencies to maturity. Instead, the feudal rulers of Japan regained their domination over Japanese society and under the leadership of the Tokugawa house succeeded in putting a halt to all the developments which were detrimental to their interests. The trend away from feudalism was checked, while in many instances earlier, obsolete, feudalistic institutions were revived.[2]

Thus the continued survival of the feudal lord, the daimyo,[3] as a partially independent political entity represented a failure to press unification to its logical conclusion. As a result Tokugawa Japan, both politically and economically, remained broken up into over two hundred feudal domains whose interests were at best competitive and more often antagonistic. The daimyo system was at the heart of the dichotomy between feudalism and centralization, since it gave to the Tokugawa Shogun [4] a double role. On the one hand the head of the Tokugawa house was the supreme ruler of Japan, responsible for the destiny of the entire nation, while on the other he represented merely the greatest of the daimyo, jealously attempting to maintain his supremacy over the others. On matters of national policy the Shogun was thus frequently torn between the conflicting interests of his dual nature.

The Tokugawa reëstablishment of a strict barrier between the warrior, or samurai,[5] and the other classes was essentially a reversion to an outmoded stage of social development. It saddled Tokugawa Japan with the maintenance of an elite military class which was to become increasingly parasitic as time went on, while it forced upon the samurai himself a fundamental personal contradiction. In his role of feudal fighter the samurai's chief purpose in life was to prepare himself for military duty, yet so effective was the stabilizing force of the Tokugawa house that he found himself living in an age in which for over two hundred years his military services were superfluous.

Finally, the deliberate sacrifice of Japan's foreign ventures to the interests of political tranquillity had the effect of dangerously reversing the course of economic development in Japan. In a country in which the seeds of commercial and capitalistic growth had already been planted, the seclusion policy denied all possibility of expansion abroad and turned the economy of the country back upon itself. The result was a dangerous accentuation of the struggle between agriculture and commerce and the conflict between feudal authority and the power of money.

It is in this sense that the regime established by the Tokugawa may be thought of as embodying a number of fundamental antagonisms which remained unresolved throughout the long interval of Japan's modern seclusion. And thus, from the moment the Tokugawa system was consummated, Japan was destined to witness a continuing struggle between the remaining vestiges of feudalism and the forces seeking to destroy them. Perhaps the most fundamental conditions underlying and aggravating this struggle lay in the nature of the economic system which supported the ruling class. The seventeenth-century feudal rulers of Japan, by basing nearly their entire economic reliance on land and the land tax, by legislating foreign trade to a mere trickle, and treating the merchant with profound contempt, created an inflexible economic foundation for a society embarking on a two-century-long period of peace and prosperity. Had the size and standard of living of the military class remained constant, and had the responsibilities of government remained unchanged, the near static rice tax might have sufficed. But neither of these conditions was maintained. The samurai grew in numbers and lived in increasing comfort in the cities. The shogunal and domain governments expanded; responsibilities for relief and national defense multiplied. Before long the agrarian base was unable to support its top-heavy superstructure. The peasant had been squeezed beyond endurance, and yet the needs of the ruling interests could not be met. From the beginning of the eighteenth century the Tokugawa shogunate consistently operated with a deficit, which it made up only by debasement of coinage and extraordinary contributions from merchants or the daimyo. The daimyo in turn found themselves unable to make ends meet and were forced to reduce the salaries of their retainers or go into debt to merchant financiers.

It is hardly an exaggeration to say that financial distress and economic suffering were at the root of nearly every sign of political and social unrest during the later years of the Tokugawa period. For while the Tokugawa government and the various feudal lords found themselves in financial embarrassment, the samurai, living on a meager rice allotment, and the peasant, crushed under the exactions of feudal tax quotas, faced outright destitution. No development revealed so dramatically the sickness of Tokugawa society as the growing discontent of the agrarian class. As the Tokugawa period continued, the long-suffering peasantry at last reached the end of their endurance. Their feeling of hopelessness showed itself in the creeping horror of infanticide, and their bitterness erupted in a series of frenzied riots against the feudal authorities.

These evidences of economic deterioration and the concomitant disturbance of the feudal harmony, while disrupting enough to the feudal regime as a whole, were doubly so for the Tokugawa house. In the first place, because the Shogun was the supreme political authority in the land, he became the universal object of popular resentment in times of depression or famine. Moreover, the Tokugawa interests, which represented the greatest agglomeration of land and economic power, stood to lose the most by the general worsening of the country's economy. Loss of financial strength quickly translated itself into declining political power. Economic decay thus weakened the Tokugawa hold over the country and served to bring into the open the latent enemies of the shogunate.

Such enemies were indeed plentiful. In a sense the whole Tokugawa regime was built up out of a balance of tensions between antagonistic forces. This is perhaps best illustrated in the manner in which the Tokugawa arranged the disposition of power and authority among the daimyo. Beginning with a basic division of the feudal houses into friendly vassals and unfriendly "allies," the Tokugawa secured their political power by an elaborate disposition of these two classes of feudal lords in such a way as to make it impossible for any one of them to move against the central authority. The unfriendly houses were largely relegated to the periphery of the islands and out of all participation in the shogunate, while the larger of the vassals and collaterals, though given positions of respect in the Tokugawa councils, were so placed that they could be overridden by officials who were chosen from among the lesser shogunal adherents. This arrangement was undoubtedly an excellent device for canceling out the daimyo against each other, but, inasmuch as it incorporated suspicion and distrust into the political framework, it invited open dissatisfaction and opposition once the central authority began to weaken. The anti-Tokugawa daimyo, especially, by nature of their exclusion from national affairs, were encouraged in a policy of watchful waiting, and it was they who eventually became the chief spearheads of attack against the Shogun.

Another problem which constantly troubled the Tokugawa was that of the *rōnin*, or unattached samurai. Tokugawa society was so tightly regimented that the unemployed warrior inevitably became a social misfit. Rōnin had been extremely numerous in the first half of the seventeenth century as a result of the extensive confiscation of domains by the first three Tokugawa rulers. By the eighteenth century, such rōnin had for the most part been absorbed into the feudal structure and had ceased to be a major threat to the peace. After the middle of the Tokugawa period, however, rōnin were again produced in increasing numbers by the growing poverty and disillusionment of the samurai class. As restricted incomes made impossible the division of feudal patrimonies among the several male members of a family, younger sons were cast adrift to make their fortunes elsewhere. As the burdensome social system restricted the energies of ambitious men of low rank, they, too, often broke with the system. These men of samurai blood and training gravitated to the large cities where the more fortunate found employment as scholars, doctors, or sometimes merchants. Here the rōnin were an ever-present potential of social and political unrest. Bitterly opposed to the Tokugawa government which restricted their every move, and to the feudal system which was the reason for their distress, they formed a core of discontent within the ruling warrior class. Ready to take advantage of any occasion to better their position, the rōnin became a most potent force in the final overthrow of the Tokugawa government.

A further source of tension in the Tokugawa system derived from the political position of the Shogun with respect to the imperial court. The Tokugawa rulers, though in reality the supreme authority in the land, accepted the theory that they were delegates of the Emperor in whom sovereignty continued to be vested. By continuing the fiction of imperial rule, they left themselves open to the eventual resurgence of imperial power. Throughout the Tokugawa period the Emperor remained a potential rallying point of discontent against the Shogun, and in the crucial years after 1854, it was the imperial court which became the center of political opposition to the Tokugawa government.

But it was over the question of seclusion that the Tokugawa system eventually came to grief. The policy of national seclusion from its very inception did violence both to Japan's economy and to the traditional sentiment of the Japanese, who historically have welcomed foreign intercourse and the possibility of acquiring new ideas from abroad. As time went on, this policy became increasingly difficult to justify. From the ideological point of view, the threat of Christianity, against which the original policy had been enunciated, paled into insignificance, while from the economic standpoint, the suicidal implications of economic isolation soon became evident. The refusal of the later Tokugawa Shogun to modify the stand taken by their ancestors placed them in an untenable position. And when, in the face of the overpowering military might of the Western nations, the shogunate eventually called for a relaxation of the exclusion laws, it merely served to inform the rest of the nation of its own weakness. In the end the whole Tokugawa system went down in confusion along with the outmoded closed-door policy to which it was committed.

Such are some of the inherent weaknesses which undermined the power of the Tokugawa shogunate and made possible the elimination after the mid-nineteenth century of the system so elaborately contrived by Ieyasu and his successors. Yet it is obvious that they offer but half the explanation of the ease with which Japan accomplished her transition from a feudal to a modern society. Clearly one of the secrets of Japan's rapid modernization was the fact that decay had been matched by the growth of anti-feudal forces of a positive nature, which aided not only in the overthrow of the Toku- gawa authority but worked to prepare Japan more directly for meeting the challenge of the modern world.

One of the first noticeable signs of such change is to be found within the feudal administrative machine. As a result of the long years of continued peace after 1600, it was inevitable that both Shogun and daimyo should shift their attention from military pre- paredness to civil administration. Government in its political sense became the chief concern of the feudal aristocracy. Under such con- ditions the samurai was offered alternative lines of action. Deprived of the opportunity to prove himself in battle, he could idealize his position as a warrior and make of it a cult,[6] or he could take his peacetime administrative duties seriously and become a bureaucrat. Both of these alternatives were followed. But the more significant from the historical point of view was the process which converted the samurai into an administrative official of the Confucian type and transformed the shogunal and daimyo administrations into civil bureaucracies. This tendency was accentuated by the influx into government service of specialists, especially in the financial field, who were men of nonmilitary background: ex-merchants, or even ex-peasants. The appearance by the late Tokugawa period of modern budgetary techniques and of a modified form of civil service train- ing indicated that the Japanese were developing many of the pro- cedures of civil government required to run a modern bureaucratic state.[7]

Powerful forces of change also struck into the economic founda- tions of Tokugawa Japan. Japan's material growth after 1600 was truly remarkable despite the restrictions placed upon it by the Toku- gawa political system.[8] The startling rise of cities and of urban popu- lation which took place in the castle towns of the daimyo domains, and especially in the two great metropolitan areas of Edo and Osaka, was accompanied by the growth of trade and commerce and the development of communication to a point where the whole of Japan was fashioned into a single economic unit. This expansion of com- mercial activity in turn encouraged the growth in size and pros- perity of the service classes. With the shift from a natural to a money economy, the city merchant found means to amass huge stores of capital wealth and thus eventually to exert a new and disturbing economic force in a feudal warrior's world.

There is danger, of course, of overestimating the power of the Tokugawa merchant. Unlike his European counterpart, the force he exerted was but obliquely anti-feudal. Though often of great wealth, he remained politically weak. Denied the opportunities of foreign trade and the benefits of legal protection, his security lay not in opposing the feudal order but in association and alliance with the privileged class. The weakness of the merchant is evident in that peculiar feature of the late Tokugawa society which has been described as the "feudal-merchant alliance "[9] in which the merchant lent to the government his business experience in return for immunity and monopoly rights. But despite the fact that the bourgeoisie did not spearhead the revolt against feudalism in Japan, they must be credited with creating conditions inimical to the feudal order and for welcoming the revolutionary changes which accompanied the fall of the Tokugawa system.

The spread of commercial economy and the concurrent decline in the economic position of the samurai class brought further results, chief of which was a blurring of the social distinction between warrior and merchant. As poverty pressed upon the warrior class, the pattern of feudal loyalties became strained. The power of money began to outweigh the call of honor. Samurai families turned increasingly to nonfeudal means of livelihood. They allied themselves to the commercial class by engaging in business, or by marrying daughters or adopting sons of prosperous merchants. This same phenomenon was noticeable in the cultural life of the country. Tokugawa Japan had started out with but one dominant social class, the feudal aristocracy, whose art and literature alone was considered worthy of attention. However the samurai-centered culture of the ruling class was soon forced to compete with the urban culture of the merchants. By the late Tokugawa period it was from this lower social group that the significant works of art and literature were coming, and the warrior himself had turned to admire the bourgeois way of life. Japanese society was to become increasingly urbanized and commercialized.

Turning to the field of scientific accomplishment we see that the Tokugawa Japanese likewise gave evidence of progress within the limitations of seclusion. In contrast to the Chinese who forgot or even consciously rejected Western scientific and geographical knowledge obtained from the Jesuit missionaries of the sixteenth century, the Japanese made diligent use of the small opening to the outside world at Nagasaki to keep in touch with developments in both China and the West. After the partial lifting of the ban on the importation of European books in 1720, study of Western methods of anatomy, medicine, gunnery, astronomy, and geography went forward at a rapid rate. During the late Tokugawa period a steadily increasing group of students made Western science their specialty and played an important part in awakening the Japanese to what was going on outside their country. When the time came, these men formed a core of technically trained personnel able to take in and apply Western industrial and military technology. Moreover students of "Dutch learning" were for the most part bitter critics of the Tokugawa regime and of the Confucian orthodoxy which it patronized. It was through such men that many of the foremost leaders and writers of the Meiji Restoration period [10] acquired an understanding of the revolutionary institutions of contemporary Europe long before the path of direct observation was open to them.

But Japan's advances along the lines of scientific development were not merely a result of the importation of Western ideas. There is noticeable throughout the Tokugawa period a change in the climate of Japanese opinion as it began to outgrow feudal trammels and take on a more realistic, positivistic guise. Concepts of scientific verification began with the lowly merchant and his abacus and eventually affected the thinking of the warrior-bred historians and political-economists. Symptoms of this change were seen in the aesthetic world where realism invaded art and literature and encouraged minute scientific studies from life.[11] The Japanese intellectual of the late Tokugawa period was an inquisitive individual, curious about nature and the world around him. And this curiosity was often at the root of his impatience with his own way of life and the system which hampered his free inquiry.

Although the religious side of Tokugawa Japan witnessed no change so revolutionary as the rise of Protestant Christianity in Europe, there were certain developments whose cumulative effects were undoubtedly comparable. At the beginning of the Tokugawa period Japan was spiritually still in her Middle Ages, dominated by the Buddhist church and its other-worldly view of life. During the

succeeding decades, however, the power of Buddhism fell before the
twin blows of Confucianism and Shinto revivalism. On the one hand,
Confucianism with its this-worldly, humanistic orientation gave to
the Japanese an essentially modern philosophy. On the other, the
revival of Shinto, both in the form of the Kokugaku [12] school and
the popular Shinto sects, brought into existence a number of nation-
ally oriented philosophical and religious movements.[13]

In the final analysis, it may well have been the growth of nationalism during the Tokugawa period which, more than any other
factor, was to account for Japan's successful transformation into a
powerful modern state. The extreme national self-consciousness of
the Japanese was nurtured in part by the sense of uniqueness which
came from isolation and by the feeling of anti-foreignism which had
grown in cumulative fashion from the experience of the thirteenth-
century Mongol invasions and the later troubles with the Portuguese
and Spanish. These attitudes were given renewed focus and impetus
towards the end of the Tokugawa period with the reappearance of
the foreign menace. They were reinforced by the Tokugawa revival
of interest in the imperial line and the concepts of political Shinto,
such as the inviolability of Japanese soil and the divinity of the ruling house. By the time of the coming of Perry, the Japanese had at
hand the ingredients of a thorough-going national resurgence capable
of meeting the threat of Western imperialism. It was in large measure
this deep patriotism of the Japanese and the sense of national emergency which united them behind the revolutionary Meiji leaders and
enabled them to move so successfully through the difficult transition
period which separated the shogunate from the constitutional government of 1889 and the Tokugawa economy from the highly developed
industrial machine which made war against Russia possible in 1905.

But while it is possible to discern certain elements of progress
within Tokugawa society, it would be a mistake to overemphasize
their actual revolutionary influence. Japan did not throw off the yoke
of feudalism without great effort and then only after the Tokugawa
structure had been forcibly torn down. The Tokugawa rulers fully
realized that the growth of anti-feudal forces in their society represented only the degree to which they had failed to maintain unaltered
the principles laid down by the First Shogun, Ieyasu. Throughout its
long history, Tokugawa policy was thus directed to the task of
holding the line against those very developments which were to be

of utmost future consequence for the Japanese people. And hence, as the Tokugawa period progressed, an ever-widening gulf was to separate the interests and institutions of the ruling house from those of the nation as a whole. This divergence between the interests of the Tokugawa house and of the nation, however, has not been adequately made clear. Historians, depicting the Tokugawa period from the viewpoint of the shogunate, have tended to share the prejudices of the ruling group and have bestowed their praise and blame in a traditional manner.

According to the generally accepted interpretation, the course of Tokugawa history is viewed as being divided rather sharply into two parts. The first, embracing the period up to about 1700, was a time during which the program of the early Shogun appeared to be going well. The second, the last hundred and fifty years, saw the eventual breakdown of the Tokugawa system. It was with the turn of the eighteenth century that the Tokugawa regime began to run into serious trouble and that countermeasures became necessary. The history of the latter half of the Tokugawa period has commonly been described as consisting of a series of routs and rallies spiraling downward in a gradual curve of decline. At periodic intervals the shogunal authorities attempted vainly to restore their system to its original form and to reimpose the feudal controls with which they had originally secured their power. These rallies, undertaken in the names of the early Shogun and of the Confucian sages, received the praise of contemporary observers and later historians. The periods of rout, on the other hand, were widely condemned as ages of luxury and corruption.

Yet in actuality, the periods of rally did very little to advance the fortunes of the Tokugawa house and almost nothing to solve the national problems of economic dislocation. The Tokugawa reformers in every case, while attacking the symptoms of decay, left the underlying disease untouched. The times of rout, on the other hand, were in many indirect ways beneficial to the future of the country and not so disastrous to the Tokugawa interests as is generally supposed. During these periods new forces of innovation were given a chance to express themselves, while the shogunate frequently showed a flexibility in its policies which might have saved it from later collapse.

This is notably true of the so-called Tanuma period, an interval of slightly over twenty-five years from 1760 to 1786, which is generally acknowledged as being the first major rout in Tokugawa history. Described in the bulk of the history books as one of the most concentrated periods of political decay and popular distress in all the two hundred and fifty odd years of Tokugawa rule, the Tanuma age nevertheless acquires new importance when viewed in the perspective of the events which occurred after 1854. For despite the undeniable evidence of political degeneracy, it was a time which demonstrated the underlying vitality of the Japanese people and revealed the growing strength of the spirit of revolt against the feudal order.

The name Tanuma has been attached by Japanese historians to the time of the Tenth Shogun, Ieharu (r. 1760–1786), and is derived from the name of the Shogun's chief favorite, Tanuma Okitsugu (1719–1788). Few Tokugawa ministers have been so maligned as this man, who is universally pictured as an incarnation of corruption and official irresponsibility. The years during which he held the ear of the Shogun and purportedly ruled the shogunate by intrigue and bribery were admittedly black ones for Tokugawa prestige. Government finances reached a new low, while economic maladjustment and natural calamity wracked the country. These evils have become synonymous in the history books with the name of Tanuma, and their cause has been laid to the laxity and corruption of the administration which he headed.

Tanuma's blame is considered all the more serious in view of the two model administrators who bracket him in history, the Eighth Shogun, Yoshimune (1684–1751), and the Regent, Matsudaira Sadanobu (1758–1829), both of whom carried out energetic programs of reform in an attempt to rally the fortunes of the Tokugawa government. Both were reformers of the accepted style who attempted to revive the conditions of former days and restrengthen the feudal aspects of society. Inasmuch as Tanuma is frequently contrasted with these men, some understanding of the nature of their political policies is essential.

With the turn of the eighteenth century it had become evident to government officials and political theorists alike that all was not well with the Tokugawa regime. Yoshimune, who succeeded to the shogunate in 1716, was a man of simple tastes and forthright character. Calling upon the name of Ieyasu, he led the Tokugawa vassals in a militaristic revival of their rigid code. By appealing to the rule of frugality and encouraging the country to Spartan reforms, he sought to bolster the weakening feudal structure.

The Eighth Shogun's policies fell roughly into two main categories, economic and educational.[14] In the economic realm, where the immediate problem was to assure the livelihood of the samurai and the solvency of the government, Yoshimune strove both to increase the national productivity and to decrease consumption. His strenuous encouragement of land reclamation and the cultivation of new food-producing plants, such as the sweet potato and sugar cane, together with his order increasing the land tax rate were conceived to benefit the feudal ruling class in general and the Tokugawa government in particular. His edicts enforcing stringent economy and his encouragement of the military virtues of self-sacrifice and frugality were calculated to assure the samurai's ability to live within his income.

In the intellectual field Yoshimune put special emphasis on instructing the military class in its position of social leadership. New schools were established and samurai youths urged to train themselves in the scholarly as well as military arts. Tokugawa regulations were systematized as a basis for correcting public morals and reinstituting the strict feudal social pattern. The lower classes, which had lately begun to show annoying signs of disregard for their inferior status, were pushed back into place by edict and censorship.[15]

Yoshimune's essentially conservative and feudalistic policies were given a saving touch by the breadth of his character and by a certain admirable pragmatism which sometimes transcended the letter of tradition. His order lifting the ban on study of Western books and his personal interest in Western style astronomy are examples. Unfortunately, his successor as reformist had less of this flexibility. Matsudaira Sadanobu, grandson of Yoshimune and chief Tokugawa administrator from 1786 to 1793, represented policies one step farther along the path of reaction as is illustrated in his slogan of "Back to Yoshimune." The spirit of formalism, which by this time had seized the shogunate, was made evident in the many sumptuary controls which he attempted to enforce, his inflexible foreign policy, his insistence on "correct" systems of philosophy, and the great emphasis placed on the compilation of official histories and samurai genealogies by his appointees to the Tokugawa Confucian college.[16]

The reforms of Yoshimune and Sadanobu are recognized as two great rallies of the mid-Tokugawa period. Yet they in no way represented permanent solutions of the problems they sought to remedy. Sadanobu's reform was especially short-lived and ran into opposition from within the councils of the Tokugawa themselves. As for Yoshimune, it is believed that toward the end of his life he despaired of his own success and gave in to the type of disillusionment which characterized the political atmosphere of the period between himself and Sadanobu.[17] The brutality of many of his methods and his dogmatic, militaristic attitude did much to antagonize his vassals and the country at large. Upon his death he left a legacy of ill will toward the shogunate.

Even the best of Yoshimune's policies seem frequently to have met with disaster or to have given rise to unforeseen difficulties. In his eagerness to build up the shogunate's financial strength, national benefit was disregarded for the selfish needs of the Tokugawa. The tightened demands which he placed upon an already overexploited peasantry were at the root of the widespread agrarian revolts which marred his shoguncy. His emphasis on material profit tended to counteract the parallel attempt to revive in the Tokugawa vassals a sense of military honor. It is an ironical fact that Yoshimune eventually aided in the commercialization of the samurai and consequently the loss of those very qualities of feudal honor and military pride which he hoped to strengthen. Yoshimune's monetary policy, which aimed at the return of all debased currency to par, and his reclamation schemes, which greatly enlarged the area of cultivated land, were backed by excellent theory. Yet the resulting scarcity of money and the overabundance of cheap rice created a disastrous situation for the warrior class, whose income was calculated in terms of rice. Likewise, Yoshimune's well-meant frugality measures were both unpopular with the samurai and a cause of deep distress to the service classes. Since the warrior class, as the chief consuming group in the country, had become the main source of profit for the merchants, Yoshimune's economy regulations, which coerced the samurai into a drastic retrenchment of their expenditures, forced the entire business world into decline.[18]

In such ways Yoshimune alienated the support not only of large segments of Japanese society but of groups close to the Shogun himself. Renewed antagonism between the Tokugawa and the imperial court is dated from the time of Yoshimune, who brusquely purged from the shogunal ritual most of the court ceremonies previously imported from Kyoto. Signs of defection occurred even within the Tokugawa ranks and flared up in the dispute between Yoshimune and Tokugawa Muneharu (1696–1764), Daimyo of Owari. Muneharu, though a Tokugawa collateral, strongly disapproved of the Shogun's restrictive frugality measures and openly flouted them in his own luxurious life. At one time he encouraged the distribution of tracts which advocated the securing of national well-being through extensive spending.[19]

Thus at almost every turn Yoshimune faced defeat and frustration, not from any lack of zeal, but because the problems which he faced were too much for him. Japanese society was no longer capable of control along the lines of the original Tokugawa system. What Yoshimune managed to accomplish by way of cleaning up the Tokugawa administration and by injecting a new spirit of urgency into its officials was soon dissipated after his death. The degeneracy which followed has often been blamed on the personalities of the men who succeeded him to authority in the shogunate.[20] But the true cause must be sought in the deeper dislocations of Tokugawa society. Yoshimune had failed to stem the tide of decay. He passed on to the generations that followed him a society which, though superficially healthy, was internally far from well.

During the succeeding decades of the so-called Tanuma period, conditions within the government and the country at large deteriorated rapidly. Scandals in the shogunate and the grasping selfishness of Tokugawa officials undermined public confidence in the government. The authorities seemed powerless to control the activities of man or cope with the forces of nature. The harassed populace, oppressed by heartless officials and goaded by famine, flood, and volcanic explosion, rose up in bloody riots against the governing class. Clearly a period of rout was at hand.

The chief accusation brought against the officials who handled the affairs of the shogunate during these years is that they did little to remedy these distressing conditions, that instead they closed their eyes to the threatening disaster and shut themselves within the capital to indulge their own pleasures. It will be the argument of this study that such was not the case, that shogunal affairs did not simply drift during the Tanuma period, but that the policy-makers applied themselves strenuously enough to the task of reviving the fortunes of the Edo government and easing the distress of the people.[21] Tanuma, while certainly not exempt from criticism, was, in his way, an able administrator. Unquestionably he suffered unduly at the hands of his opponents. Perhaps the basic factor underlying the poor press which Tanuma received is to be found in the methods he advo-cated. The policies adopted by the shogunate during the period of his active participation in government were less in keeping with the principles of Confucian theory and military precedent than those of Yoshimune, and thus they failed to evoke the support of the scholars who were the chroniclers of the time.

It is easy, of course, to point a critical finger at corruption in the shogunal administration or bemoan the frightful condition of the rural community. It is less easy to uncover the fundamental prob-lems behind these symptoms of decay. In actuality the Tanuma period was a time of major crisis in both domestic and foreign fields. At home the Japanese saw the growth of pre-capitalist merchant economy to a new point of ascendancy over the agrarian foundation of Tokugawa feudal power. The ruling interests were faced with the choice of adhering to their land-first policy or of seeking new finan-cial supports which would derive in part from the resources of com-mercial economy. In foreign relations, Japan's period of easy isola-tion came to a close, and the question of whether the country should retain or modify the traditional Tokugawa foreign policy was brought to a head.

In each of these fields Tanuma and his associates advanced posi-tively and attempted to lead the government into a course of action which would have met the challenge of the times with flexibility rather than reaction. Frankly facing the growing power of the mer-chant capitalist, they advocated a policy of commercial expansion under government control. By encouraging mining and other profit-able industries and trades which could be taxed for the benefit of the state and by developing new state monopolies and commercial taxes, they utilized the rising merchant class and absorbed a por-tion of its wealth into the state treasury. Some of the measures adopted during these years cut sharply across precedent and put the government in the forefront of innovation. In particular the en-couragement given to foreign trade at Nagasaki and the first tentative move toward relaxing the exclusion laws to permit intercourse with the Russians showed that the shogunal administrators were attempting to adjust their policies to altered conditions.

Had Tanuma succeeded, had the Tokugawa government been able to move forward without notions of precedent or social and economic preconception, the subsequent history of Tokugawa Japan may well have been entirely different. The changes which were held off until after 1854 could have taken place as a process of gradual evolution many decades earlier. The opening of Japan, the leveling of social classes, and the switch from an agricultural to an industrial and commercial economy might well have taken place peacefully and naturally. But such a transformation could hardly have occurred without endangering the very existence of Tokugawa rule. The elements in Tanuma's polices which tended to relax the framework of the Tokugawa structure were thus branded as detrimental to the future of the shogunate and were opposed by a strong party within the government. Eventually conservatism triumphed, and Tanuma was pulled down from his high office. Under Matsudaira Sadanobu, the Tokugawa structure was resolidified. The futile attempt to resist change was renewed.

The Tanuma age is thus an important pivotal period in Tokugawa history. It was a time of social and intellectual ferment when, for the first time under the Tokugawa, the forces of anti-feudalism and open curiosity about the West were permitted to express themselves. But it was also a time of terrible calamity which shocked the feudal interests to a sense of renewed urgency and drove them to the adoption of desperate countermeasures. Although hopelessly undermined, the feudal structure was to stand for yet another century. It was not to collapse until the Tokugawa policy of isolation had been shattered by Western gunboats and the Shogun's armies destroyed by the new revolutionary forces of the Meiji government.

The man who has given his name to the period of the Tenth Shogun and who forms the chief figure around which the government policies of these years revolved has never been clearly understood. Though his reputation was great, he himself has left us no written word, and only an occasional anecdote survives concerning his life. So complete was his downfall after 1786 that even this information is largely from the pens of those who opposed his policies. In these writings Tanuma is blamed as the creator of his age of extreme rout. But he was hardly that. His political ascendancy was secured only after the middle of the period which bears his name, and his influence did not radically alter the trends of his times. Rather it is these trends which are reflected in his life and in the policies which he advocated. Tanuma Okitsugu was not the creator of his age but rather its prime symbol, a forerunner of modern Japan.

CHAPTER II

The Tokugawa Administrative System

Tanuma Okitsugu lived his entire life in Edo as an official of the Tokugawa shogunate. It was his special talent that he mastered the inner workings of the shogunal administration at an early age and succeeded in advancing rapidly up the ladder of official preferment. Before taking up the story of Tanuma's public career, therefore, it is essential that we give some consideration to the massive bureaucratic machine which formed its background.[1]

The Tokugawa bureaucracy, like the rambling city of Edo, grew up, not according to some preconceived, symmetrical plan, but empirically, in response to need. The starting point of the complex political mechanism which eventually administered the entire country was the simple, feudalistic, military organization of the Tokugawa house when it was as yet master of only a minor daimyo domain in the province of Mikawa. The last half of the sixteenth century was marked by a rising crescendo of civil wars which pitted daimyo against daimyo in a ruthless struggle for survival. Feudal domains were organized primarily for warfare. Government machinery was simple and forthright, with civil functions subordinated to military. When in 1603 the Tokugawa Daimyo, Ieyasu, having quieted the civil wars, became Shogun, his house administration came to be known as the *bakufu*,[2] or shogunate, as it is referred to in English literature. Through it the Tokugawa rulers governed the entire country from their capital of Edo.

During the next few years the Edo government underwent considerable broadening and adjustment to the new civil responsibilities which accrued to the chief administrative power in the land. The shogunate, as we generally think of it, took its final form during the time of Iemitsu (r. 1623–1651), the Third Shogun. Few changes were made thereafter. The organization, which had begun as an extremely flexible mechanism, developed into a rigid bureaucracy hardened by conservatism and considerations of heredity. After 1651 minor changes of usage and function were made, but the overwhelming tendency was to keep things as they had been established by the first three Shogun.

Needless to say, the shogunate existed to carry out the administrative functions of the Tokugawa Shogun. These were defined in their broadest sense according to the Shogun's relationship to three separate groups within the country: the imperial court, the two hundred and seventy odd daimyo, and the immediate shogunal vassals and domains.

The Emperor, his court, and the whole elaborate hierarchy of court ranks and titles formed an essential part of the Tokugawa official system. The Emperor, as the ultimate source of sovereignty and the spiritual sanction to the Shogun's authority, was given a position of almost sacred reverence, while the courtiers were treated with the respect due their high rank and their proximity to the imperial symbol. Court ranks, though largely hereditary, performed a real function by defining the hierarchal position of each member of the ruling class. On the other hand the Tokugawa saw to it that the Emperor and his courtiers were carefully restricted from participation in political matters and that the system of court ranks as it applied to the military class was under shogunal control. Relations with the imperial court, therefore, required the creation of a number of regulatory and intermediary organs within the Shogun's administration, such as the Kyoto Deputy (*Kyōto shoshidai*) and the Masters of Court Ceremony (*kōke*). The functions of these officials will be discussed below.

As supreme head of the feudal-military hierarchy, the Shogun required the allegiance of all daimyo houses. Under the Shogun the daimyo were carefully arranged according to class and status. To a degree, the daimyo's position was a function of the size of his domain. Since domains were measured in terms of the assessed rice yield calculated in *koku*, the koku assessment (*kokudaka*) of a daimyo was a rough indication of his wealth and his relative position within the Tokugawa system.[3]

For certain official purposes daimyo were grouped into classes according to the types of their holdings. These, in hierarchal order of importance, were: (1) Lord of a Province (*kunimochi*), (2) Rank Equivalent to Lord of a Province (*kunimochi-nami*), (3) Lord of a Castle (*jōshu*), (4) Rank Equivalent to Lord of a Castle (*jōshu-gaku*), (5) Lord without a Castle (*mujō*).

Of greater significance within the Tokugawa system, however, were classifications which defined the exact feudal relationship of the daimyo to the Tokugawa house. These began with a broad division into three classes: (1) Collaterals (*kamon*), (2) Hereditary Vassals (*fudai*), and (3) Outside Lords (*tozama*). Each of these classes was in turn subdivided into numerous groups.

The Collaterals,[4] in Tanuma's time, were composed of two main groups. The Three Houses (*sanke*) of Owari, Kii, and Mito, being directly descended from Ieyasu, formed the first line of support for the Shogun. In the event of the failure of the main line, they stood ready to supply successors to the headship of the Tokugawa family. The Three Lords (*sankyō*), set up by the Eighth and Ninth Shogun, Yoshimune and Ieshige, formed a second line of support.[5] Of the Collaterals, only the Three Houses retained the family name of Tokugawa. The Three Lords, in order of seniority, were named Tayasu, Hitotsubashi, and Shimizu. Collaterals other than these two groups bore the special surname Matsudaira.[6]

The Hereditary Vassals of the Tokugawa Shogun were those houses which had sided with Ieyasu from an early date and had become his direct vassals. They made up the bulk of the daimyo and, although individually of relatively low income, they were entrusted with the highest official posts within the shogunate. These houses were classified and given official precedence in accordance with the history of their early relationship with Ieyasu and his two immediate successors.

The Outside Lords were those daimyo who submitted to the Tokugawa at the time of, or after, the decisive battle of Sekigahara (1600). Their status was somewhat distinct from that of direct vassalage although they too were bound by feudal oath to the Shogun. Except in unusual instances, the Outside Lords were excluded from service in the central administration; on the other hand, they retained a greater degree of autonomy in the management of their own territories.

The elaborate control mechanism which assured the loyalty of the daimyo and restricted their ability to contemplate hostile action against the Shogun has been dealt with at length by several Western writers. The relationship between Shogun and daimyo, it should be reiterated, was primarily feudal and military. Each daimyo was in fact conceived of as a military vassal accountable for a certain quota of troops. And although the unbroken peace which followed the quelling of the Shimabara Rebellion (1637–38) made such contributions of secondary importance, regular requirements for guard duty continued at such places as the imperial palace, Osaka and Sumpu castles, the port of Nagasaki, and various coastal defense stations.

From the point of view of the Tokugawa administration, the most significant duty of the daimyo was that of alternate attendance upon the Shogun at his court at Edo. This service, known as *sankinkōtai*, required that all daimyo spend every other year at Edo and the intervening years in their own domains.[7] Transfers for Hereditary Vassals were made during the fourth month of the year and for Outside Lords during the sixth month. When in Edo, all daimyo were obliged to attend the Shogun's court on the first and twenty-eighth of each month and on all other special occasions. Each daimyo was required to construct and maintain in Edo an official residence (*yashiki*) of suitable pretentiousness. In Edo, the daimyo worked through his chief representative, his Edo Deputy (*rusui*).

Attendance at the shogunal court took place according to strictly prescribed precedent worked out under the first three Shogun. Each daimyo, in accordance with his court rank, was assigned to a designated section of the great Central Citadel (*hommaru*).[8] In time these seating assignments themselves became a manner of indicating the relative positions of the daimyo within the Tokugawa feudal hierarchy. There were seven such categories. (1) The Great Corridor (*ōrōka*) was occupied by the heads of the Three Houses and certain of their immediate family, certain other Collaterals, and occasionally an honored Outside Lord. (2) In the Antechamber (*tamari-no-ma*) were seated other Collaterals and the most important Hereditary Vassals. (3) The Great Hall (*ōbiroma*) contained close offshoots of the Collaterals, Lords of Provinces and their equivalents, and Outside Lords of fourth court rank.[9] (4) The Hall of the Emperors (*teikan-no-ma*) was occupied by cadet branches of the Echizen House and Hereditary Vassals of 100,000 koku or more. (5) The Willow Hall (*yanagi-no-ma*) was taken up largely by the remaining Outside Lords. (6) In the Hall of Geese (*gan-no-ma*) were placed designated Hereditary Vassals. (7) The remaining Hereditary Vassals, of which all were Lords Without Castles, were seated in the Chrysanthemum Hall (*kiku-no-ma*).

Court titles and ranks given to the military aristocracy were limited in number and were generally assigned on a hereditary basis. Ranks were invariably linked to titles and vice versa. The Shogun himself was always of Ministerial (*daijin*) status with either the first or second court ranks (*shō, juichii; shō, ju'nii*). Of the Collaterals, it was customary for the heads of the Owari and Kii houses to rise to the title of Great Counselor (*dainagon*) and the Junior Second Rank (*ju'nii*). The head of the Mito house could become a Middle Counselor (*chūnagon*) of Junior Third Rank (*jusammi*); Maeda of the Outside Lords had the privilege of rising to Councilor (*sangi*) and the Junior Third Rank. Of the remaining daimyo, a few were especially privileged to reach Middle Commander of the Guards (*chūjō*) with accompanying rank ranging from Junior Third Rank down to Junior Fourth Rank Lower Grade (*jushii-ge*). Lords of Provinces rose to Lesser Commander of the Guards (*shōshō*) with the same scale of ranks as for Middle Commander. Those of Rank Equivalent to Lord of a Province and certain chief bakufu officials became Court Chamberlains (*jijū*) of Junior Fourth Rank Upper Grade (*jushii-jō*). The vast majority of daimyo and other functionaries remained on the two next levels of court rank, Junior Fourth Lower Grade and Junior Fifth Lower Grade (*jugoi-ge*). They bore an assortment of titles of which some derived from the central bureaucracy of the early court government but the greater portion from the earlier provincial administration.[10]

Except for those who held the upper three or four brackets of court rank, the original hereditary title was generally retained irrespective of any additional title which accompanied a later rise in court rank. Tanuma Okitsugu, for instance, though raised to the Junior Fourth Rank Senior Grade with the title of Court Chamberlain, nevertheless continued to be known as Chief of the Bureau of Palace Upkeep (*tonomo-no-kami*), the title which had come to him through his father. These titles and ranks, it should be remembered, were purely honorary in nature, though they served a purpose in defining feudal status. For this reason, court titles should be differentiated from the functional offices of the shogunate described below.

Outside of his own territories the Shogun had no direct control over military men of less than daimyo status. His own vassals of this category were, however, extremely numerous, and it is from among them that the rank and file of his officials and guards were drawn. The direct vassals of the Shogun were designated as either Bannermen (*hatamoto*) or Housemen (*kenin*). The former were distinguished by having the privilege of audience with the Shogun, the latter not. Another commonly accepted distinction between these two groups was that Bannermen received fiefs (*chigyō* or *mura*) while Housemen were supported by rice stipend (*kirimai* or *rimmai*). There were, however, exceptions to this arrangement.

As in the case of the daimyo, the lesser military houses were classed according to the size of their basic income (*hondaka*). Such income was distinguished from other temporary sources of revenue which might derive from holding salaried posts in the government. Fiefs were measured in koku, stipends in *hyō* (bales). However, the two terms for rice capacity were sometimes confused or used loosely. This was because the hyō in theory represented the tax yield from a one-koku fief.[11] A family with a 300-koku fief would, in other words, receive 300 hyō of rice annually. Thus the terms koku and hyō in certain instances became interchangeable. A third method of calculating incomes was in terms of rations (*fuchi* or *kōryō*). One ration, in other words the amount of rice necessary to support one individual for one month, was approximately .4 hyō.

One of the chief characteristics of the Tokugawa government was the strong position occupied by the Shogun himself. Once installed in his office, and provided he was of age, the Shogun was immune from outside interference except in the form of advice tendered by the Three Houses, or through the accepted channels of government. Influence over him could be gained only in so far as he voluntarily bestowed his trust upon one or another of his ministers. Nevertheless, as time went on, it became extremely difficult for the Shogun to make independent decisions. The precedent established by previous Shogun hampered his every move. His life and activities became ritualized and stereotyped, and he himself lived more and more removed from contact with conditions on his lands and the realities of state affairs.

Unless a Shogun happened to be brought in from one of the Collaterals, his whole life, except for short excursions, was spent within the confines of the great Edo Castle (*Edojō*). Upon being selected as heir apparent, he was installed in the Western Citadel (*saijō*). If he abdicated his post before his death, he spent the remaining years of his life in the Second Citadel (*ni-no-maru*). While he was in office, his activities were carried on in the Central Citadel. This spacious structure was divided into three sections: the Great Interior (*ōoku*) which housed the women's apartments, the Interior (*oku*) or the Shogun's own quarters, and the Exterior (*omote*) in which audiences were held and the business of government transacted.

Tokugawa officials performed several distinct types of service according to whether they were concerned with administration, guard duty, maintenance and upkeep, or attendance upon the Shogun. The schematic breakdown of shogunal offices which follows on pages 28 and 29 will indicate the place of the more important posts within the chain of bureaucratic command as it descended from the Shogun.

In the adjoining chart it will be seen that while, strictly speaking, the Councilors formed the apex of the bureaucracy under the Shogun, two groups of advisors could intervene between them and the Shogun. The members of the Great Corridor, generally the heads of the Three Houses, were called in for advice only on rare occasions, but the members of the Antechamber attended the Shogun's court regularly on the tenth and twentieth of the month to tender their advice on political matters and to consult with the Councilors. When important matters of state were discussed, they invariably sat with the Councilors. The Antechamber thus formed a type of supreme advisory council which could exert considerable pressure on the Tokugawa administration when it so chose.

The Councilors themselves corresponded to what might be called a cabinet. The position of Great Councilor was generally left vacant or filled on those occasions when the Shogun was a minor or some government emergency threatened. In such instances a Regent was sometimes appointed from among the close Tokugawa relations. The Senior Councilors, as may be seen from the variety of offices which came under their jurisdiction, had wide authority over matters of government policy and the administration of shogunal affairs on a nation-wide scale. The Junior Councilors were charged primarily with control of the Bannermen and Housemen and with shogunal attendants and guards.

The room of the Central Citadel in which the Councilors conducted their affairs was known as the Business Office (*yōbeya*) and

Main Offices of the Tokugawa Shogunate [12]

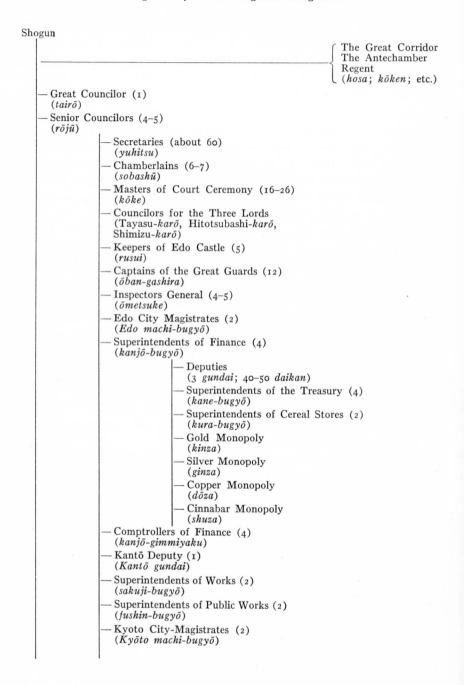

Shogun

⎧ The Great Corridor
⎨ The Antechamber
⎩ Regent
   (*hosa*; *kōken*; etc.)

— Great Councilor (1)
   (*tairō*)

— Senior Councilors (4–5)
   (*rōjū*)

     — Secretaries (about 60)
      (*yuhitsu*)

     — Chamberlains (6–7)
      (*sobashū*)

     — Masters of Court Ceremony (16–26)
      (*kōke*)

     — Councilors for the Three Lords
      (Tayasu-*karō*, Hitotsubashi-*karō*,
      Shimizu-*karō*)

     — Keepers of Edo Castle (5)
      (*rusui*)

     — Captains of the Great Guards (12)
      (*ōban-gashira*)

     — Inspectors General (4–5)
      (*ōmetsuke*)

     — Edo City Magistrates (2)
      (*Edo machi-bugyō*)

     — Superintendents of Finance (4)
      (*kanjō-bugyō*)

          — Deputies
           (3 *gundai*; 40–50 *daikan*)

          — Superintendents of the Treasury (4)
           (*kane-bugyō*)

          — Superintendents of Cereal Stores (2)
           (*kura-bugyō*)

          — Gold Monopoly
           (*kinza*)

          — Silver Monopoly
           (*ginza*)

          — Copper Monopoly
           (*dōza*)

          — Cinnabar Monopoly
           (*shuza*)

     — Comptrollers of Finance (4)
      (*kanjō-gimmiyaku*)

     — Kantō Deputy (1)
      (*Kantō gundai*)

     — Superintendents of Works (2)
      (*sakuji-bugyō*)

     — Superintendents of Public Works (2)
      (*fushin-bugyō*)

     — Kyoto City-Magistrates (2)
      (*Kyōto machi-bugyō*)

— Osaka City-Magistrates (2)
(*Ōsaka machi-bugyō*)

— Magistrates of Nagasaki (3–4), Uraga (1–2), etc.
(*Nagasaki-bugyō, Uraga-bugyō*)

— Grand Chamberlain (1)
(*sobayōnin*)

— Junior Councilors (4–5)
(*wakadoshiyori*)

— Captains of the Body Guard (6)
(*shoinban-gashira*)

— Captains of the Inner Guards (6)
(*koshōgumiban-gashira*)

— Captains of the New Guards (6)
(*shimban-gashira*)

— Superintendents of Construction and Repair
(*kobushin-bugyō*)

— Chiefs of the Pages (6)
(*koshō-tōdori*)

— Chiefs of the Attendants (3)
(*ko'nando-tōdori*)

— Inspectors
(*metsuke*)

— Chiefs of the Castle Accountants (2)
(*nando-gashira*)

— Attendant Physicians
(*ishi*)

— Attendant Confucianists
(*jusha*)

— Superintendents of the Kitchen (3–5)
(*zen-bugyō*)

— Masters of Shogunal Ceremony (20 or more)
(*sōshaban*)

— Superintendents of Temples and Shrines (4)
(*jisha-bugyō*)

— Kyoto Deputy (1)
(*Kyōto-shoshidai*)

— Keeper of Osaka Castle (1)
(*Ōsaka-jōdai*)

|— Supreme Court of Justice
(*hyōjōsho*)

Regular duty:
Superintendents of Temples and Shrines
Edo City Magistrates
Superintendents of Finance

Irregular duty:
A Senior Councilor
The Grand Chamberlain
Other Magistrates and Superintendents when residing in Edo

Assisted by:
Comptrollers of Finance
Inspectors General and others

was located in the immediate vicinity of the Shogun's daytime apartments. The office was divided into two sections, one for the Great Councilor and Senior Councilors, the other for the Junior Councilors. In the early years of the shogunate, the Shogun was in direct contact with the Councilors in the Business Office. Subsequently, however, an intermediary group of officials was employed. These were the Chamberlains.

The Grand Chamberlain held a position of extreme importance and frequently of considerable power because of his close association with the Shogun. His function was to mediate between the Shogun and Councilors. He communicated to his master the reports made by the Councilors, sometimes offering his own advice as he did so, and carried back to the Councilors the Shogun's opinion or decision. The office of Grand Chamberlain was frequently left vacant, but when filled was usually occupied by a former Chamberlain.

The Chamberlains performed much the same function as the Grand Chamberlain, but with less independence. In addition they supervised the activities of the Pages and Attendants. After the daily retirement of the Senior Councilors, they handled the affairs of the Shogun's court on the night watch. In theory the Chamberlains were under the jurisdiction of the Senior Councilors, but when a Grand Chamberlain was in office their closest association was with him. The Grand Chamberlain and the several Chamberlains thus frequently formed an "inner" group of officials close to the Shogun which competed with the "outer" group consisting of Councilors and other officials less intimately associated with the head of the Tokugawa house. The struggle between these two groups was especially acute during the Tanuma period.

Besides the Councilors and Chamberlains four other posts were placed directly under the Shogun. The Masters of Shogunal Ceremony acted as intermediaries between the Shogun and his vassals, the daimyo and Bannermen. They arranged audiences, handled the bestowal and receipt of gifts, regulated ceremonies, and the like. These officials are to be distinguished from the Masters of Court Ceremony, who performed a similar function in matters involving contact between the Shogun and the imperial court. The Superintendents of Temples and Shrines, in addition to supervising the affairs of the shrines, temples, priests, and nuns of the country, had wide judicial functions over shogunal lands of western Japan. The

Kyoto Deputy was charged with guarding Kyoto and overseeing the affairs of the imperial court, while the Keeper of Osaka Castle was made responsible for guarding the entire Kansai area.

Detailed descriptions of the function of the other lesser members of the Tokugawa bureaucracy are beyond the scope of the present outline. They were extremely numerous and, for most, the translated titles found in the above chart offer a sufficient clue to their duties. However, a few posts require special comment because of their prominence in the following chapters.

In service about the person of the Shogun were the Pages and Attendants. The former took charge of various aspects of the Shogun's daily activities and in particular attended his movements to and from the women's apartment. The Attendants took care of the Shogun's personal wants, performing such duties as serving food and dressing the hair. The several Guard groups under the Junior Council were all alike in function. They performed close guard duty about the person of the Shogun within the Central Citadel and along the route taken by him whenever he left the castle.

In the bureaucracy at large the officials in charge of finance and trade require special consideration. Superintendents of Finance were of two classes. Of the four men appointed to this post, two were strictly financial officials (*kattegata*), the other two were designated as judicial officers (*kujikata*). Within each category, the Superintendents attended to duty in alternate years. Comptrollers were established as a check on the Superintendents. They were likewise divided into financial and judicial specialists. The Nagasaki Magistrates were of considerable importance since besides administering the city of Nagasaki they handled foreign affairs, trade and customs at the one Tokugawa port open to the outside world. The post of Uraga Magistrate was set up in 1720 to guard the sea approach to Edo. At that time the shipping inspection office at Shimoda was transferred to Uraga at the mouth of Edo Bay. All ships entering and leaving the bay were inspected at Uraga.

Before leaving the subject of Tokugawa officialdom, there remain one or two peculiarities of the Tokugawa system which need to be pointed out. As indicated previously, the posts within the government were almost invariably filled by Hereditary Vassals or Bannermen and Housemen. In addition, as precedent crystallized, the holding of office became largely formalized according to family background and status. Each office became hedged around by customary requirements. This was especially true of the higher posts in the government, which tended to become hereditary within a certain limited number of houses. The post of Great Councilor, for instance, was chosen from among only four lines of Hereditary Vassals. Only thirty-five families produced Senior Councilors in more than one generation, and for the Junior Councilors this number was forty-five.

Aside from the importance of lineage, eventually all posts were classed in terms of the basic income which a candidate must possess before qualifying for appointment. Senior Councilors were generally taken from among daimyo of 25,000 koku or more. Posts of Junior Councilor and Master of Shogunal Ceremony were limited to those of daimyo rank. Bannermen of 5000 koku income could qualify for the post of Chamberlain, while 3000-koku Bannermen could become City Magistrates or Superintendents of Finance.

This arrangement naturally tended to discourage movement within the official class. However, a system worked out during the time of the Eighth Shogun, Yoshimune, helped to restore a certain mobility and made less difficult the appointment to high office of able men of low hereditary income. This was the system of temporary augmentation (*tashidaka*), which, for offices up to the 5000-koku class, permitted the granting of a temporary additional stipend so as to make up the difference between the appointee's basic income and the amount at which the office was classed. For example, a 2000-koku Bannerman, if appointed to the post of City Magistrate, would have his income raised to 3000 koku. The additional 1000 koku was a temporary augmentation which, in theory, was held only for the duration of the appointment.

In addition to this augmentation, a number of positions carried outright salaries (*yakuhō*) in either rice or money. This was an innovation of the middle Tokugawa period. During the early years of the Edo government, service for the Shogun in any capacity was considered a feudal obligation. Participation in the shogunate was thought of as an honor which required no additional remuneration. However, with the increased bureaucratization of the Tokugawa government, and especially the growing financial burden upon office-holders, a salary scale was developed for most of the positions below that of Councilor.

A final characteristic of the Tokugawa bureaucratic system which needs emphasis was the prevalence of the multiple holding of office and the sharing of responsibility. The large majority of responsible positions were held by two or more individuals who alternated in office at monthly or yearly intervals. This system, while protecting the Tokugawa from excessive exercise of power on the part of individual ministers, nevertheless seriously restricted the use of initiative or the acceptance of responsibility at all levels of the Edo bureaucratic machine. Thus it must be admitted that the predominant atmosphere which pervaded the shogunate in the mid-Tokugawa period was one of immobility. The constant adherence to precedent and to the niceties of official protocol paralyzed the activities of the Tokugawa officials, while bureaucratic inertia and the desire to avoid responsibility prevented the efficient execution of official business. As a result there inevitably developed within the administration a tendency toward behind-the-scenes manipulation and the growth of favoritism and corruption. It was at a time when such maladies had become especially acute that Tanuma began his official career.

CHAPTER III

Tanuma Okitsugu, Favorite of the Tenth Shogun

I. FROM PAGE TO SENIOR COUNCILOR

From the foregoing discussion it is evident that the Tokugawa feudal aristocracy maintained a highly formalized and in many respects artificial society in which lineage and the subtle nuances of feudal status were all-important factors in the lives of its participants. It is no accident, therefore, that the chief biographical materials remaining from this period are in the form of genealogies [1] and official registers [2] which confine themselves almost exclusively to matters of family relationship, ranks, titles, and official service. A recitation of such information, despite the tedious insistence on petty detail and an almost total absence of human interest, is nonetheless an essential starting point for the study of any Tokugawa public figure.[3]

Tanuma Okitsugu, like nearly all samurai of the Tokugawa period, claimed descent from one of the outstanding noble lines of the late tenth century.[4] His genealogy originated in a branch of the Fujiwara house,[5] from which it descended through several generations bearing the surname Ashikaga to a certain Naritoshi. The latter took the family name Sano, which he derived from the name of his castle in the district of Aso in Shimōsa province. Six generations later, a younger son of the main Sano branch, Shigetsuna (died 1265), taking up residence in the nearby town of Tanuma,[6] adopted the name of that location and became the progenitor of the Tanuma family.

The Tanuma family eventually became vassal to the Sano, but in the momentous wars which marked the close of the sixteenth century the Sano family lost its castle and was reduced to insignificance. The Tanuma family, cast adrift, attached itself first to one, then to another of the larger houses of the area and finally came to rest in the service of the Kii branch of the Tokugawa house. This event took place sometime around 1650, four generations before Tanuma Okitsugu, our chief protagonist.

The humble status of this Tanuma family may be judged by the fact that Okitsugu's grandfather, Jūemon Yoshifusa, when he gave up his feudal duties on account of ill health, was obliged to retire among the common townspeople outside the Wakayama castle. Okitsugu's father, Motoyuki, was taken in by an uncle, Tashiro Shichiuemon Takachika, and married to an adopted daughter. Motoyuki, however, retained his surname and eventually entered the service of Tokugawa Yoshimune, Lord of Kii.

In 1716, as fortune would have it, Yoshimune became Shogun, and Motoyuki followed his master to Edo in the capacity of a Page.[7] As such he was given a basic rice allotment of 300 koku. In 1724 (Kyōhō 9. 11. 15),[8] Motoyuki received the title of Chief of the Bureau of Palace Upkeep.[9] Nine years later, in 1733, he was given an additional allotment of 300 koku. At this time his total basic income of 600 koku was converted to a fief in the two districts of Takaza and Ōsumi in the province of Sagami. The next year (19. 8. 15), he was appointed to the post of Chief of the Attendants.[10] He died four months later (19. 12. 18).

Motoyuki's special duties while in office appear to have been of a scholarly nature. He was at one time placed in charge of the Shogun's library. Toward the end of his life he attended several literary parties given by Yoshimune and headed a group commissioned to make a collection of the poetry written in praise of various famous spots of Musashi province.[11]

Tanuma Okitsugu,[12] the eldest son of Motoyuki, was born in 1719. At the age of thirteen he was first presented to the Shogun, and two years later, in 1734, he was assigned to the service of the Heir Apparent, Ieshige, in the Western Citadel. His position was that of Page with a salary of 300 hyō. In this same year his father died. Okitsugu succeeded to the headship of the Tanuma family the next spring (20. 3. 4), at which time he inherited his father's 600-koku fief. In 1737 (Gembun 2. 12. 16) Okitsugu received the Junior Fifth Court Rank Lower Grade and the title, Chief of the Bureau of Palace Upkeep.

Tanuma Okitsugu moved to the Central Citadel when Ieshige became Shogun in 1745 (Enkyō 2. 9. 1). From this point on he began to rise rapidly.[13] In 1747 (4. 9. 15) he was promoted to Rank

Equivalent to Captain of the Inner Guard[14] and was ordered to familiarize himself with all matters relating to this higher post. The next year (Kan'en 1. intercalary 10. 1) he was duly installed as a regular Captain and given an additional 1400-koku basic income. The 2000 koku he now possessed were relocated in the district of Musha in Kazusa province and the districts of Soki and Katori in Shimōsa province.

Tanuma took his place among the Chamberlains[15] in 1751 (Hōreki 1. 7. 18). Four years later (5. 9. 19) his basic income was raised to 5000 koku by the addition of fiefs in Katori and the districts of Ōsumi, Aikō, and Ashigara in Sagami province. In 1758 (8. 9. 3) he was raised to the rank of daimyo by the grant of an additional 5000 koku. At the same time he was ordered to sit in on the meetings of the Supreme Court of Justice and to take active part in its hearings.[16] His status, in such instances, was to be equivalent to that of Senior Councilor.

The 10,000 koku which Tanuma now held were presently redistributed in the three provinces of Tōtomi, Sagami, and Shimōsa, the principal part of his holdings being located in the first of these provinces in the Sagara domain[17] previously the possession of Honda Tadanaka.[18] He was invested with the signet for his lands in 1760 (10. 10. 18).

In this same year the Shogun Ieshige determined to step down from his office in favor of his son, Ieharu. Tokugawa officials were put to work to prepare for Ieshige's retirement and the installation of his successor. On this occasion Tanuma won special commendation for his part in facilitating the rebuilding of the Second Citadel,[19] receiving as a token six *jifuku*[20] and a sword from the hands of the Shogun himself. At the same time (10. 5. 7) he was relieved of permanent duty with the Supreme Court of Justice and permitted to limit his attendance to occasional visits.[21]

Ieshige lived only until 1761 (11. 6. 2), but before his death he appears to have recommended Tanuma to his successor Ieharu. The new Shogun accepted this recommendation although, it is said, chiefly out of respect for his father.[22] After the change of Shogun, therefore, Tanuma continued in his capacity of Chamberlain. His last task for his former master, and the first for his new, was to take charge of Ieshige's funeral, a duty which he performed with distinction.[23]

Once in Ieharu's service, Tanuma quickly established himself as a special favorite. In 1762 (12. 2. 15) he received an additional 5000 koku in the districts of Saibara and Kitō in Tōtomi. Three years later (Meiwa 2. 4. 11) he was sent with other important officials to the Tokugawa mausolea at Nikkō to commemorate the hundred and fiftieth anniversary of the death of Tokugawa Ieyasu.[24]

Tanuma's next major advance came in 1767 (4. 7. 1) when he was appointed Grand Chamberlain.[25] Simultaneously his total holdings were raised to 20,000 koku and his court rank to Junior Fourth Rank Lower Grade. He was also granted permission to construct a castle at Sagara,[26] and his son was given a seat in the Chrysanthemum Room.[27]

Two years later, in the summer of 1769 (6. 8. 18), Tanuma made the most difficult hurdle of his career when he was appointed to Rank Equivalent to Senior Councilor.[28] On this occasion he received a further increase of 5000 koku [29] and a promotion in court title to Court Chamberlain.[30] It was further ordained that he should continue his close attendance upon the person of the Shogun in addition to maintaining the schedule of duty followed by the Senior Councilors.[31] On the days on which he sat on the Supreme Court of Justice all orders were to bear his name.[32] In his movements to and from the Shogun's court he was permitted to display two spears.[33]

It is clear that from this time on Tanuma had considerable influence in the formation of state policy. Yet this is not stated in any official sources. During the next two years the only special mention we have of him is in connection with a commendation he received for handling repairs on the Western Citadel and also for facilitating the transfer of the Heir Apparent to these new quarters (6. 12. 28) when they were ready.

Tanuma was named regular Senior Councilor in 1772 (An'ei 1. 1. 15), but he still seems to have retained his capacity as Grand Chamberlain.[34] His domain was again augmented by 5000 koku in the districts of Negata, Hōi, and Atsumi in the province of Mikawa. At the same time 5000 koku of his original holdings in Tōtomi were relocated in Mikawa. Meanwhile, in Edo, Tanuma had moved to a pretentious residence in special proximity to the Shogun's central castle, as prescribed for the highest shogunal officials. This residence was destroyed by fire in the early spring of 1772, and on this occasion the Shogun expressed his condolences with a gift of ten jifuku and a loan of 10,000 *ryō* [35] of gold to defray the cost of reconstruction.

During the next few years, Tanuma's special assignments consisted in supervising the funeral services for the Shogun's daughter, Manjū Hime (2. 3. 14), and for the Heir Apparent, Iemoto (8. 4. 23). He also played a prominent part in the shogunal progress to Nikkō in the spring of 1776. The next spring (6. 4. 21), as a special mark of favor,[36] Tanuma received a 7000-koku fief in Tōtomi.[37]

In 1780 (9. 4. 1) Tanuma was granted permission to visit his castle at Sagara for the first time. On this occasion he received several signs of marked affection from the Shogun, including gifts of travel clothing and the horse, Kuboyama.[38] During Tanuma's absence, his son, Mototomo, paid his respects to the Shogun on behalf of his father.[39]

One of the most important acts of Tanuma's career from the point of view of internal Tokugawa politics involved his part in the selection of an Heir Apparent to take the place of the deceased Iemoto. Tanuma was ordered to head a commission to investigate candidates in the spring of 1781 (Temmei 1. 4. 15).[40] The choice fell on Ienari,[41] son of Hitotsubashi Harunari.[42] On the day following the announcement of this choice, Tanuma's nephew, Tanuma Okimune,[43] was transferred from the post of Hitotsubashi-Councilor to that of Rank Equivalent to Captain of the Inner Guard attached to the Heir Apparent. This transfer, which put a member of the Tanuma family in close contact with the future Shogun, left little doubt that the selection of Ieharu's heir had been calculated to enhance Tanuma's prestige and assure his continuing influence in the central government. For his services in the matter of arranging for Ieharu's successor, Tanuma was again showered with tokens of esteem, sets of jifuku, a sword from the Shogun's own hand, and an additional 10,000 koku located in the district of Hine in Izumi province.

Tanuma reached the high point of his influence in the Tokugawa government with the appointment of his son, Mototomo, to the post of Junior Councilor. The younger Tanuma had been rising steadily "in the shadow of his father." Born in 1749, he received his first court rank and title, Yamato-no-kami, in 1767 (Meiwa 4. 12. 16). Two years later, he was assigned a seat in the Hall of Geese [44] and given the honor of being preceded by two spear bearers (6. 9. 1).[45]

Mototomo's title was changed to Harima-no-kami in 1781 (Temmei 1. 5. 11) and, the next year (2. 11. 15), to Yamashiro-no-kami. Meanwhile he had been advanced to the post of Master of Shogunal Ceremony [46] (1. 12. 15). In 1783 (3. 11. 1), he was named Junior Councilor, with a salary of 5000 hyō.[47] At the same time he began construction of his own official mansion.

Father and son now were in a position to exercise a preponderance of power in shogunal affairs, but not for long. Before half a year had passed (4. 3. 24), the young Tanuma had been assassinated by an infuriated castle guard, and the Tanuma star had begun its fall. The loss of an able son who might have carried on the Tanuma name was naturally a severe blow to the aging Okitsugu. Furthermore the circumstances surrounding the assassination greatly discredited the elder Tanuma in the eyes of the country. Happily the incident did not alter his status with the Shogun, who in 1785 (5. 1. 29) bestowed upon his favorite a final increase in revenue amounting to 10,000 koku [48] in the provinces of Kawachi, Mikawa, and Tōtomi.

The days of Tanuma's ascendancy, however, were numbered. Ieharu's health was deteriorating, and Matsudaira Sadanobu, the man who was to be Tanuma's undoing, had already made his way into the Tokugawa councils.[49] In the summer of 1786 the Shogun fell ill. The efforts of the Attendant Physicians proved ineffectual, and he died after a few months of illness (Temmei 6. 8. 20). With his passing Tanuma lost his chief support. Within a matter of hours the entire political picture had been altered. The heads of the Three Houses, seizing the opportunity offered by the accession of a minor Shogun, worked through their powers of guardianship to undo Tanuma's position. Seven days after the Shogun's death, Tanuma was obliged to hand in his resignation (6. 8. 27). He was hastily stripped of his offices and reduced to a seat in the Hall of the Geese. Three months later (6. intercalary 10.5), he was deprived of the 20,000 koku most recently granted him by Ieharu and excluded from holding office of any kind. His chief Edo residence [50] and his Osaka storehouses [51] were taken from him. A year later (7. 10. 2) his domain was entirely confiscated and his castle demolished. His family was spared reduction below the status of daimyo, however, by the allotment of 10,000 koku in the remote provinces of Mutsu and Echigo. These were assigned to Tanuma's grandson, and heir. He, himself, was ordered into retirement in his lower residence, and it was there that he died in 1788 (8. 7. 24) at the age of 69.[52] He was buried at the family temple of Shōrinji, in the Komagome district of Edo.

2. THE INNER PATH TO POLITICAL ASCENDANCY

Such is the career of Tanuma Okitsugu as described in the official Tokugawa histories and genealogies. The account is understandably sketchy, and, while it provides a chronological framework of his life as an official, it leaves unanswered numerous fundamental problems of interpretation. There is no indication, in the first place, of how his career compared with other Tokugawa officials. Are we to assume that his rise to high office was the normal expectancy of a large number of the Shogun's retainers, or was Tanuma's career unusual? There is no explanation, moreover, of how Tanuma succeeded in gaining his ascendancy over the Shogun, or what other sources of power he utilized to strengthen his hand. Nor are we told of the effects of Tanuma's rise upon Edo officialdom or on the policies of the Shogun's government. To answer such questions we must expand the horizon of our investigation to include material outside the limited official sources, to take into account the diaries, the miscellanies, and the variety of other semi-historical literature which flowed in such abundance from the brushes of Tanuma's contemporaries.[53]

Tanuma's career was unquestionably an exceptional one. Yet one must realize that it was accomplished within the framework of the Tokugawa bureaucratic system. At no point in his career did Tanuma radically depart from precedent in accepting promotions to higher posts.[54] In each case there was a well-worn path from the lower to the higher office. From Page to Rank Equivalent to Captain of the Inner Guard, from Chamberlain to Grand Chamberlain, from Grand Chamberlain to Rank Equivalent to Senior Councilor, no single step was considered unusual. Furthermore, along the way, Tanuma's landholdings were adjusted to each new official level. Thus, neither the path which Tanuma followed nor the individual steps he took were out of the ordinary. The extraordinary feature of his career derives not from these separate increments but from the total distance he traveled and the speed with which he rose.

Tanuma had few rivals when it came to the total span within

the Edo bureaucracy traversed during one lifetime. The most comparable figure in Tokugawa history undoubtedly was the notorious Yanagizawa Yoshiyasu (1658–1714),[55] who set the precedent for the leap from obscurity to the combined office of Chamberlain and chief Senior Councilor. Actually Yanagizawa considerably surpassed Tanuma in the accumulation of landholdings, for he reached the amazing total of 151,088 koku before his death, nearly three times the highest figure attained by Tanuma. But in comparing these two men we must bear in mind the relative social mobility of the ages in which they lived.

During the time of the Shogun Tsunayoshi (r. 1680–1709), when Yanagizawa was in office, the *On'ei roku*[56] records 110 grants of additional revenue ranging from 3000 to 50,000 koku. Of Yanagizawa's contemporaries, Hotta Masatoshi (1634–1684) rose from 14,000 to 130,000 koku to become Great Councilor; Makino Narisada (1634–1712) rose from 3000 to 73,000 koku in his climb to Grand Chamberlain; Akimoto Takatomo (1647–1714) rose from 15,000 to 60,000 koku. All this is in sharp contrast to the period after Yoshimune, when changes in the status and holdings of daimyo became extremely rare. During the shoguncies of Ieshige and Ieharu (1745–1786), only twenty-nine grants of additional land are mentioned[57] and none of these exceeded 10,000 koku at a time. Ōoka Tadamitsu (1709–1760), the mouthpiece of Ieshige, accumulated a mere 20,000 koku in his lifetime. Mizuno Tadatomo, who was the only other contemporary of Tanuma to make marked advances, reached 30,000 koku from an initial 7000. It is clear, therefore, that Tanuma's rise was accomplished against a greater weight of tradition than in the case of his earlier rivals. His rise from 300 hyō to 57,000 koku was a most remarkable feat in his day.

Tanuma's career becomes all the more spectacular when we consider the low social status from which he began his climb. In this respect he is comparable to Yanagizawa. But what of his own contemporaries? Mizuno Tadatomo came from a family originally of daimyo rank, which had fallen into disgrace only two generations previously and had been reduced to 7000 koku.[58] Ōoka Tadamitsu came from a family with a long history of service to the Tokugawa. In the main branch it had produced the illustrious Tadasuke (1676–1752).[59] The Tanuma family, on the contrary, had scarcely been heard of prior to the time of Okitsugu's father.

There is little doubt that Tanuma Okitsugu was made keenly aware of his low birth in a society where lineage played such an important part. This is brought out quite clearly in various incidents concerning the Tanuma genealogy which culminated in the assassination of Okitsugu's son, Mototomo. Because of the sensational nature of the attack upon Mototomo, and the shadow it cast upon Okitsugu, more has been written about it than of all the other episodes in Tanuma's life.

The Tanuma house, as we have already seen, had originally broken off from the Sano family and for some time had existed as its vassal. Knowledge of this undistinguished family background became more and more embarrassing to Okitsugu as he increased in rank and influence, and he cast about for a way to improve his genealogical standing. Fortunately for him, it happened that the existing head of the Sano family, Sano Zenzaemon Masakoto (1758–1784), was in the Shogun's service as a member of the New Guard. Tanuma presently conceived of a plan to advance his own interests at the expense of this man, who though more distinguished from the genealogical point of view was in a subordinate position within the government. First of all it appears that Tanuma put pressure on the priests of the Sano family shrine in an attempt to have its name changed from that of Sano to Tanuma Daimyōjin.[60] He then proceeded to alter his own genealogy. To accomplish this he requested an opportunity to study the Sano family records which were in Masakoto's possession. This, Sano was extremely reluctant to permit, for to a Tokugawa samurai few things were more valued than his genealogical documents. However, he called together his relatives and put the matter to them. Their considered opinion was that it would be wise to humor such a powerful figure as Tanuma with hopes of later reward. As a result Masakoto parted with his precious genealogy for what he expected to be a brief inspection.

As time went on, however, it became more and more obvious that Tanuma had no intention of returning the documents and that he was using them in order to assert the superiority of the Tanuma line over the Sano. By this time Sano's immediate superior was the newly appointed Junior Councilor, Tanuma Mototomo. Sano several times approached the young Tanuma for the return of the genealogy, at the same time expressing his desire for promotion. When neither was forthcoming he determined to avenge his honor and coolly

planned the dramatic attack in which he mortally wounded Mototomo in the Central Citadel.

From this story we gain considerable understanding of what
Tanuma must have suffered on account of his low birth. By the mid-
Tokugawa period, new daimyo were rarely created, and the high
officers of the shogunate were seldom taken from outside a select
few houses. The weight of tradition and aristocratic feeling was
clearly against a career such as his, and no amount of increased revenue or tampering with genealogies was able to erase from Tanuma
the stigma of being an upstart in society.

How, then, did Tanuma succeed in gaining such political influence? And what were the sources of his power? Obviously there is
no simple answer to these questions, for Tanuma developed a wide
range of possibilities and turned them all to his own advantage. First
of all, however, we must acknowledge his own capabilities and the
determination with which he set about his career. Even Tanuma's
enemies credited him with forcefulness and an ability to handle
people. He knew how to win the confidence of his superiors and to
encourage the good will of his inferiors.[61] It is said that his man-
ners were humble and that he showed no sign of arrogance.[62] But
behind his affable exterior there burned a fiery ambition. Even as a
Captain of the Inner Guard he is reported to have revealed his intention of one day becoming Senior Councilor.[63] In large measure
this combination of natural talent, ambition, and the ability to use
people accounted for Tanuma's brilliant rise.

Thus endowed by nature, Tanuma utilized skillfully every means
within his grasp to further his position. His chief support, and the
one without which his career would have been impossible, was, of
course, the favoritism of the Shogun. It was in the nature of the
Tokugawa system that the Shogun, whether competent or not, was
in possession of unassailable authority within his own government.
Naturally a large portion of his powers were delegated. But at any
moment the Shogun could advance his own ideas or pick favorites
through which he chose to work. Such action on his part could rarely,
if ever, be challenged. To have the complete support of the Shogun
was thus the first step toward gaining control of the Tokugawa government. Tanuma proceeded to secure this support speedily and with
the utmost ingenuity.

By mid-Tokugawa, a dichotomy had grown up between two sets

of officials who were in a position to win the Shogun's confidence. These were the Councilors and the Chamberlains. The struggle between what might be termed the "outer" and "inner" bureaucracy had become particularly acute during the time of Tsunayoshi and had continued with minor skirmishes down to the time of Ieharu. Generally the growth of authority in the hands of the Shogun's Chamberlains has been considered a pernicious development and a sign of political decay. When affairs were managed, as they were meant to be, by the Councilors in the great Business Office, they were handled with a certain impartiality according to established routine and policy. When inordinate power fell into the hands of the Chamberlains, the government took on a more personal aspect. Policy was too easily influenced by a simple word to the Grand Chamberlain, perhaps reinforced by an appropriate gift.

It was not necessarily a weak Shogun, however, who advanced the power of the Chamberlains. Even a strong one, like Yoshimune, was responsible for having taken authority from the Councilors to give to the inner officials. For, in his desire to rule forcefully and directly, he found it more advantageous to use the attendants who accompanied him from Wakayama to go over the heads of the precedent-ridden officials of the Business Office.[64] The result was that by the time of Yoshimune's death the inside route to favoritism was well developed. And since the two Shogun who succeeded him were weak personalities, it was only natural that the officials of the interior should extend their influence within the government.

The story of Ieshige's infirmity of speech is well known. Scarcely able to make himself understood, he carried out his functions as Shogun only through the mediation of those who, by close contact, had learned to interpret for him. In time Ōoka Tadamitsu became the sole mouthpiece and, as such, was able to run the shogunate singlehanded from the post of Grand Chamberlain. It was under this regime that Tanuma obtained his start and observed the techniques of government by the inner bureaucracy.

Ieharu, who succeeded Ieshige, gave promise of becoming a stronger administrator, capable of overcoming the abuses of inner-chamber politics. As a youth he had been the chief delight of Yoshimune, who had personally guided his training. Undoubtedly Ieharu was in possession of a keen mind and a reasonably sturdy body. But it took more than these to rise above the sheltered life of the

Shogun's castle or see beyond its walls of ceremony. As Ieharu came of age, he became more nervous and introverted. He took less and less interest in the affairs of the Business Office and instead retired to the company of his favorite attendants. Under him the inner officials, the Chamberlains, continued their ascendancy over the Councilors.

How Tanuma managed to monopolize the affections of the Shogun can only be surmised. No passion was involved as in the case of Yanagizawa and Ietsuna. Rather, it would seem that the Shogun recognized Tanuma's talents and trusted his ability to carry out the shogunal wishes. It is frequently hinted that Ieharu was duped by his favorite and that the true state of national affairs was kept from him, that Tanuma saw to it that the Shogun busied himself in innocuous pastimes, at archery contests or among his artists.[65] But the true state of affairs between Ieharu and Okitsugu will probably never be known. For whatever reason he had, the Shogun steadfastly stood by Tanuma up to the time of his own death.

The stages in Tanuma's rise in the Shogun's estimation are not clearly marked but can be inferred from the record of his promotions. The indications are, as already stated, that the good impression he had made on Ieshige was carried over to Ieharu. At the time of the young Shogun's accession, however, the chief of the inner officials was the Grand Chamberlain, Itakura Katsukiyo (1706–1780).[66] This man was considered a stabilizing influence in the affairs of government, having had experience in the offices of Master of Shogunal Ceremonies, Junior Councilor, and Superintendent of Temples and Shrines. The majority of his forty odd years of service had been spent under the Shogun Yoshimune. In 1767, however, Itakura was promoted to the post of Senior Councilor attached to the Heir Apparent and was replaced as Grand Chamberlain by Tanuma. There is little question that from this date Tanuma was the chief figure in the inner group around the Shogun. Meanwhile he had already begun to assert his influence over the outer officials of the Business Office.

From all indications Ieharu's first Senior Councilors were a strong-minded group. This was especially true of the two ranking members, Matsudaira Takemoto (1713–1779) [67] and Akimoto Suketomo (1717–1775),[68] who had both held office under Yoshimune. Matsudaira Takemoto, in particular, had proved a strong legacy from Yoshimune and had stood up to shogunal favorites such as Ōoka Tadamitsu on matters of policy. Several tales have come down to us which indicate Takemoto's integrity. The story of his refusal to curry favor with Ōoka Tadamitsu is well told by Titsingh.[69] Another relates how on one occasion Takemoto was approached by flattering Tokugawa officials who pointed out the poor quality of the Matsudaira domain and suggested that he have it exchanged for another of equal assessment but better quality. Takemoto stoutly refused on the grounds that he could not give up a domain which had been the hereditary possession of his family for so many generations no matter how meager its productive capacity.[70] Takemoto held the position of Senior Councilor for thirty-four years and in that time he received only 7000 koku of additional land.[71]

During the early years of Ieharu's administration, Takemoto stood out as a moral stronghold. The Shogun, while holding him in no special favor, nevertheless was constrained to respect the aged Councilor, and when it came to placing a charge over his heir, Ieharu chose Takemoto for the task. Tanuma too was forced to respect, perhaps even fear, this man. There is good evidence for believing that Takemoto managed to keep a restraining hand on Tanuma, and, while he lived, he thwarted Tanuma's plans for his son's advancement.[72]

The other ranking Councilor, Akimoto, appears to have been no less resolute in his integrity but somewhat less effectual in his ability to influence the Shogun. It is related that one day shortly after Tanuma's appointment to Chamberlain with concurrent duties on the Supreme Court of Justice, the two men came face to face in one of the castle corridors. Tanuma failed to salute his superior, the Senior Councilor. Akimoto made an immediate issue of the incident. But, in the ensuing contest for the support of the Shogun, Akimoto was no match for Tanuma, and he was eventually obliged to tender his resignation.[73]

We have in this incident some indication of the influence which Tanuma was able to exert from his place of vantage near the Shogun. Akimoto appeared keenly aware of the growing power of the inner officials, and his clash with Tanuma was apparently a deliberate attempt to bring the problem to a showdown. "If I had not brought Okitsugu to task for his disrespect," he is reported to have explained to his associates, "then there is reason to fear that his attitude would have become habitual. Were this to happen, then my office would eventually lose its prestige. I represent but a single life; the office of Senior Councilor is a thing of a hundred generations. How then could I fear the Shogun's favorite when it was a question of the honor of my office?" [74] But his courageous stand against Tanuma was of little avail.

Akimoto retired from the Senior Council in 1764; Takemoto continued until his death in 1779.[75] But how effectively he asserted his presence in his declining years is open to question. Certainly after 1769 when Tanuma combined the posts of Grand Chamberlain and Rank Equivalent to Senior Councilor, Takemoto's ability to effect policy was sharply curtailed. At any rate, following his death, Tanuma's complete ascendancy in the Business Office was assured. The majority of the Senior Councilors were indebted to Tanuma personally in one way or another. Takemoto's successor as ranking Senior Councilor, Matsudaira Terutaka (1725–1781),[76] for instance, received a 10,000-koku increase of domain only a few months after Takemoto's death as a direct result of his approaches to Tanuma.[77] Terutaka's successor as chief of the Senior Councilors, Matsudaira Yasufuku (1719–1789),[78] was even more involved, for he had given one of his daughters in marriage to Tanuma's son, Mototomo. He had furthermore been restored to his old family domain and later had received an increase of 10,000 koku through Tanuma's good offices.[79]

As for new additions to the Senior Council, these were for all intents and purposes Tanuma appointees. We get some idea of the low estate to which the outer posts had fallen from the story surrounding Ii Naoyuki's (1729–1789) [80] appointment to Great Councilor in 1784. It is quite obvious that the assignment need never have been made. The Shogun was forty-seven years old, and no government emergency threatened. But Ii was anxious to have the prestige of high office, and, if we may believe the contemporary rumor, he had himself elevated by bribing Tanuma with several thousand pieces of gold. By rights the Great Councilor should hold supreme authority in shogunal affairs. But Ii was so clearly a figurehead that it is reported that he deferred to Tanuma publicly by walking abreast of him, rather than ahead, as was proper when leaving the audience hall.[81] Thus by the middle of Ieharu's shoguncy the Councilors had been reduced to complete subservience by the Shogun's favorite. By monopolizing access to the sources of power and the fountainhead of posts and honors, Tanuma had gained unquestioned supremacy within the higher councils of the Tokugawa government.

But Tanuma was not the kind to limit his backing to a single source, even though it was the Shogun. As has been pointed out, he rose to the top in the face of tremendous opposition directed not only against him as an upstart official but against the new ideas he represented. The favoritism of the Shogun was hardly sufficient to guarantee the smooth execution of policy in a bureaucracy so compartmentalized as that of the Tokugawa. The cultivation of a wider range of influence within the shogunate was therefore essential.[82]

First of all, Tanuma was well aware of the importance of the women's apartments. We find him, therefore, through the clever use of gifts and flattery, attempting to ingratiate himself with its inmates. The political status of the Great Interior naturally varied greatly with each Shogun. In Yoshimune's time it had been severely reduced in size and stripped of its extra-legal powers, but by the time of Ieharu the Shogun's women had again become a power to contend with in the inner politics of the shogunate. Their hold on the Shogun's affection, their close attendance to his person, together with the independent status enjoyed by the Shogun's consorts allowed the Great Interior to prosper as a back room clearinghouse for favors to and petitions from the daimyo and bakufu officials.[83] The importance of the inner apartments to Tanuma's form of politics is indicated by the great lengths to which he went to win its favor.

Tanuma's chief opponent in the Great Interior was the Shogun's secondary consort, Ochio-no-kata, mother of Ieharu's ill-fated only son. It is said that Tanuma took his second wife from among Ochio-no-kata's close associates in hopes of winning the latter's good will. Later he had his wife frequent the female apartments with gifts for Ochio-no-kata.[84] Apparently this had little effect upon her. Her continued enmity was a constant source of annoyance to Tanuma and was to prove most costly to him many years later. For it was her accusation that he had poisoned the Shogun, Ieharu, that became the opening through which his enemies secured his downfall. On the other hand, among the other women of the Great Interior, Tanuma did succeed in building up a strong following. Their loyalty was demonstrated in the early days of his deepest disgrace when a group of female attendants, headed by the lady Ōsaki, petitioned Matsudaira Sadanobu for Tanuma's reinstatement.[85]

Aside from the Great Interior, direct political opposition to Tanuma could come from but two sources, namely from the Shogun-to-be and, in the event of a succession dispute, from the collateral branches of the Tokugawa. In these quarters Tanuma's success was not of the greatest. Ieharu's heir was born in 1763 and three years later was set up in the Western Citadel. There is no indication that Tanuma was able to exert his authority over this child. In fact rumor has it that, as the boy grew up, he gave signs of great ability and independence of mind and that Tanuma lived in fear of the day when he should become Shogun. Then one day in 1779 (An'ei 8. 2. 21), Iemoto suddenly became violently ill while on a hunting trip and died three days later. The Tokugawa official sources are extremely vague about Iemoto's illness, but it is clear that the suddenness of his death excited a good deal of conjecture both in and out of official circles. It was extensively rumored that Tanuma had had a hand in the matter, the supposition being that he had had the young boy poisoned.[86] Irrespective of the truth of this rumor, we cannot overlook the fact that Iemoto's elimination was of decided benefit to Tanuma and that the next settlement for the succession was clearly contrived to improve Tanuma's position. It is more than coincidence that the commission headed by Tanuma should have overlooked mature candidates from the other collateral houses [87] and decided upon an eight-year-old boy from the one house among the Tokugawa branches into which Tanuma influence had penetrated. This was Hitotsubashi Ienari, later to become the Eleventh Shogun.[88]

Tanuma went a step farther in extending his hold over the new heir by contriving to have his choice accepted for the boy's consort. This again was made possible through a fortunate coincidence. In 1776 (An'ei 5. 7. 19), Tanuma arranged the betrothal of the daughter of the great Outside Lord, Shimazu Shigehide (1745–1833), to the young Hitotsubashi Ienari. When a few years later the boy was selected to become Heir Apparent, considerable pressure was exerted by the Three Houses to break off the engagement.[89] It was their argument that it would be extremely inappropriate to have a Shogun married to the daughter of an Outside Lord. But through Tanuma's efforts the marriage was consummated as scheduled in 1781 (Temmei

1. 9. 22).[90] It is said that Tanuma earned the undying gratitude of
the Shimazu Daimyo by this action and as a token was presented
with a large model of a boat executed in pure silver.[91]

Such interference in the innermost affairs of the Tokugawa
family inevitably won for Tanuma the enmity of the Collaterals,
especially that of the Three Houses. Undoubtedly the senior Collaterals were the first to resent Tanuma's domination over the Shogun, and their opposition grew with each step he made. Their hos-
tility was the chief flaw in his attempted monopoly of shogunal power
and the ultimate cause of his fall once his protector, Ieharu, was
gone. A sidelight is shed upon this problem by yet another unsub-
stantiated story which describes at great length Tanuma's attempt
to eliminate by poisoning the chief of the Owari household, at the
time one of the strongest members of the Three Houses.[92] No doubt,
while this story itself is not to be accepted, it does reveal the strained
state of affairs between Tanuma and the senior Collaterals.

Failing any marked success in his dealings with the Tokugawa
Collaterals, Tanuma seems to have set about cultivating the support
of other powerful daimyo, both Outside Lords and Hereditary Vassals, in an attempt to extend his backing.[93] The indebtedness of the
Shimazu house to Tanuma has already been mentioned. Previous
to this the Date house sought Tanuma's help in securing the title of
Middle Commander of the Guards for its chief, Shigemura. The correspondence for this bit of inside manipulation exists today in the
published documents of the Date house and offers a vivid glimpse
into the dubious channels through which favors were secured.[94] In
this instance Tanuma as Chamberlain was able to accomplish for
Date what the Senior Councilor Matsudaira Terutaka had failed to
do.[95] It was this ability to do favors by securing the ear of the Shogun that gave Tanuma his great opportunity to ingratiate himself
with the other daimyo.

Yet another method of broadening his influence was through
the skillful disposition of the members of his own family. This was
done with an eye both to bettering his position within the administration and improving his social prestige. Tanuma's daughters were
married into the best of daimyo houses and secured marriage alliances
for him with Nishio Tadayuki (1763–1801),[96] Ii Naoaki,[97] Ōoka
Tadayoshi, and Hijikata Katsutoshi.[98] His first son received the
daughter of Matsudaira Yasutomi in marriage, while his other sons

were all adopted as heirs of other houses. One was taken by Mizuno Tadatomo, another by Hijikata, and a third by Kuki Takasada (1729–1780).[99] These were, for the most part, alliances above Tanuma's official and social status and hence added to his prestige officially, as in the case of the union with the Senior Councilor Matsudaira Yasutomi, and socially, as in the union with Ii.

Still other members of the Tanuma family entered the Tokugawa officialdom in strategic locations. Tanuma's first brother, Okinobu, entered the service of the Hitotsubashi house early in his career and eventually became one of its councilors. This man's son, Okimune (1738–1793), was attached to the service of Iemoto, the newly born heir to the Shogun, but in no very weighty capacity. The year before Iemoto's death he was transferred to the post of Hitotsubashi-Councilor. In 1781 he was commended for his part in the choice of the new heir apparent and the following year was made Chamberlain attached to the Heir Apparent, a position of considerable influence in the inner circle surrounding the Shogun-to-be. The career of Tanuma's son, Mototomo, has already been outlined. He naturally was the chief hope for the continued prosperity of the Tanuma house. His promotion to Junior Councilor was one of the major triumphs of Okitsugu's career, and his assassination hurt the elder Tanuma in a most vital way.

Aside from such family connections, we find that Tanuma was able to build up an extensive following in key positions within the official ranks of the shogunate. Here it should be noted that, other than the important central posts of the Councilors and Chamberlains, the actual business of administering Tokugawa affairs fell mainly to the revenue-collecting branches of the government. It was upon these offices that Tanuma concentrated. In these posts his appointees were nearly all men, like himself, of low status with little to lose and much to gain. They willingly became his accomplices and formed what has been described as a solid Tanuma faction within the Tokugawa government.

The most distinguished member of this Tanuma faction was Mizuno Tadatomo.[100] An opportunist like Tanuma, he seems chiefly to have desired to restore the fortunes of his house which had come to grief two generations previously, when his grandfather had been reduced from 70,000 to 7000 koku. Tadatomo started his career as a Chamberlain to Ieharu, a post he was given barely a month before the latter became Shogun. From here he and Tanuma rose together. In 1768 (Meiwa 5. 11. 15) Mizuno was made Junior Councilor in charge of financial matters. When he was appointed to Rank Equivalent to Senior Councilor in 1781 he, like Tanuma, retained his duties as Chamberlain. In addition he was made Councilor in sole charge of Tokugawa finances.[101] In 1785 Tadatomo was made regular Senior Councilor and received a final increase in income, which brought his total holdings up to 30,000 koku. For some reason, Mizuno, although clearly a willing participant in Tanuma's regime, did not share in Tanuma's downfall. Instead, he cleared himself of his association with Tanuma by giving back the latter's son whom he had adopted. He thus managed to continue as Senior Councilor until 1788, after which he retired to less important posts, apparently with little honor lost and no reduction in domain. His son was able to follow in his foosteps and eventually became a Senior Councilor with 50,000 koku income.

One less fortunate than Mizuno was Inaba Masaakira (1723–1793).[102] He, like Tanuma, came from a *kenin* house of low rank and rose through the inner offices, first in Ieshige's service and then as one of Ieharu's Chamberlains. In 1781 he was raised to the status of daimyo. What his exact position was in the Tanuma faction is hard to determine, but he seems to have played an important enough role to be considered worth purging along with Tanuma. In 1786, sharing his superior's fate, he was expelled from office and ordered into retirement, losing the 3000 koku he had received just before Ieharu's death.

In the sensitive revenue handling branches of the shogunate, four Superintendents of Finance [103] were closely linked with Tanuma. Of these, Kawai Hisataka (1725–1775) [104] became Comptroller of Finance [105] in 1765 and Superintendent in 1771. Matsumoto Hidemochi (died 1797) [106] began as a mere 100-hyō underofficial in the office of Superintendent of Finance. By 1772 he was Comptroller. Seven years later he became Superintendent, and in 1782 was given the concurrent post of Tayasu-Councilor. By this time his basic income had been augmented to 500 koku, while the stipends from his offices brought him 5000 koku a year. During his career he is said to have allied himself quite openly with Tanuma. At any rate his fate was closely tied to that of his superior, for in 1786 he lost his offices and his fief was cut in half. The following year he was reduced to

150 koku and ordered into house confinement on a charge of dishonest tax collecting. Another who shared Tanuma's fall was Akai Tadaakira (died 1790) [107] who rose to Superintendent of Finance in 1782 from the office of Kyoto City Magistrate. In 1787, his fief was reduced by half on the same charge of dishonesty. The final member of this group, Kuze Hirotami,[108] was a Bannerman of 3000 koku. Appointed Superintendent of Construction and Repairs in 1772, he later became Uraga Magistrate [109] and three years later Nagasaki Magistrate.[110] It was here that he came in contact with the Dutch factor, Isaac Titsingh, and demonstrated that remarkable open-mindedness which so impressed the Dutchman.[111] In 1784 he was shifted to Superintendent of Finance, and, somehow managing to weather the purges of 1786, he stayed on to perform many valuable services in the realm of public works and national defense for Tanuma's successor and bitter opponent, Matsudaira Sadanobu.

Doubtless there were hosts of other petty officials who should be counted as Tanuma men, but the above facts when brought together into a single frame will suffice to indicate how Tanuma was able to build up his control of Tokugawa affairs. If we take the year 1783 as the high point of his career, we are able to put together a remarkable picture of the way in which his influence permeated the government. He himself, the Shogun's favorite, combined the duties of Senior Councilor and Grand Chamberlain, while Mizuno Tadatomo, his relative through adoption, was only one step below him as Grand Chamberlain and Rank Equivalent to Senior Councilor with complete authority over shogunal finances. The other members of the Senior Council were, for the most part, incapable of acting against Tanuma's wishes. Tanuma's son was a Junior Councilor; his nephew attended the Heir Apparent, while the latter's father-in-law, Shimazu Shigehide, perhaps the most powerful of the Outside Lords, was personally indebted to Tanuma. In the inner circles of the castle the Shogun's women, with but one significant exception, were friendly to Tanuma. In the important offices of Superintendent of Finance and Nagasaki Magistrate, Tanuma had willing accomplices. Finally outside the shogunate, within the feudal nobility at large, many daimyo were allied or indebted to him.

No wonder then that Tanuma was looked upon with awe and envy. His monopoly of the means of official advancement and shogunal favors meant that the whole Tokugawa officialdom was forced to work through him, presenting to him their requests and petitions. If a man such as Ii Naoyuki found the route to high office through Tanuma, how much more did minor office seekers whose appointments required only a favorable word in the routine meetings of the Councilors. The scenes enacted each day before the Tanuma residence became one of the favorite subjects of contemporary Tokugawa writers. If we are to believe their accounts, great throngs of petitioners and well-wishers constantly frequented his door until the street before his gates resembled a busy city thoroughfare.

One extremely revealing description of the Tanuma mansion has been left us by a reliable diarist, Matsuura Kiyo, the Daimyo of Hirado. Matsuura was in his twenties when he found it necessary to make a call on Tanuma, then at the height of his power. Entering the main reception hall to wait for an interview, he found the room full with some thirty persons seated in ten rows. But even these were not all the visitors that day, for in the next room there were several more rows and beyond them row upon row of overflow. Matsuura was unable to ascertain how many rooms Tanuma had in all, but it was obvious to him that the whole residence was built on a grandiose scale. Matsuura was greatly incensed by the way the interview went. The room being so crowded, Tanuma was unable to keep a customarily decorous distance between himself and his guests, but faced them from about three feet away. Even Tanuma's retainers had accustomed themselves to what Matsuura felt was an officious treatment of their superiors.[112]

Needless to say these many callers did not come empty-handed to present their petitions. There was the usual gift presented quietly to some underling upon arrival as was customary throughout the Tokugawa officialdom. The flood of treasure which flowed in on Tanuma from this source has laid him open to the accusation of corruption and bribe-taking. But in a bureaucratic system where official preferment depended so often on the whim or favor of a superior, the practice of gift-giving had been developed to a fine art. Under such circumstances the dividing line between protocol and bribery was hard to define. By custom, presents went with each request for nomination to office or upon receipt of office, as regular tokens of appreciation. Naturally there were those who decried such practices, and frequent shogunal regulations were issued to curb their abuse. Yet there were others who even rationalized the acceptance of gifts by Tokugawa officials as a form of service to the Shogun, inasmuch as it absorbed from the daimyo their surplus wealth and lessened their ability to contemplate rebellion.

It is only natural, therefore, that Tanuma's control over the channels of preferment should have brought to him without solicitation a rich harvest of gifts.[113] That Tanuma actually cultivated this source of income, however, and thus abused the practice is one of the undeniably ugly sides of his life. When appointment to important office was decided by the size of gifts rather than the caliber of the candidates, we are coming dangerously close to outright sale of office.[114] Tanuma himself is recorded as saying, "Gold and silver are treasures more precious than life itself. If a person bring this treasure with an expression of his desire to serve in some public capacity, I can be assured that he is serious in his desire. A man's strength of desire will be apparent in the size of his gift." [115]

Countless stories are in existence which tell of the form which gifts to Tanuma took. The crowds of favor-seekers and hangers-on apparently were constantly on the alert to discover ways of tickling Tanuma's fancy and thus gaining special recognition for themselves. Since he was a man of unrefined, ostentatious tastes, the search was mainly for novelty objects, rarities from abroad, or animals which chanced to have been born on days he considered lucky.

How much wealth Tanuma accumulated during his life in high office is impossible for us to ascertain. Most accounts deal only in vague superlatives and give us very little concrete information as to his nonofficial income.[116] We know, for instance, that his Edo mansions were lavishly appointed. The apartments of one of his female favorites were built in the midst of an extensive garden, the house itself described as having ceilings set with glass through which goldfish could be seen swimming.[117] The warehouses set up at Osaka by Tanuma are said to have been one of the sights of the city.[118] Besides his official mansions, it is also known that Tanuma acquired a vast amount of real estate, some of which was put into the names of others.

Thus, our final estimate of the sources of Tanuma's political power must take into consideration the economic resources at his disposal. Just as he himself was influenced by the gifts which accompanied the petitions he received, so he in turn was able to put these gifts to use and influence others. Tanuma's economic strength derived not merely from the gifts which came his way but from his close association with the business world and the commerce-made wealth of merchant capitalists. It was frequently claimed by Tanuma's contemporaries that he profited not only from bribes but from the graft which he took from the shogunal mines or from foreign trade and government monopolies. Of this there is no direct proof, but there is little question that his opportunities of illicit gain were enormous.

The question of corruption is thus an inescapable problem with respect to Tanuma's public career. Since it laid him open to accusations he could not easily counter, it has served to cloud the judgment of history with respect to him. At best Tanuma was a controversial figure. In his own day he was both feared and hated. His enemies were legion, though they seldom appeared in the open. That a man of such low birth should make his way so rapidly to a place of power beside the Shogun was bitterly resented by those of long hereditary status in the Tokugawa hierarchy. Such men looked with suspicion on the influx into the shogunate of new personnel who shared with Tanuma his low birth and his lack of concern for the sacred precepts inherited from the Tokugawa ancestors. They watched with concern the spread of favoritism and the growth of cliques which short-circuited the customary, though more cumbersome, machinery of government. And they pounced enthusiastically upon the signs of corruption which gave them the chance of open attack.

The facts of Tanuma's meteoric rise to power are abundantly clear. But whether this was accomplished dishonestly and brought with it a moral degeneration of the bakufu or whether it created an environment conducive to healthy reform is the central problem of interpretation in our analysis of Tanuma's historical role. The answer must be looked for in a still broader consideration of the events which accompanied Tanuma's emergence to power and of the domestic and foreign policies adopted by the shogunate during his period of ascendancy.

CHAPTER IV

Filling the Tokugawa Coffers

I. THE GROWTH OF ECONOMIC REALISM

Having won nearly undisputed supremacy within the Tokugawa administration, Tanuma Okitsugu found himself in a position to influence profoundly the formation of bakufu policy. His personality set the temper of Edo officialdom, and his appointees directed the activities of key offices within the shogunate. Coming to power as he did, through the inner ranks of the shogunal bureaucracy where the ability to handle men was all important, Tanuma had little occasion to concern himself with abstract theories of government. His rapid rise from the lower ranks of the samurai class into the highest Tokugawa councils was hardly calculated to develop in him the high sense of caste and honor or the extreme consciousness of precedent and protocol which characterized the typical Tokugawa official.[1] As a result Tanuma's approach to government was largely empirical and his methods more practical than orthodox. It was in large measure this lack of orthodoxy which so aroused his conservative opponents within the bakufu.

One of the most common accusations brought against Tanuma was that he was unschooled, and hence unfit for a position of administrative responsibility.[2] Admittedly Tanuma was no scholar in the traditional Confucian sense. Yet it can hardly be maintained that he was out of all contact with the intellectual currents of his day or that he had no theoretical basis for justifying the course of action which he adopted. While there is an unfortunate scarcity of material relating to Tanuma's intellectual life, there is evidence to show that he was directly influenced by the thinking of at least two active writers of the day. These men, Seki Shōsō (d. 1801)[3] and Hiraga Gennai (1729–1779),[4] were both distinguished by their unorthodox views. Seki, though coming from a family of Confucian scholars, nevertheless laid great stress on the material well-being of the warrior class and believed that economic security must come before honor and military discipline. Hiraga, a man of many facets, a botanist, a student of Western learning, and an engineering adventurer, was obsessed with the idea of increasing the productivity of his country. During his active life he energetically studied means of improving Japan's fields and mines so as to provide the additional revenue needed to help the samurai out of his economic dilemma.

Such men may well have stimulated Tanuma's thinking and played a part in influencing his policy. But it must be understood that the theories they propounded were not necessarily novel to them alone. Rather, Seki Shōsō and Hiraga Gennai represented two facets of a trend towards economic realism which was gaining currency in the years following the failure of Yoshimune's reform. These years of political disillusionment and economic crisis had brought in their wake a profound intellectual ferment. New ideas, new political and economic formulae, had begun to challenge the accepted theories of government, whose efficacy had been brought into question. By the Tanuma age a distinct rivalry had grown up between two groups of political theorists.[5] The fundamentalists, who continued to adhere to the strict Confucian interpretation of society, were to remain the dominant school of thought in Tokugawa Japan and to retain the mark of orthodoxy. But they were brought increasingly into competition by more hard-headed empiricists who began with the problems of the day and attempted to discover, sometimes in ways considerably at variance with accepted tradition, realistic solutions to them. As we shall see, this division was fundamental to our evaluation of Tanuma's state policies.

The hold which Chinese political theory had on the minds of the Tokugawa Japanese is one of the unique features of the late feudal period. The popularity of Confucianism cannot be explained by the fact of official encouragement alone. The seed of Confucianism had been planted in Japan many centuries before the advent of Ieyasu.[6] But the conditions proper to its growth awaited the appearance of the bureaucratic Edo regime and the rigidly stratified Tokugawa caste system. Confucianism in China was preëminently the philosophy of the bureaucratic class.[7] Its theorists were at the same time men of affairs, concerned with problems of society and government. In practical application Confucianism envisaged a strict regimentation of society according to a class hierarchy derived originally from feudalistic status relationships. Above all it exalted those virtues which would most effectively secure the continuance of social stability. As Confucianism evolved during twelfth century, under the Sung School of philosophers, it fitted the earthly life and man's social virtues into an all-embracing cosmology in which the human order was given universal validity, and its strict maintenance was made a matter of religious significance.

The points of coincidence of such a system of thought with the spirit of the Tokugawa unification are not hard to see. When the Tokugawa leaders, the daimyo and their samurai adherents, laid down their arms and began to seek moral and philosophical justification for the political structure which they had created by force, Confucianism answered their need perfectly. From the early years of the Tokugawa period Japan's rulers and her political and economic theorists looked to the Confucian texts for inspiration.

One of the peculiar features of the type of thinking which emanated from this application of Confucian theory to the Japanese scene was that it conceived of the entire society in its political, social, and economic phases as being an organic whole. The modern Sino-Japanese word for economics (*keizai*) referred in these times to a broad system of political economy which concerned itself with the entire range of human activity and linked all life together into a neat chain of cause and effect. Beginning with the weighty problems of national economy, it related them finally to the personal morality of the ruler and his people.[8] To thinkers brought up in this tradition the failure of the agricultural season was as much a matter of the general moral decay of society as it was a consequence of consecutive months of drought. And the condition of society in turn was believed to reflect the private virtue of the sovereign.

Under the Confucian system the Shogun and the entire ruling class, the daimyo and samurai, were charged with the moral responsibility to lead society by good example. The selfless loyalty of the warrior to his lord and his life of strict propriety acted as the keystone of a well-ordered social structure. The fighting man, as a member of the governing class, was above all expected to maintain his virtue and sense of dignity. But dignity without visible means of support was a hollow façade. It was realized that the warrior's position at the apex of society could be maintained only if he stood at the top of the economic pyramid as well. And so he was obliged to look to his material well-being and to the productive capacity of the community over which he stood as guardian.

The economic policy of the Tokugawa Confucian theorists has sometimes been likened to that of the eighteenth-century European Physiocrats. Deriving their thought from conditions as they existed in mid-seventeenth-century Japan and from the imported tenets of Confucianism, they conceived of an ideal economy which was purely agrarian, a static organism which largely ignored the possibilities of expansion through trade and commerce. They accepted the concept that the ideal situation was for the producers to be many and the consumers few, for production to be encouraged and consumption curtailed.[9]

A necessary accompaniment of this strictly agrarian economy was the need for frugality. If the warrior was to maintain himself, he must curtail his desires and live within his means. Frugality was made a virtue along with feudal loyalty. Luxury and ostentation were not merely bad taste but positive evils. In this way the Tokugawa Confucian theorists brought themselves back to their starting point of personal virtue. Frugality, as a moral quality, rested on the personal character of the individual samurai and the Shogun. A morally good society would be, by definition, healthy and well fed.

The Confucian fundamentalist, as he met the new conditions thrown up by changes in the economic and social structure, sought to apply these abstract ideas drawn from the classics. Problems of production and demand or of the penetration of commercial economy into a closed agrarian system were attacked with well-worn concepts of the need for moral regeneration or for frugality. Japanese thinkers grounded in the tenets of Confucianism generally advocated a policy which would turn back the clock to the simple, ideal economy of former days. Two concepts in particular became the trade-marks of the fundamentalist approach. The first, a back-to-the-land policy (*dochaku ron*), advocated the relocation of the samurai out of the cities and back to the villages. There they could live on their estates in natural simplicity close to the source of production and free from the demands and temptations of city life. The second, a theory which argued the uselessness of the merchant (*shōnin muyō ron*),[10] stressed the disruptive influence of the merchant on Tokugawa society and looked for ways to eliminate or suppress the entire class.

Such views although highly unrealistic, especially when applied to the conditions of late Tokugawa Japan, nevertheless remained the accepted ideal for most of the Tokugawa administrators. Rule by moral injunction and emphasis on the agrarian economy continued to be synonymous with good government. And it was generally in the name of such principles that reform movements were undertaken.

It is in this context that the so-called empirists appear unorthodox. Less concerned with the problems of philosophical rationalization, these men started with the facts and looked for practical solutions. While they seldom threw over completely the philosophy or the logic of Confucianism, they were not afraid to advocate new or even novel policies. Their writings, which appear largely in the form of memorials to the authorities, are some of the most significant documents at our disposal for the study of Tokugawa political economy.[11]

The chief issue over which the two schools of thought differed was revealed in their conflicting attitudes toward money economy and the merchant class. The realists faced the growing commercialization of Japanese economy frankly and urged the authorities to adjust to it, not deny it.[12] They argued that the warrior class could not forever stand aloof from financial matters and that after 1700 the natural economy which the Confucianists envisaged was no longer a possibility. One of the pioneer thinkers of this persuasion, Dazai Shundai (1680–1747),[13] called for the feudal rulers to look upon money economy as a positive good and to think in terms of capital accumulation. Another, Kaibo Seiryō (1755–1818),[14] argued that the samurai, since he sold his rice for profit, was not so different from the trader. And the merchant was not so different from the samurai, for the profit from his business was in essence a type of salary. These men represent a gradual reorientation in Tokugawa thinking, a realization that trade and usury could be productive and that the ruling interests could profit from the commercial segment of their economy.

The belief that the warrior could without degrading himself participate in the field of business grew rapidly after the mid-Tokugawa period and gave rise to two controversial lines of argument which were the chief labels of the empiricists. One was a policy of state enterprise (*kokka keiei ron*) which urged the government to encourage the production of capital wealth and to use its political power to set up state enterprises and monopoly organizations.[15] The other, an anti-exclusion pro-trade policy (*kaikoku bōeki ron*), called for the revival of foreign trade as a means of bringing wealth to Japan. This second line of argument, coming as it did squarely up against the time-honored exclusion policy, aroused bitter opposition. But the policy of state sponsored trade and industry was followed to an increasing degree by the shogunate and the various daimyo in their attempts to revive their financial strength.[16]

Despite his strong feudalistic ethics, Yoshimune did much to turn the thinking of the country toward a more money-conscious solution of its economic problems. During his shoguncy the government entered into the rice market and by calculated storage, sale, and even destruction attempted to regulate the price of rice to benefit the samurai. To fill the Tokugawa coffers, the Shogun licensed commercial monopolies and levied new taxes. He regulated trade with the Dutch and Chinese to Japan's benefit and in many other ways encouraged commerce and industry.

In Yoshimune's program, however, this emphasis on mercantile enterprise was balanced by his strong insistence on feudal-agrarian principles and on the moral values of military discipline and frugality. By a life of simplicity and uprightness the Shogun himself attempted to set an example for the people. But lest they fail to comprehend this example, he showered them with moral exhortations. Neither example nor injunction, however, could arrest the trend of the times. After his death the country inherited his interest in money matters but retained little of his rigorous idealism.

Yoshimune's successors, the Ninth and Tenth Shogun, had none of the spiritual stamina required to hold the bastion of feudalism against its opponents and subverters. Moreover it was their misfortune that their administrations were beseiged by some of the worst calamities in recorded Tokugawa history. After 1745, the shogunate again was faced with declining revenues and crushing demands for relief. The momentary improvements of Tokugawa finances brought on by Yoshimune's vigorous reforms was quickly dissipated. The treasury was depleted and the government forced to retrench and to search for new sources of revenue.[17] It was at this critical juncture that Tanuma made his appearance.

It is the claim of Tanuma's numerous critics that the bakufu during the period of his ascendancy was utterly devoid of constructive leadership, that Tanuma was incapable of anything more than schemes for his own aggrandizement. This opinion has become widely accepted. Yet there are those who have refused to deny all possibility of public-mindedness on Tanuma's part and who have seen in his policies a consistent and at times far-reaching statesmanship.[18] Certainly the Tanuma period was one of decisive action on the part of the bakufu. The years from 1765 to 1786 saw the government undertake many vigorous and often courageous programs of economic reconstruction. It is in these measures that we find evidence of a considered policy rather than expediency. Tanuma, probably more than any other administrator in Tokugawa history, was attracted by the mercantilist theories of the realistic school. Under his direction the shogunate, relieved of the feudal restrictions of Yoshimune's days, embarked openly on an effort to shift the emphasis of Tokugawa finances from an agrarian to a commercial base. By land reclamation, currency reform, the multiplication of taxes on monopolies and merchant guilds, and the encouragement of foreign trade, he strove for the financial rehabilitation of his government. His initial successes were noteworthy, but they were also short-lived. Tanuma was eventually overwhelmed by calamity and destroyed by those within the government who adhered to the traditionalist point of view. After his political defeat his policy was completely discredited and his memory darkened for posterity.

2. LAND RECLAMATION

During the Tokugawa period the reclamation of new land (*shinden*) for agricultural purposes was still a feasible means of increasing the area under cultivation and thereby adding to the feudal tax receipts. From the time of its inception, the Edo government encouraged the reclamation of new land. Peasants were frequently subsidized with state funds or exempted from taxes on reclaimed land for various periods of time. In certain instances Tokugawa Deputies were permitted to draw for life 10 per cent of the income from the fields reclaimed in domains under their jurisdiction.[19] It is well known that many daimyo by extensive reclamation had greatly increased the rice production of their domains, though the koku assessment remained at the original figure.[20]

Among the Tokugawa Shogun, the one best known for his vigorous program of reclamation was Yoshimune. His various orders, which after 1722 urged the nation to riparian works of clearance and water control, won for him the name of the "Rice Shogun." Yoshimune's objectives were twofold, to broaden the foundation of government revenue, and to increase the national food supply. He appears to have been successful in both.[21] However, the people of Yoshimune's time discovered that indiscriminate reclamation was not an unmixed blessing. The rapid fall in the price of rice which followed Yoshimune's original order of encouragement showed that too sudden an expansion in the area of cultivation could be harmful.[22] Very often the new projects were injurious to the older fields (*honden*); old water rights were ignored or irrigation systems altered to benefit the new rather than the well-established lands.[23] New fields diverted manpower and fertilizer necessary for the cultivation of the older plots. Furthermore, since reclaimed land was less encumbered with taxes and non-alienation laws, it was more attractive to the peasants, who tended to neglect their former fields in favor of the new.[24] And, finally, the social status of the reclaimer was seen to determine in great measure whether the result was beneficial or detrimental to the ruling interests.

Generally the clearing of new land was undertaken by local peasant communities. Large-scale projects were directed and financed by Tokugawa Deputies or large feudal organizations such as temples or domains. By the mid-Tokugawa period, however, the majority of larger enterprises revealed, in one way or another, the growing financial power of the merchant class. Daimyo, who had the political authority to recruit thousands or even hundreds of thousands of laborers, frequently lacked the capital for wages and equipment and were obliged to seek financial assistance of merchant capitalists. But the merchants did not limit themselves to lending money for government-sponsored projects. Increasingly they themselves went into the reclaiming business and, because of their enterprising nature and their available capital, began to dominate the field.[25] Such activity on their part made possible large-scale landlordism within the framework of feudal tenure and the consequent growth in tenancy.[26] As early as 1680 shogunal edicts forbade merchant participation in the clearing of land. Similar orders were repeated by Yoshimune, but apparently to no avail.[27]

Thus after the middle portion of Yoshimune's shoguncy, the

feudal ruling class began to entertain serious doubts as to the value of land reclamation, especially when undertaken by private contractors. Numerous scholars and officials spoke out about its dangers.[28] Yet, with the steady deterioration of government finances and the constant press of population on the agrarian base, the need for new land continued.[29]

Tanuma, in keeping with his aggressive attitude toward economic problems, brushed aside whatever doubts had been raised and initiated another period of government-sponsored reclamation. In 1777 (An'ei 6. 9. 5), a bakufu order urged all daimyo to undertake riparian projects, and individuals on shogunal domains were encouraged to send in for reclamation licenses.[30] Tanuma's action was essentially a revival of Yoshimune's previous order of 1722. Though we have no indication of what prompted resumption of the program, it would be reasonable to suppose that the series of bad harvests and calamities, which had been plaguing the country since 1771, and the consequent loss of food supply were at the bottom of it. Detailed information concerning the total amount of land reclaimed under this order is lacking, but there is evidence that in the years immediately following 1777 the food shortage was somewhat alleviated, and this must have been due in part to the government policy of encouraging wider production.

Tanuma's reputation in this field of government endeavor was not favorable, however, for his name became linked with three unpopular schemes which gained for him widespread condemnation. The first of these enterprises was aimed at increasing the food supply near Edo by draining and turning into fields two sizable lakes, Imbanuma and Teganuma, which lay some twenty-five miles to the east and northeast of Edo.[31] These lakes had been studied as possible reclamation sites before Tanuma's time. Teganuma had yielded a certain number of new fields as early as 1671, but the complete drainage of the two lakes was yet to be undertaken. Such a plan was suggested in 1724 during the great reclamation drive of Yoshimune, and the shogunate spent 100 ryō subsidizing the effort before it failed.[32] But the idea was not given up. In 1780 two wealthy villagers from the district of Imba sent in a report on the possibilities of digging a ditch from Hirado to Kemigawa to drain off the waters of Imbanuma into Edo Bay. The benefits which they envisioned were, first, a large area of new agricultural land,[33] and second, a canal which would save time and expense in hauling rice into Edo from the north.[34] The drainage of Teganuma was also proposed though it was not connected with the canal. For the actual operation of the project, it was suggested that two great merchants, Tennōji-ya Tōhachirō of Osaka and Hasegawa Shingorō of Edo, be requested to put up the capital.[35]

This scheme apparently took the fancy of two Superintendents of Finance, Matsumoto [36] and Akai, and through them received Tanuma's endorsement. Considerable risk of failure was involved, but these men were the type to take chances. In 1782 (Temmei 2. 2. 20) an official of the financial office was sent to look over the situation, and seven months later work was begun. Bad weather intervened shortly thereafter, and work was abandoned until 1786 (Temmei 6. 2. 11), when it was resumed with renewed vigor. By the sixth month of that year, the ditch from Hirado to Kemigawa was complete, and there remained only the construction of dikes along the course of the canal and of a control dam.[37] But fate struck a second time. For a solid month the heavens sent down a deluge of water which brought to the Kantō area the worst flood in its remembered history. Large sections of the eastern Kantō were inundated. The Tone river went on a rampage, broke over the unfinished dam and washed out the embankments thrown up along the canal. Before the waters subsided most of the labor had been undone. In this instance natural calamity and political change came together, for two months later Tanuma fell into disgrace and the Imbanuma project was called off (6. 9. 24).[38]

The failure of the Imbanuma project was a serious blow to Tanuma's reputation. Yet it is difficult to understand why this should have been. Greater men than he had failed in the same attempt, and the project was so reasonable that attempts were to continue down to the present.[39] Furthermore there was no indication that government funds were squandered by Tanuma. But for whatever reason, the Imbanuma scheme has been added to a long list of purportedly rash projects endorsed by Tanuma and held up as an example of his maladministration.[40]

Another undertaking, for which there were clearer grounds for criticism, involved the filling in of certain low-lying parts of Edo, including sections of the central moat, in order to provide high rental land.[41] Tanuma's opponents claimed, first of all, that he had increased the fire hazard in Edo. But, worse still, this new land close to the Shogun's castle was rented out for the erection of restaurants and bathhouses, many of which carried on illicit prostitution in front of the very eyes of the government. This was one of the projects most bitterly condemned by Matsudaira Sadanobu,[42] and in 1788, after he came to power, he ordered the pleasure houses torn down and the moats redug. In the fourteen years during which the land was leased out, however, the government undoubtedly made a handsome profit from the rentals.

The third project was undertaken ostensibly to provide for the destitute and surplus population of eastern Japan. Essentially it was a program of colonization and land development which contemplated the transplanting of groups of people from the Kantō area to the comparatively uninhabited northern island of Ezo (Hokkaido). Political as well as economic motives were behind the plan, and these will be dealt with at length in a later chapter.[43] But one of the main incentives for opening up Ezo was that it would provide new land for the famine-oppressed people of the area around Edo. The matter came to a head in the spring of 1786 with the return of government inspectors from a tour of Ezo. These men, in conference with the Superintendent of Finance, Matsumoto, presented their findings on the size of the northern island and the possibilities it offered for colonization.[44] Shortly thereafter (Temmei 6. 2. 14), a plan was approved for the transfer to Ezo of over 70,000 members of the pariah class (Eta and Hinin) as pioneer colonists. The chief of the pariahs, Danzaemon, guaranteed to provide this quota. On a subsequent trip to Ezo, the inspector, Sato Genrokurō, was instructed to enter into arrangements with Matsumae, the Daimyo of Ezo, for housing and other necessities.

The Ezo colonization plan progressed this far before it too failed. It was an ambitious project which promised great benefits to all of Japan north of Edo. The opening up of a new land was envisioned, and the trade between it and the Kantō was expected to shift the entire center of economic gravity northward and bring new prosperity to the region above Edo. But, while these dreams were in the air, the sands were running swiftly out. Seven months later Tanuma was out of office, and Matsumoto shared in the fall. The colonization plan was immediately shelved by the conservative Matsudaira Sadanobu.

3. CURRENCY REFORM

One of the most controversial aspects of Tanuma's policy related to the field of currency reform. The monetary measures endorsed by Tanuma have received both praise and violent condemnation. Those who find fault with them describe them as a series of unhealthy debasements,[45] while those who praise them have asserted that Tanuma's finance officials attempted a brilliant reform which, though only partially successful, had far-reaching influence on Tokugawa finances.[46] The existence of such diversity of opinion over so basic an issue is indicative of the present state of knowledge concerning the real facts of Tokugawa monetary history. Despite the fact that a great deal has been written upon it, the subject of currency is undoubtedly one of the least understood aspects of Tokugawa economy. While there are large compendiums filled with detailed information on various issues of coins, their weights, quality, and color,[47] minute transcriptions of financial records [48] and lengthy treatises on the theory of money by contemporary economists,[49] our understanding of the basic principles underlying Tokugawa currency or of how to interpret the available data remains inadequate. It is for this reason that any absolute judgment of Tanuma's currency policy can hardly be made at this time.

The Tokugawa currency system [50] is generally described as a unified tri-metal system in which gold and copper circulated by piece and silver by weight.[51] The ratio of exchange between these metals was set by law upon an absolute gold base. After 1700, silver was generally set at 60 *momme* to the gold ryō and copper at 4 kan to the ryō.[52] In practice, however, the system operated quite differently. Tokugawa currency was far from unified. Nomura Kanetarō, in his provocative article on Tokugawa currency,[53] suggests that it would be more realistic to consider the entire circulating medium of this period, with the exception of paper and the possible exception of copper, as commodity articles rather than unit tokens. This was certainly true in the case of silver. As for gold, it is known that very soon after the middle of the seventeenth century gold coins, because of damage and counterfeiting, no longer circulated as unit pieces, but by weight.

Actually, in the years immediately after their unification of Japan, the Tokugawa did manage to create a single nation-wide system of currency, but as time went on, because of shifts in the economic basis of the country and the damage and debasement of coins, a rapid regression took place. The once unified currency became decentralized. Once the backslipping had begun, the Tokugawa government never recovered complete control. Government edict had little effect upon the exchange rate or the manner in which Japanese merchants conducted their financial transactions. Gold came into favor in the Edo area, silver in the Osaka-Kyoto area. The basic financial calculations were carried out in each locality according to the favored metal. Gold and silver were actually exchanged or moved about as little as possible. Instead, bills and notes took over much of the circulating function of the precious metals,[54] the latter serving as media of accumulation rather than exchange. Between Osaka and Edo financial transactions took on the nature of a foreign exchange operation handled by the shogunal treasuries and commercial exchange houses. These transactions were clearly affected by the daily fluctuations in the gold-silver exchange rate.

Altogether during the Tokugawa period, the government issued sixty-six varieties of coin in gold and silver alone.[55] The motives which prompted these various issues are generally reducible to three. First, and most general, was the use of debasement as a means of augmenting the government revenue. This expedient became one of the most important sources of government income during times of financial distress.[56] Secondly, the Tokugawa bakufu frequently reacted to pressure from the expanding commercial world for the creation of a greater volume of currency. And thirdly, a most vital reason for recoinage was that it formed one of the only known tools of government financial manipulation. New currency issues frequently marked Tokugawa attempts to deal with general monetary problems.

The mid-Tokugawa period saw two such significant attempts. The first, carried out by Yoshimune between 1714 and 1716, was an idealistic endeavor to return to the original monetary standard of Ieyasu's days. By recoining existing money to standard purity, Yoshimune proposed to re-unify the currency system. But in so doing he shrank the volume of currency and brought disaster upon the financial world. He admitted defeat in 1736 when he permitted the re-issue of debased coins. The Tanuma period witnessed a second and even more significant chapter in the Tokugawa monetary reform.

Tanuma's financial advisors struck out in another direction in an effort to effect a unified currency and to stabilize the gold-silver exchange rate. Essentially their policy sought to introduce bi-metallism into the Tokugawa system. Had their program been applied uniformly, it would have expanded significantly the currency base of the country [57] and brought many benefits to the Tokugawa financial world. As it was, it too was no great success, but not, as Tanuma's critics have claimed, because the program was purely a selfish scheme for Tanuma's personal enrichment.

The name most closely associated with the new currency policies is that of Kawai Hisataka, Comptroller of Finance from 1765 to 1771. It was he who originated the program, and although he died in 1771, his ideas were carried on by the Tanuma faction within the bakufu. Kawai's new policy was initiated in 1765 (Meiwa 2. 9. 1) with the issuance of a five-momme silver piece (*go-momme gin*).[58] In this coin the quality of silver was identical with that of the debased silver lumps put out by Yoshimune in 1736, but a revolutionary step was taken by minting the silver into pieces of uniform weight.[59] Two years later the government took the further step of ordering the five-momme pieces to exchange at a fixed ratio of twelve pieces to the gold ryō.[60] Thus, within the course of two years, the shogunate attempted to convert silver from a commodity article into true money, circulated by piece and used as an auxiliary to gold. Unfortunately the reform was not carried out on a wide enough scale to accomplish its purpose. Only some 1806 kan 400 momme were coined [61] and the old lumps were never taken out of circulation. Many areas of the country never saw the new coins.[62] Because of the government's attempt to make the silver pieces circulate at an artificially high rate with respect to gold (the real value at this time was approximately 14 five-momme pieces to the gold ryō), there was great reluctance on the part of the public to accept them. The issue was discontinued in 1772, at which time the government relaxed its attempt to control the exchange rate.[63]

But the revolutionary ideas begun in 1765 were not abandoned. In the year 1772 (An'ei 1. 9. 7), a new two-*shu* silver coin, the famous *nanryō nishu* piece, advanced the program a step further.[64] The nanryō was of excellent quality, being 98 per cent pure silver, and its issue incorporated two new ideas which were an advance over the former five-momme coins. First, the name silver was avoided

altogether, the characters nanryō [65] being substituted. Secondly, the
face of the coin was stamped with the words "Eight pieces of nanryō
will exchange for one ryō *koban*." [66] Thus the shogunate attempted
to force the public into accepting the new coins at face value as true
auxiliaries to gold. Along with the minting of these new coins, the
Edo government embarked on a strenuous program to encourage
their circulation. The use of nanryō was made mandatory in all payments to the government.[67] Quantities of it were shipped to Osaka
for use in the Kansai area.[68] Eventually the coin was absorbed into
the economy, and the two-shu piece became an established part of
Tokugawa currency, where it performed a useful function as a coin
of medium size.[69]

How this came about and whether it succeeded in creating a true
bi-metallism are still matters of scholarly dispute. Apparently, in
this case, the writings of two contemporaries of Tanuma were to
become the basis of later conflicting opinions. Getaya Jimbei in his
widely quoted memorial of 1787 [70] was extremely critical of the
government attempt to force circulation of the coin at an artificial
rate and reported that the program threw the commercial world into
turmoil. On the other hand Nakai Chikuzan (1730–1804), in his
Sōbōkigen,[71] stated that the coin met with favor and circulated well.
The truth would seem to be that neither of these statements is incor-
rect if consideration is given to the dates at which they were written.
Getaya, writing in 1787, was still able to feel the popular resistance
to the new issue. Nakai, writing in 1789, saw a change in popular
attitude toward the coin. This change occurred in 1788 when the
public finally realized the excellent silver content of the coin and
acknowledged its convenient size. Fortunately, too, a slump in the
price of gold at this time brought the market value down as low as
56 momme of silver per gold ryō, even lower than the officially
adopted exchange rate.[72] In this way the coin came into favor. But
it is probable that it never circulated according to the embossed
legend on its face. A study of contemporary business transactions
shows that it continued to be used for the intrinsic value of the
silver it contained, and its value fluctuated according to the market
value of silver. In other words, it circulated in much the same way
as the former lumps.[73]

A second aspect of the shogunal currency program of the Tanuma
period dealt with *zeni*, or cash. These small coins of common use

were a most important feature of the Tokugawa currency system, since they were in constant demand for the daily monetary transactions of the people. By the middle of the eighteenth century a decided increase in demand for this low denomination of money came from two causes. Following the debasement of 1736, the populace had avoided accepting gold and silver and preferred payment in zeni.[74] At the same time the rapid spread of money economy created new uses for coins both in the metropolitan districts and in the rural areas. By 1738 the scarcity of zeni had pushed the value of copper cash to the point where 2800 or 2900 were equal to the gold ryō. The official rate, it will be recalled, was 4000 to the ryō. Although periodic issues of cash were brought out after 1736, zeni still continued to circulate at a premium. It was thus realized by the Tenth Shogun's finance officials that the public would welcome a large increase of these low denomination coins. But since the shogunate was faced with a shortage of copper, it tried the novel expedient of minting zeni of iron and brass.

In 1765, branches of the Gold Monopoly (*kinza*) in Edo and Fushimi were ordered to strike iron cash.[75] In 1768 a mint for the making of iron and copper cash was set up at Nagaski.[76] During this period the shogunate was constantly under request from the various daimyo for licenses to mint cash within their domains.[77] To meet this demand for money in the outer areas, the central government first of all lifted its restrictions on the export of cash from Edo [78] and later permitted the private minting of iron zeni by the Lords of Sendai and Mito.[79]

While these measures augmented the supply of the one-*mon* cash, the government, once again at Kawai's suggestion, put out a new type of coin. This was the brass four-mon piece (*shimon sen*), issued by the Silver Monopoly (*ginza*) from 1768.[80] While we hear that the single-mon coins invariably met with the displeasure of the populace because of their poor quality, the four-mon coins had a mixed reception. There appears to have been a good deal of grumbling at first because of a feeling that they were not worth the face value of four-mon. Furthermore, because the reverse of the coin was decorated with a wave-like pattern, it was widely rumored that Kawai had put his own crest on the coin and that private corruption was somehow involved.[81] But on the whole the new issue seems to have met with favor.[82]

In this way the volume of small denomination currency was greatly augmented, so much so in fact that the government soon overstepped itself and created a surplus. In 1773 the market value of zeni fell to 5780 the ryō. The following year the minting of iron coins was discontinued and the output of four-mon coins cut in half.[83] Still the value of cash continued to drop, causing a consequent rise in commodity prices and the loud complaint of the people. The surplus of zeni cannot, of course, be given as the sole cause of the increasing cost of living during the 1780's, but it certainly added to the upward trend and hence to the distress of the populace.[84]

Perhaps an even more unfortunate result of the indiscriminate minting of zeni came from the multiplication of types and qualities of the small denomination coins. Whereas zeni had previously circulated as true token coins, now the public was disposed to revalue the new against the old. Some coins were circulated at a premium; others were devalued. Thus even in the world of petty finance, in the small purchases of daily necessities, the people became burdened with a disunified currency.

In summary, it would appear that Tanuma's financial policies were not successful in their more idealistic objectives of bringing new order to the Tokugawa monetary system. As already indicated, one of the reasons for this was his inability to go far enough in dealing with the forces of decentralization. But of more immediate cause was the shogunate's refusal, in the face of a constantly shrinking treasury,[85] to abandon the idea of making profit from its minting operations. Although we have no accurate data on the extent of the government intake from new coinage at this time, we may perhaps gain some idea of its magnitude by reference to a later period. In the 1830's, for instance, the profit from recoinage averaged one-third of the total government revenues.[86] The Tanuma administration, by putting overvalued money in circulation, must also have reaped immense profits, and this act, while of short-term benefit to the treasury, was in the long run damaging to the purchasing power of the common people and to the confidence of the business world in the Shogun's government.

But on the other hand, it must be acknowledged that reforms were attempted. The minting of silver into coins was from the theoretical point of view a great step forward. Despite the fact that these coins circulated at a discount, they nevertheless added a new, convenient form of coin to the existing currency structure. Nor must it be supposed that Tanuma's financial policy was conceived in isolation. It was intimately tied in with his encouragement of mining and his successful program of foreign trade, which reversed the balance of trade in Japan's favor. Much of the silver which went into the five-momme and the two-shu pieces was imported from China. (From about 1750 to 1780 such imports had amounted to over 8000 kan.) Some of the iron and copper used for the new zeni came from newly developed mines. Thus in contrast to a policy which rested solely on debasement of existing money, Tanuma's policy actually increased the amount of precious metal in circulation and hence had a stimulating effect upon the commercial economy. It is here that we can see the consistency of Tanuma's currency program as part of his overall policy of economic expansion.

4. GUILDS, MONOPOLIES, AND TAXES

Tanuma's mercantilist ideas were nowhere better illustrated than in his handling of government monopolies and licensed merchant guilds. It is chiefly from his activity in this field that he won the reputation of being the extreme example of commercial-minded Tokugawa official. While Tanuma held the reins of power in the shogunate, schemes of all types were put forward in order to squeeze wealth from the merchant class. New government monopolies were set up, new guild licenses were issued, and new taxes were placed on whatever appeared to be taxable.

Merchant organizations as they developed under the Tokugawa were of various types, according to their relationship to the government. There were the direct government monopolies, or *za*, which were closely supervised by the Tokugawa authorities. They handled the manufacture or distribution of special products monopolized by the Shogun. Similar to the za were the factories, or *kaisho*, which were placed under shogunal superintendents to handle the monopoly purchase and sale of other similar commodities. Less closely associated with the government were the *kabu nakama*, or merchant guilds licensed under special government charters, and finally there were the *nakama* and *kumiai*, which were privately organized guilds or unions.

It can be seen that these organizations were of two broad types:

those organized by the merchants themselves and licensed by the government, and those which to greater or lesser degree involved the direct participation of the bakufu. The latter class, the various forms of za and kaisho, grew up in those fields of commercial activity such as mining, coinage, and foreign trade in which the Tokugawa held special prerogatives. The Gold Monopoly (kinza) and Silver Monopoly (ginza) each performed two functions. They acted first as agencies for the monopolization of gold and silver by the Tokugawa and secondly as government mints. These two organizations were of early origin and were placed directly under the Superintendent of Finance. A third agency, which handled the minting of copper cash, the *zeniza*, led an unsteady existence until its final abolition in 1772. Thereafter, and at times even before this date, zeni were minted under the control of the Gold and Silver Monopolies. Previous to this, in 1738, a government Copper Monopoly (*dōza*) had been set up to take over the function of cornering the nation's copper production for currency and for the Nagasaki foreign trade. In 1750 the Copper Monopoly was converted to a factory attached to the Silver Monopoly office in Osaka.

By Tanuma's time these organizations were firmly established, but to anyone with a business sense it was clear that they were not operating at full efficiency. Government and private mines alike were ignoring monopoly regulations and selling their ores illegally. Mining operations had become stagnant, so that the mints and government export monopolies were starved for raw materials. This was especially evident in the case of copper. Despite the small amount of copper provided for export to the Dutch and Chinese at Nagasaki, the Japanese were frequently unable to meet their commitments. Domestically the dearth of copper forced the price of cash distressingly high.[87]

The scarcity of copper was one of the first concerns of the shogunate during the Tanuma period. In 1763 (Hōreki 13. 3. 22) a government order exhorted the copper mines to greater activity and urged the country to begin a search for new ore deposits.[88] Likely sites were to be reported to local officials, who in turn were to pass on information to the Superintendent of Finance. Simultaneously, the shogunate attempted to get its hands on some of the better mines which lay outside of the Tokugawa domain. Chief of these was the Ani mine of Akita district in Dewa province. Though this mine was in the domain of the Satake family, steps were taken to have the surrounding lands declared shogunal property. It was only through the most strenuous opposition of the Satake house that the plan was frustrated.[89]

In its own mines the government strove to step up production by reorganization of the operating personnel.[90] The monopoly system whereby all copper was to be sold to the government was tightened to eliminate leaks.[91] In 1766 (Meiwa 3. 6. 3), by Tokugawa order, the Copper Factory at Osaka was made into an independent monopoly with full powers to act as the sole purchasing agent for copper. All merchants engaged in the copper transport business and all retail dealers in copper goods were put under its jurisdiction. Private sale of copper by mine owners or by shippers was prohibited. Copper ore, no matter where mined or by whom, was first to be sent to the copper depots at Osaka or Nagasaki, where fair prices were to be set for its purchase by the government. The Copper Monopoly further had the power to require detailed production inventories from the mine owners and even estimates of future production.[92] The organization thus reconstituted was naturally a great improvement over the previous factory system, and, although there appears to have been little fundamental change in the country's overall copper output, the amount which was available for government use did increase.[93]

Throughout the remaining years of the Tanuma period the government continued to encourage further efforts to track down new deposits of ore in the hope of finding a permanent solution to the copper problem. An order in 1767, which emphasized the need for mines of all kinds, gold, silver, copper, iron, and lead, placed all existing and future mines under the jurisdiction of a newly created Superintendent of Mines (*kinzan-bugyō*). This officer was ordered to travel the country on a tour of inspection and encouragement.[94] Naturally with such constant insistence by the government, the entire nation became mine conscious, and countless schemes, both legitimate and otherwise, were suggested. The Tanuma period is often referred to as a time of wildcat adventures, when the public and the government were taken in by unscrupulous charlatans.[95] But not all of the schemes proposed during these years were reckless nor the men involved in them irresponsible. One man of apparent integrity was the well-known Hiraga Gennai, who, with his genius for engineering and his smattering of Dutch learning, toured the country to give much needed advice on better mining techniques.[96]

In addition to this major effort to stimulate and control copper production, the Edo government after 1767 put its attention on the task of tightening up the monopoly of silver. Causes for loss of silver by the government were investigated, and the domestic use of silver was severely curtailed. Orders of this nature were repeated in 1775 and again in 1785, which would lead one to suspect that the efforts to maintain an effective silver monopoly were not altogether successful.[97]

In 1780 (An'ei 9. 8. 28) an Iron Monopoly (*tetsuza*) and a Brass Monopoly (*shinchūza*) were also created, the first attached to the Osaka branch of the Silver Monopoly, the other to the Silver Monopoly headquarters in Edo. From that time on, all the country's iron and brass pig was ordered to be sent to Osaka where Tokugawa agents would make arrangements for its purchase. At the same time new factories for the refinement of brass were increased. Whereas formerly this had been done only in Kyoto, now Osaka, Fushimi, and Sakai were permitted to build refineries.[98] The establishment of the Iron Monopoly met with considerable opposition from the various merchants and artisans engaged in the iron trade, especially over the matter of price fixing. In 1784 certain modifications were made in the operation of this agency.[99] Both the Iron and Brass Monopolies were abolished in 1787, when Matsudaira Sadanobu systematically reversed all of Tanuma's policies.[100]

While the above organizations grew out of the Tokugawa privilege of controlling the mines and precious metals of the country, another group of monopolies were based on the Tokugawa right to regulate foreign trade. The Cinnabar Monopoly (*shuza*) was one of the oldest of these, having been established in 1609 to handle the cinnabar imported from China and the Ryukyu Islands. Since that time, Japan had developed her own source, and the agency took over the sale and distribution of the domestic cinnabar as well. In 1738, under Yoshimune, and again in 1759, the regulations of the Cinnabar Monopoly were reinforced. During the Tanuma period renewed efforts were made to tighten the monopolistic nature of this organization and to prevent leakage through illegal sales. This is indicated by two shogunal orders, one in 1777, the other in 1782.[101]

Three other monopolies based on articles of foreign importation dealt with ginseng, alum, and camphor. The Ginseng Monopoly (*ninjinza*) was established in 1763 through the efforts of the Superintendent of Finance, Isshiki Masahiro (died 1770),[102] who appointed the distinguished government physician and botanist, Tamura Gen'yū (1718–1776),[103] as its superintendent. The monopoly was designed to control the sale of both imported and domestic ginseng[104] and to regulate prices and quality.[105] Its offices were established at Kanda in Edo, and twenty-eight licensed retailers were distributed throughout Japan. In this way this extremely popular drug was made available over a wide area and to all classes of society.[106]

The Alum Factory (*myōban-kaisho*), with branches in Edo, Kyoto, Osaka, and Sakai, was established in 1758.[107] These branch factories were empowered to buy up all domestic alum and handle its retail sales.[108] Later, in 1782, a second line of factories was set up to handle alum imported at Nagasaki from China, together with that brought in by the Satsuma Domain from the Ryukyus.[109]

The Camphor Monopoly (*ryūnōza*) was a new idea of the Tanuma period. Established at Nagasaki in 1768, it was apparently brought into being to handle the distribution of domestically manufactured camphor as distinguished from the imported variety.[110] The organization was abolished in 1782 perhaps, as Dr. Tsuji suggests, because of the failure of the manufacturers at Nagasaki to produce camphor which could compete with that which entered from abroad.[111]

Aside from the above government monopolies, Tokugawa interference in the business world was frequently justified as a necessary means of regulating the distribution and price of certain vital commodities. The government's attempt to stabilize the price of rice, for instance, had been a matter of basic concern from early Tokugawa days, and numerous restrictions had been placed upon the free use of rice throughout Japan. Characteristic of the Tanuma treatment of this problem was a tendency to balance the requirements of control with the opportunity for government profit. Thus while on the one hand the Tanuma period witnessed a closer supervision of the rice market at Osaka, it also saw the removal of restrictions on the use of rice for commercial purposes.[112] The search for profit is perhaps best illustrated in Tanuma's attitude towards sake brewing, which, in spite of the high price of rice, continued to be permitted without restriction. The shogunate at the same time

revived an earlier tax on breweries. One of the first of Matsudaira
Sadanobu's reform policies after the fall of Tanuma was to impose
a 50 per cent reduction on the diversion of rice for brewing purposes.[113]

Another product the control of which the shogunate considered
essential was coal. A factory for the monopolization of coal (*sekitan-
kaisho*) was set up in 1762.[114] In 1773 measures were taken to reduce
the price of coal, while two years later a second factory was established to take care of the expanded coal trade. All coal sold within
Edo was to bear the mark of one of the licensed organizations and
come under the Tokugawa price controls.[115]

Perhaps the most ambitious of the Edo government's regulative
ventures was the attempt to control the manufacture and sale of lamp
oil. Owing to the importance of this commodity to the populace, it
was argued that the government should do everything possible to
keep down its price. An early move in this direction was taken by
Yoshimune, who had sought to lower the price by encouraging production. Another step was taken in 1759, when the manufacture and
sale of oil was put under state control, a government wholesale
agency (*tonya*) being organized for the purpose.[116] Since oil was
manufactured in a great number of widely scattered localities, the
government had considerable difficulty in enforcing this plan. The
many orders regarding this problem put out during the Tanuma
period give us an excellent insight into the techniques employed by
the government monopolists. All seed for squeezing was to be bought
up by specially licensed wholesalers, who shipped it either to Edo or
Osaka and turned it over to designated oil manufacturers. Several
areas outside of the two big cities were given permission to squeeze
oil, some by the use of water wheels. All oil, no matter where manufactured, was then to be shipped to the wholesale distributors in
Osaka and Edo. Even a village which engaged in the refining of oil
could not use its product directly. It was required first to send it to
the city and then to buy it back.[117]

It is obvious that by the time such regulations came into being,
profit through monopoly control rather than price reduction had become one of the major concerns of the government. The above enterprises, involving as they did the active participation of the Edo government in business, yielded a direct profit to the Tokugawa treasury. This was delivered to the government in the form of a yearly

payment of a certain percentage of the profits of the enterprise. Profit was also found in the issuance of licenses to various merchant associations and occupational guilds. Organizations such as the nakama and kumiai were primarily products of the mid-Tokugawa period and came to their first peak of development under Tanuma's encouragement. By 1780 Edo and Osaka each had over a hundred such associations, chief of which were the Ten Guilds (*Tokumi-donya*) of Edo and the Twenty-four Guilds (*Nijūshi-gumi*) of Osaka. All of these organizations paid to the government a yearly tax (*unjō* or *myōga*). Although there was little uniformity in the rate of assessment, and few merchants were taxed systematically according to what they were able to pay, by the mid-Tokugawa period the shogunate was adding appreciably to its income through this method of extracting revenue from the merchants.

While the Tokugawa government never evolved a systematic means of taxing income or commercial transactions, it tried in somewhat haphazard fashion to extract what it could from such sources. By the Tanuma period taxes were being levied on wine, vinegar, oil, water wheels, and even houses of prostitution and temples which kept prostitutes.[118] Some of the revenue from the above sources was turned back to provide better service for the public. As an example, a tax on ships entering Nagasaki harbor was used for dredging and repair work.[119] But on the whole such income was used to fill the depleted Tokugawa treasuries.

In actuality the bakufu policy under Tanuma's direction was distinguished chiefly by the extent to which the government was ready to go in its search for tax revenue. Unfortunately, it discovered that the tax limits were easily reached. When in 1772 a registration tax was imposed on all articles taken to pawn shops in Osaka, the townspeople put up strong resistance.[120] Nor was the peasantry any more disposed to accept extra impositions from the government. When in 1785 the shogunate put out an order requiring all farmers who transported their tax rice to Edo by boat to register their boats and pay a fee for such registration, the farmers rebelled.[121] They saw no justice in having to pay a tax on the very boats in which they were carrying their own tax rice to the government storehouses. A group of Kantō farmers banded together to resist this order and forced the government to back down on its plan.[122]

A similar but even more humiliating experience was encountered when the Edo government attempted to put through a plan for the state inspection and taxation of all silk thread and cloth made in the provinces of Kōzuke and Musashi. The tax itself was levied, not on the peasants, but on the great city-wholesalers who, it was felt, would be willing to pay the fee in return for the assurance that they were receiving material of good quality at a standard price.[123] In 1781 ten inspection stations were set up in the silk markets of these two provinces, but their presence frightened away the wholesalers, who went elsewhere to purchase their yearly supply of silk. The peasants, who waited in vain for purchasers, finally rose up in an armed riot and destroyed the office of the Local Deputy and the houses of the three wealthy villagers who first suggested the tax. Later a group of 3000 peasants besieged the castle of Takasaki [124] and refused to disperse even under gunfire. These threatening conditions forced the authorities to back down. The inspection scheme was given up and order was again established.[125]

The failure of these tax schemes contributed greatly to Tanuma's bad reputation, but a final plan approved by him in the last desperate years of his official career collapsed with even more disastrous results. This idea, which was essentially an attempt at credit control, was in many ways far in advance of the times. Its avowed objective was to ease the financial distress of the daimyo. In these years of economic distress, the feudal lords had been going in debt to the merchant financiers at an appalling rate. The shogunate itself was in the habit of providing extra capital for emergency purposes. But with its own weak financial condition it became increasingly difficult to meet even the emergency needs of the daimyo.[126] It was thought, therefore, that an excellent solution to this problem would be to create a floating reserve fund (*yūzūkin*) under Tokugawa control from which the daimyo could borrow whenever they needed. Thus the daimyo would be enabled to keep free of the humiliating entanglement with the Osaka banking houses, while the shogunate could benefit from the interest accumulated from the fund. The merchants who were to provide the capital also would benefit, since the government would stand behind their loans. To initiate this scheme the Edo government undertook in 1785 to float a loan among the wealthy merchants of Osaka. The program was called the Thrice Beneficial Law (*santoku-hō*), since it was to benefit the merchants, the daimyo, and the shogunate. The loan was to be collected by the

Osaka City Magistrate. Daimyo loans were to be made from the fund as though directly from the Shogun. Hence repayment was a feudal obligation. The government, for its part in securing the loans, was to take one-seventh of the interest; the rest would go to the merchants [127] who provided the capital. Feasible as this plan appeared on paper, the government met with immediate resistance from the Osaka businessmen, who questioned the shogunate's ability to operate the program without loss to themselves. Thus the majority of merchants avoided contribution on one pretext or another.[128]

Balked in this attempt, the shogunate, in the last months of Tanuma's career (Temmei 6. 6. 29), made another desperate try at putting the reserve fund into operation.[129] The order which came out at this time was quite similar to demands for compulsory government loans in our day. All persons and institutions throughout the land: temples, shrines, farmers (whether in Tokugawa territories or daimyo domains), merchants, and artisans, were required to subscribe an amount of money according to their property holdings. This money was to be loaned to the government for five years. As security the lenders were to receive Osaka or local rice certificates, and these would be redeemable in rice at Osaka or by the nearest Tokugawa Deputy in five years' time. The loans were to accumulate 7 per cent interest per annum, from which the shogunate would deduct one-seventh for expenses. The government set strict time limits for the collection of the contributions, which were to be paid to the local Deputies, lords of the various domains, or, in the metropolitan areas, to the government's financial agents, the Mitsui and Ueda companies.[130]

This was undoubtedly one of the most audacious plans conceived by Tanuma in his attempt to stem the progress of financial decay. Whether it was as impractical as its detractors claimed is hard to determine, for the plan never had a fair trial. By 1786 the country was in no mood for additional imposts from the government. Continuous years of bad harvests had created a condition in which not only the shogunate, but the entire country, was without financial margin. As it was, the rains and floods of the summer of 1786 interfered with the collection of funds, and as the rains let up Tanuma and his party went out of office. One of the first acts of Tanuma's political opponents was to call off the reserve fund plan.[131]

These spectacular failures should not blind us, however, to some of the more positive results of Tanuma's domestic policy, a policy which was characterized by open encouragement of mercantile activity and a shrewd, even ruthless, program of taxation. In terms of immediate short-term objectives we must admit that Tanuma was far from being a failure. His were years of famine and extraordinary expenditure. The ability of the shogunate to weather the stormy period from 1781 to 1787 without serious deficit undoubtedly owed a great deal to his aggressive money-making program.[132] But Tanuma's political downfall put an end to any hopes of bringing about a fundamental change in the financial attitude of the Tokugawa authorities. After his fall the mercantilist leanings of the government were "corrected" and the traditional land-first policy reaffirmed.

5. FOREIGN TRADE

Despite the restrictive seclusion policy adopted by the Tokugawa after 1633, the Edo government seems to have had no fundamental ideological antagonism against foreign trade itself. Intercourse with the "safe" traders from China and Holland continued to be encouraged so long as it was under careful regulation at the port of Nagasaki, where it would yield a handsome profit to the Shogun. Thus, during the latter half of the seventeenth century, the Nagasaki trade steadily increased, and little restriction was placed on the number of foreign ships or the volume of trade permitted to them. The Dutch and Chinese merchantmen brought with them Chinese silk, Formosan sugar, Manchurian ginseng, and many other minor rarities. They took away principally Japanese silver and copper. Eventually the latter commodity became the great staple of Japan's foreign export and the chief source of profit for the Dutch and Chinese.

Before the seventeenth century was out, however, Japanese copper production had begun to decline. This was dramatically brought to light in 1698 when the Nagasaki copper merchants had to default on their contracts, and the foreign traders were obliged to wait over a year for their cargoes.[133] It was this incident which brought the Nagasaki trade to the attention of the bakufu official Arai Hakuseki (1656–1725), who was at the time engaged in a general clean-up of the Tokugawa administration.

Arai, in his study of the Tokugawa foreign trade, arrived at some

startling conclusions which, though highly exaggerated, had a sober-
ing effect upon the shogunate's trade policy.[134] He claimed that the
Nagasaki exports since 1601 (he wrote in 1707) had drained from
Japan 7,192,800 ryō of gold and 1,122,627 kan of silver. He might
have added that in the year 1698 alone Japan exported over 8,000,-
000 *kin* of copper [135] and that Japan's copper mines were rapidly
nearing exhaustion. Arai's chief concern, however, was the loss of
specie abroad and the serious effect this was having on Japan's
finances. He recommended a drastic curtailment of the Nagasaki
trade and a complete embargo on the export of gold and silver. This
plan was adopted in 1715. In that year the Chinese were limited to
30 vessels a year and a 6000-kan trade volume. They were prohibited
from taking out silver altogether and permitted only 3,000,000 kin
of copper. The Dutch were cut to ten vessels and a 3000-kan trade
volume, with a limit of 1,500,000 kin of copper.[136]

Yoshimune continued this physiocratic trade policy by further
cutting down on the volume of foreign trade and strenuously push-
ing the domestic production of all commodities imported from
abroad. Silk manufacture was already well advanced in Japan, but
it made great strides under his encouragement. It was he who obtained seeds of the ginseng for planting in Japan, and he also who
promoted the production of Japanese sugar. During these years
Japan's copper mines steadily deteriorated, and the volume of exports was repeatedly cut down, so that by 1743 only ten Chinese
merchantmen were permitted to trade at Nagasaki, and their copper
exports were cut to 1,500,000 kin. The Dutch had been limited to
one ship annually and 600,000 kin of copper. Even this combined
quota of 2,100,000 kin was sometimes not fulfilled by the Japanese
copper merchants.

This sorry state of foreign trade continued to the 1760's. But
with the appearance of the Tanuma faction in the shogunate, a more
positive, expansive trade policy was again commenced.[137] Though
severely handicapped by the lack of adequate copper supplies,
Tanuma and his financial officials managed to make out of the
Nagasaki trade something much more profitable than had been
thought possible, and for a time the balance of trade was even reversed in Japan's favor.

The first step in this direction was taken in 1763, when the Chinese requested an increase in their copper exports. Taking advantage

of this request the Tokugawa government signed a twenty-year agreement with the Chinese permitting the latter to take out of the country an additional 300,000 kin of copper annually, while they in turn were to leave in Japan 300 kan of silver.[138] This same year, it will be recalled, the government sent out its first general plea for greater copper production. Two years later in 1765, the government issued its first new currency, the five-momme silver piece. These events were all intimately related. The copper was needed for export, while the five-momme and succeeding silver issues were largely made possible by the silver imported from China.[139]

Tanuma achieved further success in the field of foreign trade through his ability to develop acceptable substitutes for copper at Nagasaki. The Japanese had previously discovered that an extensive foreign market existed for certain dried sea products such as tangle (*kombu*), sea-ears (*awabi*), sea slugs (*iriko*), and sharks' fins. Since these products were put up in bales, they were called bale goods (*tawaramono*) by the Japanese. The export of bale goods had first assumed importance in the year 1698, when the Japanese had failed to fulfill their copper contracts. Thereafter, as the copper supply dwindled, its place was gradually taken by the more abundant dried sea products.[140]

Bale goods came largely from the northern island of Ezo, although certain coastal areas in the main Japanese islands also contributed to the national supply. Several merchant firms were organized to handle the collection and transportation of sea products to Nagasaki. In 1743 five merchant houses were given exclusive rights in the bale goods export business and were authorized to set up factories at Osaka and Nagasaki for the purchase of sea products for export. These five houses in turn operated through a number of wholesalers with headquarters at Osaka, Shimonoseki, Nagasaki, and later Matsumae in Ezo. In the northern island, a group of Ōmi merchants had taken over the collection of sea products and had developed an elaborate contract system whereby individual merchants bid for the right to exploit certain areas. These contractors were eventually organized into a single wholesale house.

In 1754 the entire bale goods business from Ezo to Nagasaki was converted into a single monopoly. The government began a campaign to educate the villagers of coastal areas in Tokugawa domains on how to prepare sea products for export, while the daimyo were urged to push production in their respective territories.[141] Apparently this first monopoly system was no great success. Its failure became apparent after 1763, when the government initiated its policy of importing gold and silver from abroad, and the need for bale goods became acute. Renewed efforts by the government to increase the supply of bale goods proved ineffectual. The merchants constantly complained of their inability to make ends meet because of the low price at which they were committed to sell to the Chinese. By 1786 they had accumulated a debt to the government of 3900 kan of silver.

In that year the shogunate reorganized the entire business by converting it into a government operated monopoly.[142] A Bale Goods Office (*tawaramono-yakusho*) was set up at Nagasaki under the direction of Tokugawa officials. Merchants formerly engaged in the trade were converted into government agents, and even at the extreme local level village headmen were brought in as representatives of the government. The shogunate supplied capital when needed and set the prices. Production was encouraged by the offering of bounties for those who went over their quotas. Domestic consumption of exportable sea products was strictly curtailed. It appears that this new organization was a decided success. Within a year production had increased by a quarter, and the Nagasaki authorities were able to import not only the 300 kan of silver delivered according to agreement by the Chinese but also additional amounts of gold and silver from both the Chinese and the Dutch.[143]

But as in the other aspects of his domestic program, Tanuma was unable to secure a lasting modification of the Tokugawa trade policy. His successor to power, Matsudaira Sadanobu, was openly critical of the effort needed to keep the Nagasaki trade going and claimed that Tanuma was ruining the country's economy by sending abroad copper which was all too scarce in Japan. He therefore reversed Tanuma's trade policy and began a period of retrenchment. In 1790, he broke off the export agreement with the Chinese. The number of Chinese ships permitted to trade at Nagasaki was again reduced to ten a year. Dutch trade dwindled of its own accord. For as a result of the French Revolution, during nearly three decades after 1789, hardly a Dutch vessel entered Nagasaki harbor. Tokugawa foreign trade reached the lowest point in its history.[144]

CHAPTER V

The Dutch and the Russians

I. THE EVOLUTION OF THE SECLUSION POLICY

For nearly a hundred years after the confirmation of the Tokugawa seclusion policy, Japan was left in comparative isolation by the rest of the world. After the middle of the seventeenth century, Portuguese and Spanish power in the Far East declined; the Dutch were cut back to their East Indies bases by the loss of Formosa, and the British turned their attention to the conquest of India. Japan's Asiatic neighbors, Korea and China, both followed their own policies of exclusion and were anxious to minimize foreign contacts.

It was during the Tanuma period that Japan's dream of national seclusion was finally broken, at first gently by the slow stirring of the Japanese people, who began to waken to the dangers of continued isolation, and then more rudely by the startling news of Russian penetration in the islands to the north of Japan. Once again the problem of Japan's attitude toward the outside world was reopened for critical appraisal and the seclusion policy brought into question. The Tanuma period, standing as it does between the early years of easy seclusion and the later period of increasingly mounting pressure from abroad, marks a turning point in the history of Tokugawa foreign relations.

Although Tokugawa foreign policy was characterized after the 1630's by rigid control of the country's foreign contacts, it should not be supposed that the seclusion policy came full blown into being or that once established it underwent no modification. As in the case of other Tokugawa institutions, the evolution of foreign policy involved a number of changes which served to both strengthen and weaken the Japanese determination to keep the world from her doors.

It is perhaps natural that a tendency to strengthen the seclusion policy should manifest itself first. The passage of time alone was a factor in confirming the Japanese in the belief that foreign contacts were a baneful influence. This was especially true in a society such as that of Tokugawa Japan where the weight of tradition played so all-important a role. Thus the ultimate sanction for the seclusion policy became the fact that it had been in operation for many generations and that it had become part of the fundamental law of the Tokugawa. But aside from the forces of pure conservatism, new ideological supports were added to the belief in the benefits of seclusion. Whereas the original policy had been aimed at eliminating certain political and religious dangers, before long economic reasons were advanced for the maintenance of the closed door. These were the physiocratic ideas already referred to, which were given such vigorous expression by the old-style Confucianists. A majority of the political theorists of the late seventeenth and early eighteenth centuries came out for either the reduction or total elimination of the Nagasaki trade. By the mid-Tokugawa era seclusion had become an essential part of the thinking of the fundamentalist school.[1]

After this time, however, a growing number of voices were raised against seclusion. The earliest champions of this opposition were the theorists who advocated the acquisition of wealth through trade.[2] These members of the realistic school of political economists based their reasoning primarily on Japan's pressing economic needs. But they were soon joined by others who argued from actual knowledge of world affairs and from the conviction that Japan was suffocating herself intellectually by refusing to open her doors. The open expression of such ideas indicated the beginning of a fundamental change in the Japanese attitude toward the outside world.

The realization that Japan could profit intellectually by an association with the Occident came as a definite rediscovery in the early years of the eighteenth century. Ironically, the discovery was made by one of the most outspoken opponents of Japan's foreign trade, Arai Hakuseki.[3] It is generally acknowledged that the beginning of a new attitude toward the West dates from Arai's interviews with the Italian priest Sidotti, who was captured off the coast of Satsuma in 1708 while attempting to smuggle his way into Japan.[4] Such an incident should normally have caused considerable agitation within the Tokugawa government and alerted its officials to a renewed vigilance against the Christian religion. But, as Murdoch points out, the authorities took the news of Sidotti's capture with remarkable calmness, in fact with more curiosity than panic, so remote were the days of the active Christian menace. Arai Hakuseki was commissioned by the Shogun to examine the priest and to make an investigation of the history of Christianity in Japan. The outcome was his *Seiyō kibun*, in which he not only inquired into Sidotti's religious convictions but added whatever information he could garner on the geography, history, and science of European countries. In his usual objective fashion, Arai expressed unconcealed admiration for the priest's scientific knowledge, while his Confucian background caused him to look at the supposedly subversive religion of the foreigner as more of an absurdity than a potential national threat.

In his *Seiyō kibun*, Arai asserted categorically that the Christian nations were no longer a danger. Apparently this mild treatment of the Christian problem had an immediate effect on the Tokugawa intellectuals, for within a few years Ogyū Sorai (1666–1728), another prominent Confucian scholar, was writing that the government should permit scholars to judge for themselves the doctrines of the alien religion.[5] The sting had been taken out of Christianity, and the chief argument for seclusion had been weakened.

Another incident of equal importance in preparing the new attitude toward the West occurred in 1720 when Yoshimune relaxed the ban on the importation of books dealing with Western subjects and encouraged certain of his officials to take up the study of the Dutch language and Western science. Although up to this time a small group of Japanese had acquired a limited knowledge of European languages, it was only after 1720 that the serious study of the Dutch language and of Western scientific writings was begun by those outside the official circle of Deshima translators. This date thus marked the beginning of the so-called Dutch Learning (*rangaku*) in Japan.[6]

The results of Hakuseki's mild attitude toward Christianity and Yoshimune's utilitarian view of Western science became apparent during the Tanuma period. At no time within the seclusion period was Japan as open in her foreign contacts and in the free consideration of the possibilities of renewed foreign intercourse as the period from 1760 to 1786. During these years a new interest in things Occidental was evidenced by the great fad for imported novelties. The markets of Edo were full of objects imported from Holland, and such curiosities as barometers, thermometers, and clocks were avidly collected by those of means. The chief collector of such objects appears to have been Tanuma himself.[7] Taking their cue from him, Tokugawa officials relaxed their attitude toward foreigners. The Nagasaki Magistrates became more easy-going with the Dutch. Contact between the Dutch and their interpreters became more friendly. On their official visits to Edo the Dutch were visited freely by daimyo and scholars, both out of curiosity and genuine scientific interest. Information concerning the "Red-Haired Ones," formerly banned from publication, now circulated for popular consumption.

It was in the midst of this period of unsuspicious interest in the foreigners who came to Nagasaki from the south that news reached the Japanese of the approach of the Russians in the north. The news was not immediately disturbing. The Russians did not at first appear to be a threat to Japanese peace. Although in a few decades the Japanese were to be exercised into a near state of panic over the Russian menace, during the Tanuma period the Russians were looked upon as a new opportunity. The possibility of opening the doors of trade in the north, both as a means of securing new wealth and meeting the Russians before they had advanced to the point of demanding concessions, was considered seriously by the shogunate.

The Tanuma period thus offers us the prospect that Japan might have abandoned her seclusion policy voluntarily over a half century before she was eventually forced to do so. It is this attitude toward the West which was perhaps the most significant aspect of Tanuma's policy. Yet again forces of reaction were overwhelmingly arrayed against any fundamental departure from the laws of the Tokugawa forefathers. After Tanuma's fall the seclusion policy was reaffirmed, and the conflict over foreign policy which marked the last years of the shogunate became inevitable.

2. DUTCH STUDIES AND THE NAGASAKI TRADE

Fortunately for our study of Tokugawa foreign relations we are seldom entirely dependent on the meager accounts which have survived in Japan. Generally we are afforded some check or elaboration through the writings of foreign visitors at Nagasaki. This is particularly true for the Tanuma period when, by coincidence, the state of new Japanese interest in the West was matched by the arrival of two well-informed and interested Dutch agents. The first of these was the Swedish physician, Karl Thunberg, who arrived in Nagasaki in 1775. The other was Isaac Titsingh, the Dutch factor, whose presence in Japan between 1779 and 1785 spanned the high point of the era of liberal foreign policy.

Thunberg, who has left some excellent observations on the Japanese scene and on the state of Japan's knowledge of the West, was the first to call attention to the new attitude toward foreigners.[8] His report on the cordial treatment of the Dutch mission to Edo in 1776 shows that Japanese students of Western science had acquired comparative freedom in their intercourse with the outsiders. In his interviews with the Japanese, Thunberg remarks that they gave evidence of familiarity with Dutch works on botany, medicine, and surgery. Already the stimulus given by Yoshimune to serious study of the Dutch language and the various branches of Western science had begun to have results. Moreover it is clear from Thunberg's writings that, by this time, knowledge of the West was not limited to any obscure group within the government but was widespread among the educated class. Perhaps the most significant piece of information revealed by Thunberg is that he was able to correspond by letter with some of his Japanese associates after his departure from Japan in 1776. This, of course, was in direct violation of the seclusion regulations.

Titsingh's account of the expanded state of Western studies in Japan, though cryptic in spots, is even more revealing than Thunberg's.[9] According to him, not only in Nagasaki and Edo but also at Osaka and Kyoto, persons of quality attached themselves to the Dutch mission in order to acquire a familiarity with the Hollanders and to learn to read their books. A number of these persons he records by name. It should not surprise us to find heading this list one of the chief figures in the Tokugawa feudal hierarchy, Shimazu Shigehide, Daimyo of Satsuma and father-in-law of the Heir Apparent, the future Shogun Ienari.

The Shimazu house had long been interested in overseas affairs. This interest was sustained in part by the trade which the Shimazu maintained with the Ryukyu islands. In the long history of the Shimazu family, Shigehide was especially notable for his progressive views.[10] Born in 1745, he succeeded to the position of head of the

Shimazu house at the age of ten, though he was placed under guardianship until 1760. In both his personal life and his administration he was extremely original and unconventional for his times. Although well versed in Chinese studies, he nevertheless showed an unusual interest in things Western and frequently visited the port of Nagasaki to inspect Dutch ships and associate with foreigners. Titsingh asserts that Shigehide was able to "use our alphabet to express in his letters what he wished a third person not to understand." [11] Although none of these letters has been preserved as proof of the Satsuma Daimyo's proficiency in Dutch, we know that he continued to patronize Dutch studies down to his death in 1833 and that all of the arrivals at Deshima learned to expect his call when they visited Edo. Doeff in 1806, Fisscher in 1822, and Siebold in 1826 all record association with him.[12]

As daimyo of one of the largest domains in the country, Shigehide had ample resources with which to encourage study and research among his retainers. A long list of works came out under his patronage. Works on the Chinese language or on the geography of Satsuma and the Ryukyus were in the native scholarly tradition. But his studies in botany, medicine, taxidermy, and other scientific fields owed a great deal to his associations with the Dutch. The *Seikei zusetsu*,[13] which was completed in 1804, is one of the best known of such studies. The work was a detailed encyclopedia of agricultural plants and medicinal herbs, collected and described in a scientific manner. In addition to encouraging such publication, Shigehide contributed liberally to the educational and research facilities of his domain. In 1773 he founded colleges for training in military and literary arts. The next year he set up a medical college and five years later an institute for astronomy and mathematics.[14] In Edo and Kagoshima he built botanical gardens to aid in the study of herbs and drugs.

All of this activity plus his own luxurious mode of living was a heavy drain on the Satsuma treasury. Shigehide is said to have left a five-million-ryō debt at the time of his death. Yet, before he died, he succeeded in laying the foundation for the eventual recovery of the Satsuma fortunes. A vigorous expansionist in his economic policy, Shigehide was especially attracted by the doctrines of Satō Nobuhiro (1769–1850), one of the most famous of the realistic school of political economists and a foremost advocate of domain industries and

monopolies. It was Shigehide who after 1830 placed Satsuma finances
in the hands of Chōsho Shōzaemon, the man who devised the policy
of domain operated trade and industry which eventually wiped out
the Satsuma debt. By the 1850's Satsuma was one of the most prosperous domains in Japan.[15]

Another of Titsingh's aristocratic associates was Kuchiki Masatsuna (born 1744) [16] who, though a less imposing figure in the Tokugawa hierarchy, was a more talented scholar. His association with
Titsingh was particularly intimate, and several of his letters written
to Titsingh in excellent Dutch exist today to substantiate the Dutch
factor's statement that Kuchiki was able to express himself in Dutch
more clearly than many Portuguese, born and bred among the Dutch
at Batavia.[17] Kuchiki's two works on Western subjects, his *Taisei
yochi zusetsu*,[18] a voluminous study of the geography and customs
of European countries, and his *Seiyō sempu*,[19] a work on European
coins, both attest to the lively exchange of information which went
on between himself and Titsingh.

Shimazu Shigehide and Kuchiki Masatsuna, both men of daimyo
rank and both students of Western science, were, to be sure, exceptional individuals. But they were illustrative of the growing interest
in the physical sciences and other aspects of Western culture among
the ruling class in Japan. It is important to realize that the larger
part of the new Dutch studies was conducted by order of, or under
the patronage of, one or another of the daimyo. Few of the so-called
Dutch Scholars (*rangakusha*) were isolated individuals. The fact is
that once the trend of interest in Western science was started, few
of the daimyo could afford to neglect the new branch of learning.
Thus Maeno Ranka (1723–1803) and Nakagawa Junnan (1712–
1781) were physicians to the Daimyo of Nakatsu, Sugita Gempaku
(1737–1817) to the Daimyo of Wakasa, and Ōtsuki Gentaku (1757–
1827) to the Daimyo of Sendai.[20] The shogunate also patronized
such scholars, and, even in the years after Tanuma's fall, when
Dutch studies were looked on with suspicion, it was obliged to cultivate the new source of information both from considerations of defense and for the purpose of keeping abreast of the times. In 1811,
for instance, a translation office was attached to the Bureau of
Calendars of the shogunate, and Ōtsuki Gentaku and others were
commissioned to make translations of works on Western nations.[21]
Previously, in 1808, the college of interpreters at Nagasaki had been

instructed to take up the study of Russian, and the next year of English.[22]

Titsingh lists a host of individuals of lesser rank who were associated with him during his stay in Japan. The greater portion of these were interpreters at Nagasaki, but two Edo physicians, the previously mentioned Nakagawa Junnan and Katsuragawa Hoshū (1751–1809), were singled out for their excellent command of Dutch. These men had both studied under Thunberg during his visit to Edo and had received from him certificates of proficiency in medicine. Nakagawa is the man who obtained the original copy of the Dutch translation of Kulmus' *Tabulae anatomica*. This was translated into Japanese by Maeno and Sugita in 1774 under the title *Kaitai shinsho*. Katsuragawa had a good deal to do with having the translation received favorably by the Shogun and the Senior Councilors. The circulation of this book without suppression together with the publication of Ōtsuki Gentaku's *Rangaku kaitei* (Introduction to Dutch Studies) in 1783 marked two great milestones in the popularization of Dutch studies. The former placed Japanese medicine on a new and more scientific footing; the latter made possible the first public circulation of a book containing Dutch writing.[23]

Titsingh's contacts in the Japanese art world also had important repercussions. His particular associate in this respect was Shiba Kōkan (1747–1818), who is often considered the originator of Western modes of art in Japan. Actually Shiba was preceded in his study by the erratic genius, Hiraga Gennai, who appears to have worked on the techniques of oil painting and copperplate etching. Shiba was originally an artist of the Kano school who later went over to the Harunobu school of wood-block printing. A side interest in astronomy took him to Nagasaki, where he made the acquaintance of Titsingh and exchanged his knowledge of Ukiyoe prints for some Dutch books on painting and etching. From this point, Kōkan went on to perform a pioneer work in familiarizing the Japanese with Western painting. In 1783 he collaborated with Ōtsuki Gentaku in printing a number of copperplate etchings of maps and various Western subjects.[24]

These few examples of the outstanding contacts which Titsingh records suffice to give us an idea of the intimate associations which the Japanese had established with the Dutch at this time, associations from which the Dutch were also to gain a great deal. Titsingh's

Illustrations of Japan shows the result of careful translation from Japanese sources, as does also the posthumous *Annales des Empereurs du Japon*, which is a translation of the *Ōdai-ichiran*. Titsingh's ability to take away without molestation numerous books on Japan as well as maps and drawings of the Japanese islands illustrates the liberal state of affairs at Nagasaki.

This change to an attitude of friendly interest and coöperation toward the Dutch, we must assume, was to a large extent a reflection of official shogunal policy, an assumption which Titsingh bears out. It is through him that we are informed of the existence of a liberal group within the government which desired to "widen the road" of foreign intercourse. This party he links to Tanuma, and especially to the son, Mototomo, whose death in 1784 was, in his opinion, a mortal blow to the liberal cause.

The elder Tanuma's attitude toward the field of Western studies is perhaps best revealed through his association with Hiraga Gennai.[25] Hiraga was one of those unusual characters of the Tanuma period who in his diverse activities in the scholarly and literary worlds was as much a mirror of his age as Tanuma himself. He was born in 1729 at Shidoura in Sanuki province, the son of a minor samurai in the service of the Daimyo of Takamatsu. At the age of thirteen he began the study of botany under the local physician. Six years later (1748) he was given a salary of four rations and ten pieces of silver and employed as a pharmacist to his lord Matsudaira Yorimasa. In 1752 Hiraga made his first trip to Nagasaki, where he picked up a smattering of Dutch and a store of scientific knowledge. From here he went to Edo and placed himself under instruction in botany to Tamura Gen'yū. The latter, it will be recalled, was destined to make his name by heading the shogunal experiments in the production of ginseng, eventually becoming the superintendent of the Ginseng Monopoly. Tamura's botanical researches carried him over a wide area of Japan. In 1757 he opened an exhibition in Edo to display the many natural products he had collected. Being the first of its kind in Japan, it excited widespread interest throughout the country. Two years later Hiraga opened his own exhibition, at which he placed on display a number of rare products which he had discovered.

It is believed that Hiraga came into association with Tanuma at about this time, having been brought to the latter's attention by the chief retainer of the Tanuma house, Miura Shōji. If we can believe the accounts which tell of this meeting, Tanuma showed Hiraga immediate partiality and, after the first interview, frequently invited the young scholar to report personally on what he had learned at Nagasaki or from his Dutch books. It is also stated that Hiraga was involved in the falsification of the Tanuma genealogy.[26]

It was about the time of this supposed meeting with Tanuma that Hiraga appears to have begun harboring the desire to free himself from his feudal duties. In 1760 his lord had commissioned him to compile a work on the medicinal herbs to be found within the Takamatsu domain. Perhaps Hiraga felt that such restrictive labors would never offer him an opportunity to express himself adequately, or perhaps he had definite hopes of subsequently attaching himself to the Tanuma establishment; the reason is not clear. But shortly thereafter he asked to be released from service and was detached from the Takamatsu domain in 1761.

By this move Hiraga secured for himself greater freedom of movement, but if he had hoped to reënter feudal service for some other lord, his wish was not fulfilled. Hiraga remained a rōnin. From this point on, his life was directed to free-lance writing and acting as consultant on various engineering projects. His writings ranged from treatises on dinosaur bones, asbestos, and electricity to humorous writings for the popular stage and the bourgeois city audience. His scientific activities took him to Nagasaki where he continued his studies of Dutch, built himself a thermometer and an electric sparking machine, and even experimented with constructing a balloon. While at Nagasaki, Hiraga also conceived of a plan to export Japanese porcelains. Later he traveled to Sendai and Akita as a consultant for the copper mining operations in those localities. This was the unusual life which came to an end in 1779 in the Edo jail, where Hiraga had been confined for having killed one of his own pupils in a fit of anger.

Though the real conection between Tanuma and Hiraga is somewhat obscure, it is most natural to link the two together. Tanuma, representing the new iconoclastic spirit within the Tokugawa government, rose from the lowest level of officialdom through the use of new ideas and new methods. Hiraga, an example of the new spirit of restlessness and dissatisfaction which was affecting the samurai class, made his way by the mastery of an unorthodox branch of learning. Both were men out of the ordinary tradition of Tokugawa society, and both came under attack by the vested political and intellectual interests of the day.

What Tanuma's exact policy was toward the Dutch at Nagasaki is revealed by Titsingh himself, although his remarks must be taken with a certain degree of caution. We have already seen that Tanuma had approved an increase of trade with the Chinese for the purpose of importing gold and silver for the Tokugawa mints. Similar concessions were offered the Dutch, which, though slight, were nevertheless all that the Japanese at the time were able to give. How much farther the liberal shogunal authorities contemplated going is a matter of speculation which rests primarily upon a single passage in Titsingh's *Illustrations of Japan*. Since this passage has been the basis of so much reinterpretation by both Japanese and Western historians, it may be worth while to quote its main portions at length:

When they [the Japanese] turn their eyes to neighbouring nations, they observe that the admission of foreigners is not injurious to the government; and that a similar admission of strangers into their own country would furnish them with the means of studying a variety of arts and sciences of which they have but vague notions. It was this that induced Matsudaira-Tsou-no-Kami, the extraordinary counsellor of state, to propose in 1769 the building of ships and junks calculated to afford the Japanese facilities of visiting other countries, and at the same time to attract foreigners to Japan. This plan was not carried into execution in consequence of the death of that counsellor.

Though many Japanese of the highest distinction and intimately acquainted with matters of government, still consider Japan as the first empire in the world, and care but little for what passes out of it, yet such persons are denominated by the most enlightened as *Inooetzi-no-Kajerou*, or *frogs in a well*, a metaphorical expression, which signifies that when they look up, they can see no more of the sky than what the small circumference of the wall allows them to perceive. The eyes of the better informed had been long fixed on Tonoma-yamassiro-no-kami,[27] son of the ordinary counsellor of state Tonomo-no-kami,[28] uncle to the Djogoun,[29] a young man of uncommon merit, and of an enterprising mind. They flattered themselves that when he should succeed his father, he would as they expressed it, widen the road. After his appointment to be extraordinary counsellor of state, he and his father incurred the hatred of the grandees of the court by introducing various innovations, censured by the latter as detrimental to the welfare of the empire. He was assassinated on the 13th of May, 1784, by Sanno-Sinsayemon, as related in my *Annals of Japan*. This crime put an end to all hopes of seeing Japan opened to foreigners, and its inhabitants visiting other countries. Nothing more, however, would be required for the success of such a project, than one man of truly enlightened mind and of imposing character. At present, after mature reflection on all that is past, they are convinced that the secret artifices and intrigues of the priests of Siaka were the real cause of the troubles which for many years disturbed the peace of the empire.

In 1782 no ships arrived from Batavia, on account of the war with England. This circumstance excited general consternation not only at Nangasaki, but also at Osaka and Miyako, and afforded me occasion to stipulate with the government for a considerable augmentation in the price of our commodities for a term of fifteen years. Tango-no-kami,[30] the governor, with whom I kept up a secret intercourse, proposed to me in 1783 to bring over carpenters from Batavia to instruct the Japanese in the building of ships and smaller vessels, a great number of barks employed in the carriage of copper from Osaka to Nangasaki having been wrecked on their passage, which proved an immense loss to the government. Knowing that it would be impossible to comply with his request, because none of the common workmen employed in our dock-yard in the island of Java possessed sufficient skill, and the masters were too few to allow any of them to be spared for even so short a time; I proposed to Tango-no-kami to send with me, on my departure from Japan, one hundred of the most intelligent of his countrymen to be distributed in our yard, assuring him that pains should be taken to teach them all that was necessary to qualify them for carrying into execution at their return. The prohibition which forbids any native to quit the country, proved an insurmountable obstacle. On the arrival of a ship in the month of August, I caused the boats to manoeuvre from time to time in the bay with Japanese sailors on board, which much pleased the governor, but did not fulfill his intentions. I then promised that when I reached Batavia, I would have the model of a vessel built, and present him with it on my return, together with the requisite dimensions, and all possible explanations: this, I accordingly did in August the following year. The death of Yamassiro-no-kami, of which I received information immediately after my arrival at Batavia, annihilated all our fine schemes. Having finally quitted the country for Europe in the month of November in the same year, I know not whether my instructions on this point have been followed or not.[31]

The information contained in this passage is precisely the kind least likely to find confirmation in Japanese sources. To date no corroboratory Japanese documents have been discovered, so that we must try to assess without such aid the reliability and the full implication of Titsingh's statements.

Our first step should be to note that the facts given us by Titsingh are of two types, those actually experienced by him and those obtained at second hand. His story concerning "Matsudaira-Tsou-no-Kami" would come under the latter category. The official in question was most probably Matsudaira Settsu-no-kami Tadatsune,[32] Junior Councilor from 1747 to his death in 1768. Titsingh's corruption of this man's title, together with the obvious impossibility that Matsudaira should have made his proposal in 1769, one year after his death, immediately casts doubt upon the rest of the story. The crucial point at issue, of course, is whether Matsudaira was a man capable of having the ideas with which Titsingh credits him. Although there is no conclusive evidence on this point, his earlier positions in the shogunate as Master of Shogunal Ceremonies and Superintendent of Temples and Shrines were certainly not calculated to make him the "leader" of the liberal party as Murdoch would have it.[33] Professor Shimmura Izuru in his study of the problem believes it extremely unlikely that a proposal so openly in violation of the seclusion policy could have been made in public, especially by a man of Matsudaira's background.[34]

Titsingh's conversations with Kuze Tango-no-kami, however, were a matter of firsthand experience and hence may be given more credence. Since Kuze was one of the Tanuma group, what Titsingh tells us of him is extremely important in revealing Tanuma's own views on foreign policy. There is no question but what Kuze showed a remarkable open-mindedness in his attitude toward the Dutch by permitting the free exchange of correspondence between Titsingh and his Japanese friends and in conceiving of the plan to have Dutch shipwrights sent to Japan. But whether this demonstrated anything more than a desire to improve the method of shipping copper from Osaka to Nagasaki is again a matter of conjecture. Kuze did not need to go beyond the legitimate limits of domestic policy in wishing to improve Japanese knowledge of shipbuilding. To say that he conceived of this as the first step in the breaking of Japan's political isolation would be a dangerous conclusion.

But the fact remains that Titsingh left Japan with a belief that changes were in the air. There were certainly others, translators and students of the Dutch language, who talked to Titsingh openly of "widening the road." The willingness of the government to permit the circulation of such ideas without suppression was itself of major significance. That this freedom derived from the presence of the Tanuma faction in the shogunate is also clear, for with the fall of

Tanuma the era of liberal foreign policy came to an abrupt end and friendship again gave way to suspicion. Matsudaira Sadanobu as a matter of course tightened the traditional controls which had been relaxed under his predecessor. He was later to feel fully confirmed in this conservative policy by what he believed to be the menace of the Russians in the north and by political dangers which he foresaw in the spread of Western learning in Japan. Not only did he make certain that all thought of abandoning the traditional seclusion policy was carefully repressed, but he strove to keep Dutch studies from leading to the spread of dangerous ideas. During the late Tokugawa period, study of Western languages and sciences was tolerated purely as a technical means of keeping abreast of the outside world. Such study was conducted under careful control which divorced it from its disturbing anti-feudal implications.[35]

3. THE NORTHERN PROBLEM

Relations between the Japanese and Russians in the waters to the north of Japan began in comparative obscurity. During the seventeenth century contacts were occasional and haphazard. The main Russian interest in the Far East at that time was confined to Siberia and the attempted southward penetration into the Amur region. With the signing of the treaty of Nertchinsk in 1689, however, the Russians were forced to abandon their plan for the Amur. They consequently placed their major emphasis on the China fur trade at Kiakhta. As a result Russian expansion in quest of fur and empire was deflected eastward. After the beginning of the eighteenth century the Russians began the active exploration of the waters off the Siberian coast. The penetration of Kamchatka was followed by probes into the Kuriles. Bering's expeditions of 1728 and 1741 greatly increased Russian knowledge of the northern waters and made possible the exploration of Alaska and the northwest coast of America.

Throughout this period the Russians were aware of Japan and the advantages which trade with that country would hold for them.[36] The first concerted attempt to explore the Japanese islands and to investigate the possibility of trade seems to have been the Spanberg expeditions of 1738–1742. From this date the Russians began a slow descent of the Kuriles. As they went they established bases on some of the islands from which they traded with the native tribesmen for fur and food.

The Japanese, meanwhile, had only the vaguest knowledge of these northern islands. The scattered reports of Russian approaches took shape as a connected picture only after long delay. The suspicion by the Tokugawa authorities that Japan was being placed under aggressive foreign pressure came slowly during the sixth and seventh decades of the eighteenth century and was hampered by the lack of coöperation between Edo and Matsumae. The Japanese feudal representative in Ezo, the Daimyo of Matsumae, was in a singularly favorable situation. His lands were unassessed and he himself exempted from regular Alternate Attendance and the usual shogunal control. It was in 1759 that the authorities of the Matsumae domain received information of the actual settlement by the Russians on some of the Kurile islands, but the information was not passed on to Edo. The arrival of a Russian vessel in the port of Nemuro in 1778 was handled with extreme caution by the Matsumae Daimyo. The Russian request for trade was met by the usual reply that all the foreign trade of Japan was conducted through Nagasaki, but again the incident was not reported to the shogunate. Secrecy was doubtless maintained for a purpose, for already a brisk trade seems to have sprung up between the Japanese and the Russians. Moreover, the Matsumae officials were fearful of Tokugawa interference in their domain affairs.

The news of these events in the north could naturally not be kept from Edo for long. The incident which did most to dramatize the coming of the Russians was the strange case of Count Benyowsky.[37] A Hungarian by birth, he was captured by the Russians while serving in the Polish government. He managed to escape from exile in Kamchatka in 1771, and subsequently sailed the seas bordering Japan and the Ryukyus until he finally reached Canton. In the course of several landings on the Japanese coast he communicated with the Dutch at Nagasaki and warned them of the Russian activity in the north and of the secret trade relations which existed between the Russians and the Japanese of Ezo. At about this same time the Dutch also became apprehensive of the Russian Far Eastern policy, having been informed of Russian research in the Japanese language and other signs of Tzarist interest in Japan.[38] They thus passed on a series of warnings to the Japanese authorities.[39]

For various reasons, the shogunate paid little heed to these early communications. It was not until news of these events leaked out to the nonofficial world and aroused the concern of the students of foreign affairs that the government seemed to show an awareness of the significance of the Russian menace. In the atmosphere of liberality toward foreign studies referred to above, it was not long, of course, before the Russian problem became a matter of common knowledge among the Japanese Dutch scholars. These men were quick to point out the urgent need for the government to formulate a definite northern policy. The first significant outcry came from the Sendai physician, Kudō Heisuke.[40] Kudō learned of the existence of the clandestine trade with the Russians and of the gradual Russian exploration of the Kuriles from the Magistrate of Finance of the Matsumae domain. By piecing this knowledge together with what he gathered from his friends among the students of Dutch Learning, he was able to come out in 1783 with his famous *Akaezo fūsetsu kō*.[41] This essay, which was presented to the Edo authorities as a memorial, came out clearly in favor of the economic development of Ezo and the legalizing of trade relations with Russia. Because of the comprehensive nature of Kudō Heisuke's report and because of its effect upon shogunal policy, it deserves to be outlined at greater length.

First of all it should be noted that in urging the development of Ezo, Kudō argued from two basic points of view, one political and the other economic. He visualized both the necessity of increasing Japan's national production and the need for building a strong defense against the Russians. Yet of these two points of view the economic predominated. Kudō was a decided moderate. Unlike the alarmist Hayashi Shihei, he harbored no fanatic distrust of the Russians. His ideas were couched in a quiet logic attractive to government officials.

Kudō believed Ezo to be a land of opportunity, rich in precious metals [42] and fertile plains for colonization. Development of the Ezo mines would, he maintained, provide goods for export to either the Russians or the Chinese and Dutch. In either case it would enrich Japan.[43] The colonization of Ezo would not only provide room for Japan's surplus population but would act as a defense measure against the Russians. The Russians, he argued, were desirous only of trade; by meeting them openly and trading with them, the Japanese could satisfy the Russian desires. From such intercourse two benefits would be derived. Not only would Japan improve her economy, she would be able to acquaint herself with Russian policy and internal conditions and thus place herself in a better position to meet any subsequent Russian advance. Kudō pointed out that trade with the Russians already existed despite the stringent laws to the contrary, and that rather than attempt to suppress it, the government should profit by legalizing and controlling it. Since this trade was mainly in foodstuffs, rice, wine, and marine products, it was by nature well calculated to bring profit to Ezo as well as to the Japanese mainland. From this point he went on to argue for a more liberal trade policy for the rest of the country, the opening up of ports other than Nagasaki on the main island, and for the enrichment of Japan through trade.

Thus Kudō advocated departure from the traditional seclusion policy, but primarily for economic reasons. The political implications of such a move were minimized to a point where the thesis sounded relatively harmless. The *Akaezo fūsetsu kō* was completed in 1783, but Kudō was more circumspect than his associate Hayashi Shihei. Instead of publishing it, he presented it to Tanuma through the good offices of the chief Tanuma retainer, Miura Shōji.[44] Tanuma in turn brought it to the attention of his Superintendent of Finance, Matsumoto, who called in its author for further questioning. Matsumoto readily saw the seriousness of the northern situation and the opportunities for government profit. After consultation with Tanuma, he sent an order to the Matsumae Daimyo for a report on the mining potentials of the Ezo and on the current state of trade with Russia. This report when received contained information which varied considerably from that in Kudō's previous memorial, and it was therefore decided that an official commission should be sent to Ezo and the northern islands to investigate directly the true state of affairs in that region.

The expedition which got under way in the early months of 1785 was an elaborate affair for those days. Besides Yamaguchi Tetsugorō, an official of the Tokugawa Public Works Service (*fushin-yaku*), it included six shogunal appointees. Two vessels were especially constructed for the mission. The merchant Tomaya Kubei was ordered to take charge of transportation and procurement. The expedition first went to Matsumae, after which its members split up into several parties and proceeded to explore Ezo, the Kuriles, and Sakhalin.

As might be expected, the Tokugawa commissioners were given a cool reception by the Matsumae officials and the bale-goods contractors, who had been immune from government interference up to this time. Apparently the northern faction did everything to thwart the investigation, even to the point of threatening the natives of Ezo with death if they should reveal the existence of the illegal trade with Russia. The members of the expedition, however, uncovered enough evidence to prove without a doubt that Kudō Heisuke's contentions had been true. Their findings may be summarized as follows: [45]

1. The contract areas held by the bale-goods merchants had taken on the nature of security on the debts of the Matsumae domain, so that the daimyo himself had little control over these areas.

2. The Matsumae Daimyo and the contract merchants attempted to keep the Ainu as undeveloped and ignorant as possible in order to exploit them for their own advantage.

3. The inhabitants of eastern Ezo communicated with the Russians and imported silk, brocade, cotton, sugar, and medicine.

4. The inhabitants of western Ezo traded with Manchuria and imported jade, brocade, and eagle feathers.

5. This trade did not appear to be direct. The Japanese of Ezo used the Ainu as middlemen.

6. The Kuriles north of Itorup (Etoru) were occupied by Russians.

7. The Russians were constantly on Itorup in order to secure seal and sea lion furs and to trade with the Ainu. Frequently they passed the winter on the island.

Being apprised of these facts, Matsumoto presented to the higher Tokugawa authorities a number of recommendations.[46] The first was that the illicit trade should be searched out and stopped. He envisaged a three-year control plan wherein government stations would be set up to keep an eye on activities of the contract merchants. Secondly he argued against legalizing trade with the Russians, not out of any ideological objection, but because he felt the Nagasaki trade was enough to supply Japan's needs of foreign imports.[47] Furthermore, he feared such additional trade might reverse the balance established at Nagasaki and deplete Japan of her precious metals. On the other hand, Matsumoto recommended the long-range development of Ezo, and he went ahead on plans for the settlement of several thousand pariah in the northern island. But as we have already seen, the Tanuma faction was never given time to carry out its policies in the north.

The Russian question, more than that of the Dutch at Nagasaki, offered the Japanese the opportunity to make a new departure in their foreign policy. The Russians did not at first arouse the fear of the Japanese, and the shogunal officials, as they met the northern problem, could ignore the political implications of the situation and concentrate on the economic. It is significant that, while for various reasons Tanuma and his advisors did not openly advocate a lifting of the seclusion controls, they were able to face the problem logically and dispassionately. Had there been more time and had the views of such men as Kudō Heisuke gained greater currency, their eventual decision may well have been more daring.

But in the policy of Tanuma's successor, Matsudaira Sadanobu, the political and defensive aspects of the foreign problem eventually drove out every other consideration.[48] Emphasis was placed on military preparedness, secrecy, and absolute seclusion. Interest in foreign affairs among those outside the government was discouraged, and men such as Hayashi Shihei paid dearly for attempting to bring into the open the foreign question.

CHAPTER VI

Political Decline and Social Unrest

Our survey of the domestic and foreign policies of the bakufu during the administration of the Tenth Shogun has revealed some of the more positive results of the rise of Tanuma Okitsugu to power within the Tokugawa government. During these years, shogunal policy was characterized by a new interest in mercantilistic ventures and a tendency to relax the disciplinary and restrictive side of the administration. Through Tanuma's influence new men were brought into office and new ideas, many of which held encouraging promises for the future, were put into operation. But Tanuma has been remembered in history for the negative rather than positive aspects of his influence. The same freedom from restraint which in his day made possible an experimentation with new lines of state policy encouraged also the spread of license and bureaucratic negligence. This was the reverse side of the coin, the life of extravagance, the corruption of officials, the growing poverty and discontent of the lower classes, which is more often remembered as characteristic of the Tanuma period.

In the final analysis, the failure of Tanuma's policies was a product of his own personal defeat, for his political fall obscured the benefits his programs might have brought. This personal failure had a double origin. It was public, in that he was unable to stem the tide of decay within the official class or alleviate the misery of the people. It was private, in that he was unable to avoid the accusation of self-interest and corruption. In all fairness to Tanuma, it should be pointed out that he himself was not to blame for many of the evils heaped upon his head. The social and economic aberrations of his day were the outcome of many deep contradictions inherent in the Tokugawa system itself. Yet to his contemporaries, so quick to take a moralistic view of life, he became the scapegoat for conditions which were beyond his control. In the end he and his policies were overwhelmed in a wave of reaction and moral indignation.

I. THE AGE OF LUXURY

To the Confucian-trained warrior-aristocrat of the Tokugawa period one of the most grievous of social ills was what he termed luxury. In a status-bound society, based on a rigid landed economy, for the samurai to live beyond his income or the lower classes beyond their status was a matter of serious concern and the root of numerous sumptuary edicts issued by both the bakufu and the daimyo. The Tanuma age gained a reputation for being one of the most notorious periods of luxury and ostentation in Tokugawa history. It is matched in popular legend only by the earlier Genroku (1688–1704) and the later Bunka-Bunsei (1804–1829) eras. It is not easy to do justice to this aspect of the Tanuma age, not for any lack of material, but because of the superabundance of minute details which fill the pages of the native commentaries on the life of the period. There appears to be nothing the Japanese enjoyed so much as to set down in picturesque detail the many examples of novelty and unusual behavior which they noted among the samurai or townsfolk. A few of the more typical illustrations will thus have to suffice to convey the scene of luxurious living for which the Tanuma period is known.

Luxury started at the top, with the Shogun. It will be recalled that, upon becoming Shogun, Ieharu had excited hope among Tokugawa officialdom that he would be a man of strong character. In his first years he had undertaken a reform of the judicial organs of the shogunate and had inspired a revival of interest in the military arts. No physical weakling like his predecessor, he led the Tokugawa vassals to the hunt and held tests of archery and swordsmanship in front of the ancestral Ueno shrine. Thus the Bannermen and Housemen were put on their mettle and encouraged to follow the Spartan way of the warrior.

Unfortunately, as time pased, Ieharu did not insist on keeping these functions within the bounds of frugality. Hunts and contests became increasingly spectacular and extravagant, so that they eventually became a drain not only on the Tokugawa treasury but on the samurai who received the dubious honor of attending them.[1] In the end the trend toward pomp and pageantry affected every aspect of the Shogun's life and every function of the Shogun's court. The rebuilding of the Second Citadel at the time of Ieshige's retirement in 1760, the elaborate memorial service for Ieyasu in 1765,[2] the great progress to Nikkō in 1776,[3] were but the beginning of a series of heavy burdens which fell on the shogunate under Ieharu.

While the Shogun thus showed no inclination to check the heavy spending of his government, his chief favorite, Tanuma Okitsugu, is more generally accused of setting the tempo of high living among bakufu officials. We have already touched on the matter of Tanuma's wealth and his propensity for rare and costly gifts. We have seen how the custom of giving and receiving gifts had grown to immense proportions, and that Tanuma was the central figure in this business.

But the trend toward luxury was not dependent upon the conduct of individuals alone. As the warrior-aristocrat accustomed himself to life in the city, and as Edo official society became larger and its social functions more elaborate, an increasing strain was placed on the samurai's pocketbook. The custom which required new shogunal appointees to entertain all members of the official unit to which they were appointed was one of the great burdens for Edo officials. It did much to implant in the feudal class a habit of high living. Moriyama Takamori, a contemporary Tokugawa official, has left us a revealing description of the elaborate outlay for entertainment required of new appointees.[4] The particular post to which he was named obliged him to provide a banquet for his twenty-three new colleagues. This feast could be no ordinary affair, nor was it possible to keep expenditures within Takamori's means, since it was established by custom that the cakes must come from the high-priced Echigoya and the wine from the exclusive Sukiya. Thus the entire function cost him 48 ryō, a sizable sum for those days. Moriyama went on to say that one of his colleagues once attempted to substitute less costly fare but was so abused by his guests that he had to apologize publicly to them. These stories give us some idea of the social pressure under which the members of Edo officialdom lived.

Moriyama ended his discussion with a grateful word for Matsudaira Sadanobu who, he felt, had put an end to such enforced entertainments. But the shogunate in Tanuma's day also attempted to prohibit the abuse of junior officials by their seniors,[5] and, had Moriyama written a few years later, he would have known that Matsudaira Sadanobu was ultimately no more successful than Tanuma.

In matters of dress and behavior, shogunal warnings and sumptuary laws revealed how universal among the upper class was the desire for conspicuous display. Daimyo were cautioned to use palanquins only on specified occasions, to limit their attendants to the number due their status, and to refrain from dressing them in unusual habits so as to catch the eye of the people.[6] An order in 1764 complained that many of the feudal houses were in the hands of youths who dressed gaudily and set luxurious examples for their followers.[7] The form which such love of ostentation took can be illustrated by a few of the better-known stories of the period.

The first of these concerns one of Mizuno Tadatomo's retainers by the name of Hijikata. At a party given by Hijikata, the guests were startled to find the tearoom decorated with rare and costly objects worthy of a great lord. Two sketches by the famous artist Kano Motonobu [8] adorned the pillars of the *tokonoma*.[9] In front of these was an incense burner executed in pure gold and silver. For the ceremony, Hijikata used a silver kettle, a water jar of excellent Nanking ware, an incense box of yellow Annam ware, and a tea caddy of incised gold.[10]

Of Tanuma's Superintendent of Finance, Matsumoto, it is told that in summer he enclosed the several passageways from his quarters to those of his concubines with mosquito netting so that he could pass without annoyance to their apartments. Matsumoto also is said to have had a phobia against the sound of rain, so that he had a great awning constructed over the entire roof of his residence to keep the sound from penetrating to his rooms below.[11] It is further related of this same man that on one occasion a favor seeker came to him with a life-size Kyoto doll done up in a wooden box and gift wrapper. When the box was opened, however, it was discovered that the doll was alive and that Matsumoto had actually been presented with a dancing girl.[12]

We need not multiply these stories in order to visualize the extravagant gaiety of the life of Edo officialdom during these years. But even more astonishing displays of conspicuous consumption were seen among the city mercantile class. The townsfolk, because of their exclusion from political or social recognition, turned to the only form of self-expression available to them, the search for money and entertainment.[13] It was they who took the lead in inventing novel ways to display their wealth. Their courtesans, their literature, and their music became the chief elements of luxury and license in the life of urban society.

In Edo the most influential members of the merchant class were the Rice Brokers (*fudasashi*), who amassed great wealth by handling the collection of the rice tax and the conversion of rice to money for the Shogun and his retainers. It was a common occurrence to find Tokugawa Bannermen and Housemen so financially involved with these merchant houses that they were literally on allowance from them. Thus the Rice Brokers obtained a certain amount of political influence, or at least immunity, along with their economic power, for the authorities found it inconvenient to deal too harshly with the men who had their hands on the source of government income. This was illustrated in 1776, when the shogunate attempted to suppress some of the less desirable activities of the Rice Brokers by ordering them to put down interest rates and to desist from manipulating the rice market. When the merchants countered by discontinuing their services, the government was obliged to back down.[14]

Led by the Rice Brokers and other monopoly merchants, Edo bourgeois society rose to new heights of extravagance during the Temmei (1781–1788) period. It was then that Edo came into its own and captured from the Osaka-Kyoto area the leadership in the world of plebeian art and literature. These were the years of the so-called "eighteen men about town" (*Jūhachi daitsū*), the eighteen dandies who set the style of the times. Most of these men were Rice Brokers, and their world of activity was the theater quarter and the "nightless city" of Yoshiwara.

While the basic motives of this bourgeois culture were frivolous, it should not be supposed that the life of the *tsūjin*, or dandy, was coarse or vulgar. The key term in the culture of the Temmei period was *sui*, "elegance" or "sophistication." The gaudy first bloom of bourgeois culture which took its name from the Genroku period had by now matured into something more subtle and cultivated. These merchant dandies found pleasure in restraining their zeal for show and limiting their display to forms which only the cultivated eye could appreciate.

The luxurious life of the townsfolk of the Tanuma period have been generally described in terms of changes in their clothing, food, and other articles of daily use. Elaborate female hair styles with a profusion of combs and pins,[15] the increased use of silk and brocade, the added length of kimono sleeves and of the *haori*,[16] the expanded width of the *obi*,[17] were all held up as indicative of the greater wealth possessed by the merchant class. In matters of food the Tanuma period witnessed a sudden growth of restaurants equipped in a variety of ways to please the bourgeois taste. Novel dishes were imported from China and Holland, and many houses offered elaborate menus in place of the previous practice of serving only one set course for all patrons.[18]

Domestic life also reached new standards of comfort and luxury. Domestic architecture became more substantial.[19] The wealthy merchants were able to provide gardens for their pleasure and fireproof storehouses for their protection. Yearly festivals and ceremonies were celebrated with increased costliness. Weddings became more elaborate. New games enlivened the leisure hours of the people. The three-stringed *shamisen* became popular throughout the entire nation.[20]

In the entertainment world, the theater quarters and the Yoshiwara took on a special brilliance. It was at this time that the geisha first made her appearance.[21] The Kabuki theater reached a high point in lavishness of production. A large number of excellent actors supplied the needs of a growing audience among all classes, high and low.[22]

It will be argued that not all of these developments in city culture were indicative of what we would term extravagance. Much of this so-called luxury found among the lower classes was merely the sign of a rising standard of living. But in the formalized Tokugawa class society even the normal progress toward better dietary and living conditions was looked on with distrust by the authorities. A static theory of society required unchanging habits within each of the status groups. Thus among the merchants and tradespeople, better living standards and the display of greater wealth was decried as luxury, while among the samurai, the quest for entertainment was branded as a sign of moral decay.

2. AN AGE OF MORAL DECAY

The Tanuma period has been described as an age of general moral decay. Like the charge of luxury, this charge has a social rather than individual connotation. For immorality, as applied by the Tokugawa Japanese to their society, generally took on the meaning of transgression of status, of behavior unbecoming one's class. Defined in this way, the Tanuma age was undeniably a time of moral degeneration for all classes: warrior, peasant, and merchant. It was a time of loose social conduct, when the samurai lost their sense of honor and military spirit, when townsfolk aped their betters, and when villagers abandoned their farms and flocked to the cities.

One of the chief complaints of Tokugawa moralists who surveyed the life of ease lived by the city-bred feudal class was that it was losing its virility. Sugita Gampaku, himself a most unwarlike samurai, has left us a vivid description of the degeneracy which he saw around him. He writes:

> On looking at the condition of the present day military class, I observe that its members have grown up in a most fortunate age of prosperity which has continued for nearly three hundred years. For five or six generations they have had not the slightest battlefield experience. The martial arts have steadily deteriorated. Were an emergency to occur, among the Bannermen and Housemen who must come to the Shogun's support, seven or eight out of ten would be as weak as women and their morale as mean as merchants. True martial spirit has disappeared completely.[23]

The shogunate was, of course, not unaware of this loss of military vigor among its vassals. It will be remembered that Ieharu had encouraged the arts of swordsmanship and archery in his early years as Shogun. But the cultivation of the warlike virtues became an increasingly artificial pastime in an age of peace, while on the other hand the attractiveness of urban social life was a pull too great to resist. The pages of the *Tokugawa jikki* are full of entries which record the punishment of shogunal retainers who behaved in a manner unbecoming their position as samurai and as officers of the Shogun. The phrase "conduct in disregard of one's status," *mi wo wasuretaru furimai*,[24] was frequently used in condemning these unfortunate men to expulsion from office or to lifelong banishment. A few examples from the *Tokugawa jikki* will give us an idea of what was considered culpable conduct.

In the summer of 1764, four low-ranking officials of the Edo government went to the Kuroda river in Edo, ostensibly to practice the manly art of swimming. However, they took along with them a boatload of geisha and a quantity of sake. The party caroused late into the evening and finally returned. It was not until the next day, when the men had sobered up, that it was discovered that one of their party had been left behind, drowned in the river. When brought to judgment, the three officials at first tried to conceal the event, then behaved in an insolent fashion before the members of the Supreme Court of Justice. For this crime the three officers were expelled from the samurai class by being stricken from the roster of *bushi*. The townspeople involved were also punished.[25]

In 1766, two separate instances are recorded of Bannermen who were convicted and banished for gambling.[26] The following year a Tokugawa official was punished for brawling in the streets of Edo, another for befriending suspicious characters and for going about town without his swords.[27] In 1771 an official in the service of the Heir Apparent absconded after having spent his substance in high living. For a time he hid in a prostitute's house, then drifted about the outlying villages, gambling with the common people. Upon being picked up by the shogunal police, he was banished.[28] A few years later another official, driven to extreme poverty, dressed himself as a menial and disappeared. In the course of his wanderings he stole money from a merchant.[29] Another, after stealing clothes from a second-hand clothing dealer and pawning them for money, spent the proceeds on a prostitute and then absconded.[30]

Murdoch has described one of the most sensational orgies of the time when in 1787 Mikami Mino-no-kami, a 3000-koku Bannerman, held a party for seven of his colleagues, also Bannermen of 5000-, 6000-, and even 7000-koku.[31] As might be suspected, this was one of those enforced banquets which followed a promotion in the Shogun's service. In the course of the evening the interior of Mikami's house was completely wrecked, and the participants moved on to spend the rest of the night at the Yoshiwara. The next day none of the officers was able to report for duty and severe punishments were handed out. Another story which scandalized the people of the time was a love suicide between a prostitute and a 4500-koku Bannerman.[32]

These incidents, taken from the annals of the Tanuma period, are sufficient to give us an understanding of what the Japanese have meant by the charge of moral decay. A dispassionate view of these breaches of discipline will reveal, in nearly every case, problems deeper than individual weakness. In many of the incidents cited, there is evidence of the general economic decline of the samurai class and of the inevitable process whereby city-living undermined the

zeal of the fighting man. The same pages of the *Tokugawa jikki* from
which we have just drawn yield numerous illustrations of the economic causes behind the misbehavior of the Tokugawa officials. In
1762, for instance, one of the Osaka City Magistrates was relieved
of duty for borrowing large sums of money from Osaka merchants
and failing to make good on his debts.[33] In the same year, one of the
Edo City Magistrates was convicted of fraudulent financial dealings
with other Tokugawa officials.[34] In 1771 a minor shogunal official
was banished and his son executed because the latter had been convicted of theft.[35] The record of the following year tells of a Bannerman who borrowed money from the villagers of his fief and then
refused to return the sum. The villagers rose up in a mass protest
and thus forced the matter to the attention of the government.[36]
There is also the pitiful story of another minor official who was too
poor to provide himself with suitable attendants and so claimed illness in order to avoid having to appear for duty. But tiring of his
voluntary confinement, he at length took to drinking and eventually
ended up in a brawl which indicated to the authorities that he was
not the invalid he claimed to be.[37]

Among the daimyo there were many signs of financial difficulty.
Some found the burden of the Alternate Attendance system too
heavy, and on occasion requested to be relieved of the duty.[38] The
feudal houses had neither the means nor the desire to maintain their
full military strength. Some houses faced outright bankruptcy. For
example, in 1782 Sakakibara Masanaga, a 150,000-koku daimyo of
Takada in Echigo, had to request financial aid of the shogunate to
rehabilitate his bankrupt domain. The Shogun granted him 30,000
ryō, but simultaneously reduced Sakakibara to the status of a 50,-
000-koku daimyo until he should get back on his feet.[39]

The tendency of the samurai to become urbanized was in many
ways an unavoidable result of the system whereby daimyo and their
attendants congregated in castle cities. In particular it was accentuated by the enforced residence of a large portion of the feudal
aristocracy in Edo, where they were constantly exposed to the debil-
itating enticements of bourgeois society. The samurai, of course, had
his own pastimes, his own art and literature proper to his class, but
it took either a dull or an overly serious mind to be content with
the strictly manly exercises and the morally uplifting Confucian
classics. As decades of peace dissipated all memory of military alarm,

and as the bourgeois culture grew in variety and sophistication, it is not strange that there should have been a growing defection within the ranks of the military class, that the art, literature, and the night spots of bourgeois origin should have appealed to an increasing number of the warrior-aristocrats.

It is said that, by the middle of the eighteenth century, 70 per cent of the patrons of the Yoshiwara were samurai. Although we cannot verify this statement, a glance back at the stories of the delinquent Bannermen will show that nearly every one involved a trip to the "nightless city." In 1753 the shogunate issued a warning that every daimyo must take a legitimate wife at least once during his life. This has been interpreted to mean that the daimyo were in the habit of limiting their relations to the more exciting company of concubines taken from the gay quarters.[40]

Bourgeois pastimes became the delight of the warriors. In the houses of the samurai the once despised shamisen was now frequently heard, and the singing of the plebeian *jōruri*[41] and popular songs replaced the more proper excerpts from the classical *nō* drama. Of the eighteen dandies of the Temmei period, two were samurai, one the scholar Murata Shunkai, the other the famous physician and expert in Dutch studies, Katsuragawa Hoshū.[42] Samurai read and sometimes wrote the plays, the novels, the risqué stories, and poetry of the bourgeois circle. The Tokugawa official Ōta Nampo (1752–1826), whose work in a serious vein has already been referred to,[43] was one of the chief figures of the *kyōka*[44] school of humorous poetry in Edo. Hiraga Gennai wrote *kabuki* plays and originated the comical *sharebon*.[45] Ōta reports that the Superintendents of Finance, Kuze and Kawai, neglected their serious studies for the writing of comical poetry.[46]

Tanuma himself seems to have been more at home in this hybrid society than in the strictly aristocratic environment which he, as a daimyo, should have cultivated. He is frequently accused of having set an example of lax behavior and of having condoned, or at least ignored, the gross breaches of conduct which so shocked the old-line military men. The *Tokugawa jikki* is full of complaints concerning the disregard of rules and regulations among the Tokugawa officials. In the ceremonial functions of the Shogun's castle, proper seating arrangement was ignored. The daimyo, when leaving the assemblies, lifted their voices or jostled each other unbecomingly as each tried to make his exit ahead of the others.[47] Outside of the castle, daimyo failed to carry their proper regalia, and retainers went about without swords. Guards on night duty at the castle were observed to lock the doors and spend their time within, carousing in groups rather than going their rounds in military fashion.[48] In the streets of Edo the government had difficulty in finding retainers who were capable of performing the duties of policemen.[49]

Urbanization of the warrior was further reflected in the closer financial dependence of the daimyo on the merchant financiers and the growing participation of samurai in commercial activities. In view of the accepted tradition that the samurai was to maintain honor and dignity without regard for his physical well-being and that he was not to touch money or consider financial gain, Tanuma's money-conscious policy was certainly a departure from the principles of military government. The entire mercantile program was held in suspicion by a large proportion of the feudal aristocracy because it put money before rice and soiled the hands of the fighting class. But neither the central nor the domain governments could afford to be particular about how they filled their treasuries. And the poverty-stricken samurai was only too glad to find ways of augmenting his insufficient salary. At this early stage the individual opportunities of the samurai to enter business were not yet well developed. It is known that some Housemen engaged in reclamation projects and that an increasing number bought agricultural land to supplement their feudal holdings.[50] The *Tokugawa jikki* informs us that samurai were in the habit of renting out their town houses to merchants,[51] and many of the more businesslike apparently made a profitable enterprise out of their rentals. But the large-scale participation of samurai in domestic industry and handicrafts which was characteristic of the late Tokugawa period was only just beginning.

The military class lost prestige not only by abandoning its strict code of behavior but by the increased concessions it was obliged to yield to the lower classes. The government itself, having succumbed to the practice of encouraging and utilizing the merchants, was scarcely able to restrain their growing power. We have already referred to the government's defeat in its skirmish with the Rice Brokers. In 1765 a Tokugawa order attempted to regulate the interest rates of the moneylenders and to curtail the practice of dunning before the gates of the samurai residences, but such orders were ignored whenever they were put out.[52] During the Tanuma period a large number of merchants were employed by the shogunate to run government monopolies or to act as special financiers; many of these were favored with the privilege of bearing a surname and wearing the long sword.[53] The two-sword townsman became a familiar feature of Edo bourgeois society. It is stated that the great merchants lived like daimyo, possessed innumerable residences, and regulated their houses as would a member of the upper class. To the disgust of the samurai, merchants were heard to call their wives and children by terms reserved for use by the daimyo or even the Shogun.[54]

Thus forced by economic necessity and lured by new pleasures, the warrior-aristocrat began to lose his high sense of caste. A life of comfort and leisure replaced the rigors of the battlefield. Money gained ascendancy over considerations of loyalty and feudal duty. The samurai, his morale undermined and his income depleted, became an easy victim of hypocrisy and corruption.

3. AN AGE OF OFFICIAL CORRUPTION

The charge of corruption has already been met in our discussion of Tanuma's career. We have seen that in a society in which the practice of present-giving was a matter of long-established custom it is extremely difficult to ascertain the dividing line between etiquette and bribery. There is little question, however, that the giving of gifts developed out of all proportion during the Tanuma period. Tanuma, himself, often mixed public and private affairs. When official appointments were decided according to the size of a contribution, when matters of state policy were influenced by private interest, when money replaced the customary token gift, then the accusation of corruption cannot be avoided.

Kanzawa Tokō in his *Okinagusa* has painted a vivid picture of the abuses which he saw in the Tokugawa official circles.[55] He writes that bribery and flattery took the place of honest administration and that each official sought by the use of gifts and favors to improve his private interest. The dominant ambition of most officials was to rise to a position where they in turn could become the recipients of such gifts, but the majority went through their incomes before such appointment came.[56] According to Kanzawa those who refrained from bribe-giving were treated with scorn, and for them even the life of a rōnin would be considered happy.

Matsudaira Sadanobu had only harsh words for the corruption of his predecessor's age.[57] In typical Confucian style he frequently repeated the pious warning that reform would have to come from the top, that with the Shogun and his chief ministers lax in their behavior, one could hardly expect better conduct from the lesser officials. Specifically he attacked the habit of cultivating the women of the Great Interior, the endless requests for favors from people in high places, and the corruption of the Tokugawa local Deputies, the *daikan* and *gundai*.

These, of course, are chronic problems of any bureaucracy which has attained its maturity. But what especially condemned Tanuma in the eyes of his moralistic contemporaries was not so much the fact that these excesses existed but that they believed he did little to stop them. In contrast to Matsudaira Sadanobu, he issued no flood of hortatory injunctions, and made no pretense at acting the good example. Thus, when in 1773 an order came out against the habit of making petitions outside the regular bureaucratic channels,[58] and when in 1777 the practice of working through the female apartments was singled out for condemnation,[59] few people listened, for Tanuma himself was the worst offender in these matters. Of the common accusation that Tanuma practiced private corruption and made huge profits out of the financial transactions of the government, there is no positive evidence. But the information that we have concerning his colleagues makes such a charge plausible enough. It will be recalled that two of Tanuma's Superintendents of Finance, Akai and Matsumoto, were convicted of dishonest tax collecting. In the early years of the Tanuma period two officers of the Tokugawa treasury in Osaka were exiled for accepting bribes from the local merchants. These officials had given out information that the government was about to buy gold, and thereby made immense profits for themselves and their merchant accomplices.[60]

Among the host of lesser Tokugawa officials the existence of corruption, while not excusable, was perhaps more understandable. Of all the bakufu officials the local Deputies seem to have been the most constant source of concern. Murdoch has several lengthy paragraphs describing the increased corruption among these officials following the death of Yoshimune. But corruption was no sudden development in the Tokugawa local administration. Yoshimune himself was certainly not immune to it.[61] As in the case of so many of the accusations leveled at the personnel of the Tanuma period, more than personal morality was involved.[62] This becomes evident when we look into the various entries in the *Tokugawa jikki* in which deputies were cited for irregularities. In 1770, for example, a Deputy by the name of Ikeda Kihachirō Tokiyasu was convicted of using tax money to pay off his own debts and of putting government tax funds out for usury. His punishment was to have his meager 150-koku salary reduced to 50 and the confiscated portion applied in yearly installments to wipe out his indebtedness.[63]

This story reveals a condition which underlay the whole Deputy problem, namely the low salary which these officials received. The local representatives of the shogunate were customarily chosen from among Bannermen of low rank. Their personal salaries were small and the funds allotted them for official expenses were insufficient. Yet each one administered a domain of some 100,000 koku. Moreover, since the larger portion of a Deputy's duties involved his presence in Edo, such officials often were obliged to cut expenses by remaining permanently in Edo, leaving the actual supervision of the peasants to subordinates. As the number of intermediary officials increased and as the Deputies lost touch with the localities under their jurisdiction, opportunities for corruption and inefficiency naturally multiplied. Tanuma did not entirely neglect this problem, and it was under his direction that Deputies were organized into mutually responsible groups of three or four in which the members of each group were set to check on each other.[64] But corruption in the ranks of Tokugawa officialdom stemmed not so much from the attitude of the higher authorities or from any lack of restraints as from the fundamental inequalities which were part of the feudal system and from the worsening economic conditions which the maintenance of an anachronistic system made inevitable. Such conditions were further aggravated by the cycle of natural calamities which periodically plagued the Japanese islands.

4. THE JUDGMENT OF HEAVEN [65]

With a regularity which seemed hard to explain as coincidence, times of serious political decline during the Tokugawa period appear to have invited the retribution of heaven.[66] This was true of the declining years of Tsunayoshi's administration, during the luxurious Genroku era (1688–1704). It was also true of the last years of Ienari's shoguncy, during the corrupt Bunsei (1818–1829) and Tempō (1830–1843) eras. But it is doubtful if either of these periods matched in fury and devastation the succession of calamities which descended upon the Japanese of the Tanuma period. By some strange fate Tanuma seemed doomed to have his policies wrecked and his name blackened by the whims of nature. In the minds of the people his influence in the shogunate was believed to account for the disasters which descended upon them from above.

Underlying the troubles which plagued the last fifteen years of the Tenth Shogun's administration was drought. Beginning with 1770, nearly every year saw the withering of crops in one part of the land or another because of the lack of rain. In some areas, for eight consecutive years severe drought parched the land. In the cities, food became scarce and water almost nonexistent.[67] Fire raged unchecked, and disease spread with alarming suddenness. On top of this was added the terror of heavenly portents. In 1770 a hurricane leveled the newly built imperial palace in Kyoto. A great comet, with a tail which spread over half the heavens, lit up the sky throughout the summer and autumn.[68]

The year 1772 (Meiwa 9. 2. 29) started off with the second largest fire in the history of the city of Edo. The greater portion of the city was burned to ashes, including a large number of daimyo residences. According to unofficial reports the fire cut a path nearly five miles wide and fifteen miles long.[69] It destroyed 178 temples and shrines, 127 official daimyo residences, 878 nonofficial residences, 8705 houses of Bannermen, and 628 blocks of merchant dwellings. It is estimated that there were over 6000 casualties, a large portion of which were deaths.

The human suffering which such a fire brought to the great capital of the Tokugawa is easily imagined; yet beyond this was the staggering cost of reconstruction, much of which fell upon the shogunate. After the fire, the Shogun was immediately besieged by feudal lords and retainers for funds to rebuild their residences, and the shogunate was obliged to set up a graduated scale of amounts which could be borrowed from the Tokugawa treasury.[70] The Edo government was further burdened with the expense of repairing the damage to its own official buildings.

Throughout the spring and summer of 1772 drought conditions continued. Then suddenly in the autumn (9. 8. 2) a tempest hit the Kantō area causing floods and ruining crops. In Edo many of the residences, newly rebuilt or still building after the fire of the previous spring, were blown down or ruined by the water, and the great Eitai bridge was knocked askew. Hardly had the people of Edo recovered from this calamity when a storm of equal intensity struck again (9. 8. 17) and blew down an estimated 4000 houses.[71]

Such was the terrible ninth year of Meiwa. Before long the people began to pun upon the year name (*nengō*), calling it the year of calamity.[72] The government in the eleventh month had the year name changed to An'ei (eternal tranquillity).[73] This act had little effect on the course of nature, however. During the second year of An'ei (1775), from early spring into summer, epidemic diseases spread over the country. In Edo alone some 190,000 persons are estimated to have perished, and, as the epidemic spread from townspeople to aristocracy, death struck the ranks of the Tokugawa Collaterals and took the heir to the Owari house.[74]

In 1774 conditions became somewhat better. The harvest was normal, and gradually the price of rice, which during the years of drought had soared to great heights, came down to a reasonable level. The Tokugawa government was able to order its local officers and the daimyo to put aside rice for future trouble.[75] But relief was only temporary. By 1777 bad harvests had again made rice scarce, so that storage was impracticable. Few areas had been able to build up any appreciable reserve.[76] The next few years thus saw a general worsening of the agricultural base of the country, while catastrophe struck in isolated spots throughout the land.

In 1778 Kyoto was visited by a destructive flood. The following year the volcanic island of Sakurajima, just a mile from the city of Kagoshima in Satsuma, erupted and rained destruction onto that populous city. The dead were counted at 16,000.[77] In 1780 heavy rains and floods in the Kantō district necessitated extensive government relief in the stricken areas.[78]

But this was only a prelude to what was to befall the country. In the early summer of 1785 (Temmei 3. 7. 6) the great volcano of Asama in the province of Shinano, some eighty miles northwest of Edo, erupted. For four days it never ceased pouring out lava and throwing up rocks and ashes. The skies over Edo darkened and a gray rain of ashes descended upon the city. In the areas between Asama and Edo, destruction was appalling. The immediate loss of life was estimated at over 20,000.[79] Large areas around the foot of the mountain were scorched, while the entire provinces of Shinano, Kōzuke, and Kai were buried under ashes.[80] In these areas the agricultural crop was ruined, roads became impassable and rivers were clogged so that they overflowed their banks.

Not only did this catastrophe cut deeply into the rice income of the shogunate, but relief and rehabilitation bore heavily on the Tokugawa, for these provinces were the heart of the Shogun's own lands. Once it was realized that the local officials were unable to cope with the situation, the shogunate moved to the scene and put its funds behind the tremendous task of clearing the ashes from the fields.[81] The Superintendent of Finance, Matsumoto, was ordered personally to supervise the work, and eventually the entire peasant population was mobilized and paid and fed out of the government treasury.[82] This work of clearance went on into the next year, but it is said that much of Shinano and Kōzuke remained unproductive for four or five years.

The year 1783 did not need this special catastrophe to make it one of the blackest ones in Tokugawa history. Throughout the country there was an almost complete crop failure and, coming as it did after a succession of poor years, this failure brought in its wake famine and pestilence. The center of the famine area was in northern Japan, where it was reported that nearly half of the entire population died.[83] The people resorted to cannibalism, and lawlessness went unchecked.

In 1786, the last year of the Tanuma period, the entire nation's agricultural production was cut by two-thirds; famine and plague were almost universal. The Kantō area was swept by one of the worst storms in its history, and floods reached record height. It was this storm which wrecked the Imbanuma project, destroyed bridges, and played havoc with the city of Edo.[84]

5. THE JUDGMENT OF THE PEOPLE

These are the principal calamities of the Tanuma period, the terrible works of nature which descended upon Japan in the short space of sixteen years. No one living through such experiences could refrain from asking the reason for such a convergence of disaster upon Japan. Few doubted that in some way or other it was connected with Tanuma's unusual rise to political influence. The belief that maladministration could bring on visitations from heaven is a common concept throughout the world. It is especially prevalent in the Far East among those people influenced by the Confucian view of the relationship between heaven and human society. In actuality a society such as that of Tokugawa Japan, which was still largely agrarian in nature, with a population expanded to the limit of its capacity to support it, was especially vulnerable to sudden changes in the agricultural yield or to widespread natural calamity. And this vulnerability was doubtless accentuated during periods of political or economic instability. It is impossible, of course, to credit Tanuma's unorthodox policies or the laxity of his officials as the cause of a volcanic eruption, of a storm, or a succession of droughts, for these are directed by forces outside the realm of human interference. But when we come to the secondary disasters, the famines, the fires, the spread of pestilence, then the government and the people themselves may be brought to account.

The great fire of the ninth year of Meiwa was started by arson and, from a small blaze which might easily have been put out,[85] developed into the second largest fire in the history of Edo. From the Tokugawa orders to its fire fighters after the event, we can ascertain that the Edo fire patrols had declined in spirit and efficiency.[86] They wasted precious time disputing over matters of jurisdiction. Samurai and merchant units refused to coöperate and often fell to quarreling. It must also be remembered that the Edo of Tanuma's time was a city whose growth had made the current methods of fire, flood, or disease control grossly inadequate.[87] People lived in unhealthy concentration; they built their houses too close together; areas once left vacant had been built over to meet the constant pressure of an expanding population. During the Tanuma period, Edo paid not only for ineffective official control but for the cumulated social dislocations of previous generations.

Disasters in the countryside have frequently been blamed on inadequate preventive measures by the local officials or failure to bring prompt and adequate relief. Japanese historians have generally contrasted the poor state of affairs in the Tokugawa domains with the ideal conditions created in the lands of three model administrators of the period.[88] These three daimyo, Hosokawa Shigekata, Uesugi Harunori, and Matsudaira Sadanobu, through a combination of economic retrenchment, state aid, and moral exhortation, are said to have brought their fiefs through the series of droughts and famines with a minimum of suffering and loss of life. But judgments in this matter should be withheld until more penetrating comparative studies have been made. Certainly many factors besides government administration were involved. The size of administrative areas, for instance, their relative economic development, or the past history of agricultural conditions [89] had much to do with the applicability and effectiveness of the administrative techniques then in favor. Thus while Matsudaira Sadanobu had singular success as a daimyo, he found the running of the shogunate another matter. The reforms which had worked so well in his domain had little effect on nation-wide problems.

The people of the Tanuma period, however, were scarcely able to assess the great calamities of the 1770's and 1780's objectively. To the contemporary peasant or citizen of Edo, or even to the intellectuals, these disasters were taken as a reflection on Tanuma himself and on the shogunal administration.[90] Directly or indirectly these natural disturbances undermined the public trust in the Tokugawa government. Dissatisfaction expressed itself in all classes of society, and at the lowest level broke out in open revolt.

Numerous detailed studies of the peasant uprisings (*hyakushō ikki*) of Tokugawa Japan have been made by native scholars, and since their results are available in English,[91] no lengthy treatment of this subject is necessary here. It can well be imagined, however, that the years of financial distress and natural calamity which marked the Tanuma period, should have witnessed an unprecedented number of mass protests and uprisings among the peasantry and the city poor. The causes of these uprisings were not necessarily uniform. Not all of them were directed against the government. But it is undeniable that a large percentage were brought on by the unreasonableness of the official class or the unwillingness or inability of the government to relieve popular distress.

Two mob protests against the shogunate have already been referred to, the revolt against the boat tax of 1785 and the larger uprising against the silk inspection scheme of 1781. Other uprisings protesting exactions of the central authorities occurred in the spring of 1764, when the peasants of the shogunal domains opposed an emergency tax levy to defray the expenses of entertaining envoys to the Shogun from Korea,[92] and in the winter of 1764–65, when a levy of men and horses was made in preparation for the great anniversary service for Ieyasu at Nikkō. In the latter instance an estimated 200,000 villagers converged upon Edo. They marched in angry mobs oblivious of the gunfire of the government guards and were dispersed only after reassurances were offered by the respected Kantō Deputy, Ina Hanzaemon Tadasuke. The peasants were granted their petition that the additional tax be repealed. But several hundred of their leaders were later imprisoned on the grounds that the mobs had behaved in an unruly fashion and had wrecked and plundered the houses of wealthy merchants along the way.[93]

More numerous than these uprisings against the actions of the central government were those of local origin. The Tokugawa Deputies were under constant pressure to squeeze from the peasants all that they would yield. Such pressure, together with the growing private corruption among the local Tokugawa officials, accounted for many small disturbances, particularly during times of poor harvest or famine when the tax collectors refused to ease the tax burden. Troubles in the Tokugawa lands of Hida appear to have been endemic as a result of the exactions of the Deputy, Ōhara Hikoshirō. These matters came to a head between 1771 and 1773, when the farmers several times resorted to violence in protesting the Deputy's methods of taxation. In 1773 a group of farmers proceeded to Edo to put their case before the highest shogunal authorities. In Hida at the same time 10,000 farmers banded together in insurrection. The peasants were finally quieted when the Deputy called upon the troops of neighboring domains to come to his aid with cannon and guns.[94]

During these same years the domains of the Tokugawa collateral, the Lord of Mito, were disturbed by mass uprisings over the minting of iron coins. The people, angered by the rise of prices, which they blamed on the new issue, rioted and destroyed one of the mints. The Mito authorities gave up their attempt to issue coins in 1775.[95]

These are but a few of the better-publicized uprisings against the Tokugawa authorities during the Tanuma period. Many similar disturbances troubled the domains of the daimyo. But it must not be supposed that the feudal class was the only object of peasant protest. The wealthy landowning peasant and the merchant frequently shared the enmity of the lower classes. A secondary aspect of most of the uprisings here described was the wrecking and looting of the houses of the wealthy and the destruction of the record books of the moneylenders.

Riots stimulated by the economic oppression of the landlord-moneylending class became more frequent in the years of famine after 1783. In the fall of that year, after the eruption of Asama and the destruction of the rice crop, the entire area north of Edo seethed with angry mobs of starving peasants. One such mob, 1000 strong, from the town of Annaka in Kōzuke, stormed their lord's castle in an effort to secure relief. On being repulsed, they turned on the houses of the wealthy, breaking into storehouses and distributing rice and treasure.[96] Such a pattern was often repeated.

Although the rural population was most immediately affected by conditions of drought and famine, as food became scarce and the price of rice soared, the city poor were also reduced to misery. Their desperation led to destructive riots known as *uchi kowashi*. Between 1785 and 1787 the price of rice rose from 61 momme to 187 momme of silver per koku.[97] A series of severe rice riots in 1787, though coming after Tanuma's fall, were a result of these conditions. Rioting began in Osaka in the spring of 1787 and spread to Edo, where for three days mobs of citizens wrecked and looted the premises of rice dealers and wealthy merchants. The shogunate, unable to stop the lawlessness, waited for the riots to expend themselves and then instituted relief measures.[98]

While the incidence of popular violence showed undeniable signs of increase during the Tanuma period, it is well to remember that serious uprisings did not necessarily begin at this time. They were, in fact, a disturbing feature of the administration of the model Shogun Yoshimune as well.[99] Many of the troubles which came to a head in Tanuma's time had their origin in Yoshimune's policies. Yoshimune's "bakufu first" attitude, as it was termed, had done much to worsen the public attitude toward the Tokugawa. It was he who had raised the rice tax from 40 to 50 per cent of the crop in the shogunal lands.[100]

Furthermore, it is possible to see beneath the varying circumstances which gave rise to these uprisings the same deep-seated economic problems which lay at the bottom of so many of the other signs of Tokugawa decay. The rioters themselves made this clear when they attacked the premises of moneylenders and sake merchants. During the calamitous last years of the Tanuma period, the one group which was able to come out ahead was the merchants. Their ability to manipulate the rice market, to foreclose on mortgages, or buy up land cheaply [101] earned them the hatred of both the peasantry and the warrior class. They symbolized the growing penetration of money economy into rural life which, more than any other factor, accounted for the decline of the village community and the disruption of the feudal rice tax system.

Whatever the root of the problem, however, it must be admitted that the severe uprisings of the mid-Tokugawa period did nothing to enhance the prestige of the shogunate or of the administrative class. Once all-powerful, the authorities now appeared unable to cope with the angry peasants and townsfolk. As uprisings became more numerous and more violent, the shogunate tried by edict and military force to suppress the unrest among the lower classes. In 1734, the central government gave orders that its Deputies should call on neighboring daimyo for reinforcements in order to bring back tranquillity to their lands.[102]

The order was reinforced in 1769.[103] Local officials were ordered to suppress mob protests at any cost. In 1770 offers of money and the privilege of bearing the long sword and a surname were made to villagers who would give information leading to the suppression of uprisings.[104] Nevertheless, revolts increased, and although in most instances the authorities took a number of token heads, the peasants generally won their petitions. It is clear that the feudal authorities, caught between the alternatives of ruthless suppression and maintenance of the productivity of the agricultural community, hesitated, and in their indecision lost what to them was most precious, their prestige.

While riots and mob appeals were the peasant's most aggressive means of protest against government oppression and unbearable conditions, quiet but more insidious action on their part undermined the productive capacity of village economy. By the mid-Tokugawa period the voluntary limitation of the size of peasant families by abortion or infanticide [105] and the escape of the rural population to the city [106] were becoming serious problems. Both movements had a dangerously depressive effect upon the agricultural manpower and the productive capacity of the countryside.[107] The shogunate clearly understood this, and through edicts and instructions to its local officials attempted to counter the threat to its income, but to no avail. The traditional relationship of feudal power to land economy was becoming hopelessly undermined by forces too large for bureaucratic control.

Although the relationship of the merchant class to the feudal aristocracy produced no such visible disturbances, by the Tanuma period certain subtle changes had become apparent in the attitude of the merchants to feudal authority. As the commercial houses increased in financial power, and as they became more essential to the welfare of the government, they won numerous privileges and immunities which lessened their cause to fear official displeasure. The growing lack of respect for feudal authority among the bourgeois class was amply illustrated in their literature, in which the government and officials were frequently lampooned.[108] We see this trend in their plays, novels, poetry,[109] and especially in the comic jottings, known as *rakushu*,[110] which were placed anonymously in public places in the principal cities. Understandably, some of the most open criticisms of the government were made by the samurai patrons of bourgeois society. Hiraga Gennai satirized the official world of his day in his work *Nenashigusa*.[111] Ōta Nampo, one of the "eighteen men about town," frequently ridiculed the government. His poem comparing the irritation of officials to the buzz of mosquitoes is perhaps the best known example of humorous anti-government sentiment to come out of the Tokugawa period.[112]

Tanuma was the butt of more than his share of satirical literature. During his years of bakufu service, the government was ridiculed for its attempt to enforce frugality[113] and for its currency issues.[114] Official corruption and loss of military spirit were satirized in popular songs. Tanuma himself was lampooned for his greed.[115] The assassination of his son was made the subject of numerous plays, stories, and comic songs.[116] After the mid-Tokugawa period no Tokugawa official, it seemed, was immune from popular satirization. The prestige of the feudal government continued to diminish.

While the existence of discontent among the nonofficial classes should excite no great surprise, defection within the ranks of the ruling class will be recognized as something more serious. The Tanuma period witnessed two incidents of deep significance which brought to light a new and dangerous trend in the thinking of the samurai class. These were the so-called Hōreki and Meiwa affairs, which mark the genesis of the late Tokugawa imperialist movement.[117]

The first of these incidents, which came to a head in 1758, involved a samurai of Kyoto, an instructor in military science by the name of Takenouchi Shikibu. This man, in the course of his studies, became attracted to the brand of Shinto revivalism originated by Yamazaki Ansai. He presently began to give lectures on the old Shinto texts. In these he recalled the idyllic past of the Japanese people, when the emperors supposedly ruled through virtue. He pointed to the evil times which had befallen Japan since the establishment of military rule and called for an imperial restoration. Takenouchi obtained a following among young court nobles, and they in turn managed to excite the interest of the Emperor. But at this point, high court nobles, fearing possible reprisals, reported the matter to the Tokugawa authorities. The bakufu did not take a very serious view of the report. For several years Takenouchi went about his activities unmolested, but finally, in 1758, he was banished from Kyoto and other centers of Japanese population.[118]

The second incident was also incited by a lecturer on military science, a samurai by the name of Yamagata Daini. Yamagata had become a rōnin and had taken up the scholarly profession for his support. His early training was begun in Kyoto, where he appears to have absorbed some of the imperialistic dreams of the courtiers together with an interest in Shinto. In 1756, at the age of thirty-one, Yamagata proceeded to Edo where he set up a school and soon gained a wide following. The evils which he saw about him in the capital of the Shogun made a deep impression on him, and he shortly began to criticize the shogunate for its responsibility in bringing such things to pass.

In 1763, Yamagata published a treatise entitled *Ryūshi shin-ron* [119] in which he daringly advocated abolition of the dual form of government. In this treatise he criticized the Shogun's usurpation of imperial power and pointed to the corruption of the Tokugawa military government. The warrior class, he said, had lost its vitality through years of peaceful and luxurious living. In official places bribery and corruption were the rule, while throughout the land a spirit of materialism had seized the people. But all this would be remedied, he believed, if the rule of the Emperor were restored together with a civilian government staffed with men of ability.[120]

Whether Yamagata ever contemplated a plot against the Shogun is still a matter of conjecture. However, he talked frequently of the vulnerability of the Edo castle's defenses and thereby alarmed some of his pupils, who denounced him to the authorities. He and his chief associate, Fujii Umon, were arrested and accused of planning a conspiracy to overthrow the government. The trial of Yamagata and Fujii lasted eight months during the year 1767. The government admitted finding no evidence of a plot but considered that the open criticism of the Tokugawa voiced by the men constituted grounds enough for punishment. Yamagata and Fujii were executed. Takenouchi Shikibu, who had been picked up on suspicion of complicity, was exiled to the island of Hachijō and died on the way there.

Among the serious repercussions of this incident was the suspicious association between Yamagata and the Daimyo Oda Nobukuni. The records do not make clear what Nobukuni was accused of, but it is obvious that the shogunal authorities questioned his loyalty to the Tokugawa. Nobukuni was ordered into retirement, his lands removed to Dewa, and his status within the shogunal hierarchy severely reduced. Nobukuni's natural father, the Master of Court Ceremonies, Oda Nobushige, was removed from office and his domain was passed on to his heir.[121]

The involvement of court nobles and daimyo in these admittedly immature conspiracies against the Tokugawa were, nonetheless, indicative of the feeling of protest which was rising against the shogunate. Disillusionment had begun to penetrate the official class. The movement begun by Takenouchi and Yamagata was to grow rapidly from its first stirrings in the early years of the Tanuma period. Eventually the desire to restore the rule of the Emperor became one of the strongest factors which led to the overthrow of the shogunate.

CHAPTER VII

The Triumph of Reaction

To a large number of Tokugawa officials and diamyo whose interests were closely identified with those of the shogunate, the state of affairs as they appeared in the last years of the Tenth Shogun's administration must have excited deep concern. All about them they saw signs of declining Tokugawa power. At the center of authority, the Shogun appeared to have retired into the company of his favorites, to whom he left the conduct of state affairs. The management of the shogunate was thus almost completely in the hands of Tanuma and his faction. These men, many of them like Tanuma, upstarts in the Tokugawa hierarchy, conducted not only their personal lives but the government in ways which were unfamiliar and often shocking. The traditional precepts of the Tokugawa forefathers were ignored. Frugality and military discipline were given but lip service. Bribery, favoritism, and behind-the-scenes rule corrupted the morale of the Tokugawa vassals. As if in judgment of this state of moral decay, heaven itself it seemed had hurled down a series of catastrophes, surely a warning that some deep soul-searching was in order. Yet it was believed that all this had been kept from the Shogun by the clever Tanuma, who allowed the Tokugawa and the national interests to advance to the brink of destruction. To those who looked upon the state of affairs in this light, it was clear that a day of reckoning must soon come, that a complete house-cleaning within the Tokugawa administration must be undertaken.

In the course of Tokugawa history, violent political change has often followed periods of corrupt government or serious natural disturbance. Yet in each instance political change had to await the advent of a new Shogun.[1] Under the Tokugawa system, only with a change in the Shogun could sweeping modifications in administrative personnel or policy be brought about. To Tanuma's political opponents it must have been some consolation that the Shogun Ieharu's health was deteriorating, but it was impossible to know when his end would come. Furthermore, Tanuma had managed to weave his influence around the Heir Apparent, while his young and active son, Mototomo, seemed ready to effect a political carryover into the next generation. Matters as they stood in the early 1780's must thus have appeared desperate to those who were opposed to Tanuma Okitsugu.

Within the shogunate it is evident that an undercurrent of resentment and opposition to Tanuma had grown in proportion to his rise in influence. The centers of such opposition were readily discernible and have already been pointed out. First and foremost were the chief collateral branches of the Tokugawa, the Three Houses and the Three Lords, who were keenly sensitive to any decline in Tokugawa fortunes and in their own prestige. There were also the various daimyo, and especially those of Senior Councilor rank, who, though they may have fawned on Tanuma or obtained favors from him, would have been only too glad to see him eliminated from the center of the political stage. Within the Great Interior, the lady Ochio-no-kata seems never to have reconciled herself to Tanuma. Her enmity must have been doubly great if she credited at all the rumors that Tanuma had a hand in the death of her son, the former Heir Apparent.

Besides these specific political opponents, Tanuma excited the intellectual antagonism of the Confucian scholars and the Confucian-trained members of the Tokugawa bureaucracy. These men who saw the ideals of Confucian society disregarded, who saw the unorthodox school of Dutch studies gaining in favor and influence, could not but be bitter over the low estate to which the traditional philosophy of the Tokugawa had fallen.

Opposition to Tanuma naturally did not express itself openly, but it ran close to the surface. As the state of the nation went from bad to worse, matters of personal grievance were extended into a righteous conviction that the elimination of Tanuma, his party, and all that he stood for was the only salvation of the country. As so often happens in Japanese politics, the first step in this direction took the form of assassination. The assassin was a minor figure in the Shogun's court, and his motives seem to have been more personal than political.

I. THE AFFAIR OF SANO MASAKOTO

There is no evidence in Japanese sources to confirm any suspicion that Sano Masakoto had anything more than personal reasons for his assassination of Tanuma Mototomo. The elder Tanuma's attempt to use the Sano genealogy for his own benefit has already been cited. It was this which stood at the bottom of Masakoto's grievance. Tanuma Mototomo had acted for his father in this affair, and, having been in actual contact with Sano, was in a position to receive full blame for what was primarily the elder Tanuma's doing.

But Sano had other grievances against Mototomo.[2] As an officer of the New Guard he came under the jurisdiction of the Junior Councilors, of which the younger Tanuma was one. Sano, whose income was extremely low, had urgent hopes of obtaining a promotion. During the course of two years, he presented Mototomo with some 620 ryō in gifts along with his petitions for higher office. All through this period Sano was made to believe that a promotion was in the offing, but each time an opening occurred someone else obtained the position. A final grievance was added during a hunt which took place in the neighborhood of the Kinoshita river in 1783 (Temmei 3. 12. 3).[3] Sano was one of the fortunate ones to bring down a bird. But the younger Tanuma, who reported the shot, gave the credit to another.

Thus Sano's resentment grew until he determined to kill Mototomo. Realizing that the only place where he could get close enough to his victim was within the central castle itself, he determined to attack while on guard duty despite the death penalty against drawing a sword within the castle precincts.

Whether anyone else was aware of Sano's intentions we shall probably never know. Titsingh, whose information in this instance most probably came from conversations with his Japanese associates, claims that "several persons of highest rank were privy" to Sano's design and urged him on.[4] Titsingh goes on to state that the original intention was to murder the elder Tanuma, the plan to eliminate the younger having been adopted because the father was already nearing the end of his life while the son was young and vigorous. That such a well-thought-out plan ever existed is indeed hard for us to believe. Especially is it hard to accept the view that there had been a deliberate choice made between possible victims. Sano clearly had but one immediate enemy, the younger Tanuma, his direct superior in office and the one he considered personally responsible for his many grievances. But this does not mean that there were not those who would have gladly seen Tanuma Mototomo eliminated and that they did not indicate this by their actions at the time of the attack.

On the twenty-fourth day of the third month of Temmei four (1784) Sano Masakoto, from his vantage point in the guardroom, watched the Junior Councilors as they retired from the Business Office.[5] Tanuma Mototomo came last; his three other colleagues had walked ahead more briskly. As Tanuma drew opposite him, Sano jumped from his post, and, accosting the Junior Councilor in a loud voice,[6] began to slash at him with his sword. Tanuma, mortally wounded, fell to the floor but managed to crawl into a dark corner and elude Sano's pursuit. All of this took place in full view of a large number of officials, yet, through surprise or calculated delay, not a one raised a finger to protect Tanuma. Not until Sano had struck several blows and was vainly searching for his victim was he finally caught and disarmed. The first man to reach him was the aged Inspector General, Matsudaira Tadasato, whose seat was one of the farthest away of those who actually witnessed the incident.[7]

It would be hard to prove that, as Titsingh suggests, there was any ulterior motive in the slow reaction time and the cowardice shown by the officials and guards. The shogunate itself never found grounds for prosecution on such a charge, although the greater portion of the inactive onlookers were convicted of negligence.[8] Matsudaira Tadasato was rewarded with a fief of 200 koku. Two Inspectors General and three Inspectors were relieved of their posts. Sano's colleagues in the guard company were demoted, while a City Magistrate, two Superintendents of Finance,[9] and several other officials were reported for negligent conduct.

Tanuma Mototomo died one month after the attack, and Sano was sentenced to death by his own hand. The event stirred the entire nation. Sympathy was uniformly on the side of Sano, who, it was felt, had struck a blow for the people, then suffering from famine and the high cost of living. When in the next year (1785) the price of rice fell to half of the 1784 level,[10] it was widely believed that Sano's spirit was responsible. People began to call him the Great Rectifying Spirit (*Yonaoshi-daimyōjin*) and flocked to his grave in Tokuhonji temple in such large numbers that the Superintendent of Temples and Shrines had to order the gates of the temple closed.

Even then, in defiance of this order, people broke into the temple grounds to place flowers in front of the grave.[11]

At the same time, in the literature of the common people, numerous plays, stories, and songs took up the subject of the Sano attack. A play of this nature entitled *Inabikari tagoto-no-tsuki* is said to have been performed in Osaka only four months after the event,[12] while the popular contemporary writer Santō Kyōden wrote a story in the form of a *kibyōshi*[13] on the subject in 1788. This work, entitled *Jidai sewa nichō tsutsumi*, is quoted in full in Tsuji's *Tanuma jidai*.[14]

Most interesting among the literary by-products of this incident is the so-called *Seventeen Articles* (*Jūshichi-ka-jō*),[15] which Sano Masakoto is said to have left in his house at the time of his execution. This document luridly enumerates the crimes of the elder Tanuma, not those of the son. For various reasons Tsuji considers this work to be spurious, and there is little cause to disagree with this opinion. However, no evidence better illustrates how Tanuma Okitsugu suffered for the fate of his son.[16] Whether Sano had meant to do so or not, his sword struck the first blow in the downfall of the Tenth Shogun's favorite minister.

2. THE APPEARANCE OF MATSUDAIRA SADANOBU

While the Sano incident helped to discredit Tanuma in the eyes of the nation, it does not appear that the Shogun altered his opinion of his favorite on account of it. It will be recalled that after the event Tanuma was given a final 10,000-koku increase in his landholdings and that during the next two years the Shogun backed Tanuma in the most daring of his domestic measures. The years 1785 and 1786 were feverishly active ones for the shogunate. Whether in a desperate attempt to break through the encircling ring of natural calamity and economic distress or because of the realization that the Shogun and Tanuma himself had not much longer to live, Tanuma put into operation in quick succession the most controversial of his many schemes. The Imbanuma project was begun anew, expeditions were sent to the Kuriles and Sakhalin, the colonization of Ezo was considered, and the ambitious "Thrice Beneficial" loan scheme was attempted. But while these last efforts were being rushed, the internal political scene was shifting irrevocably in the direction of reaction.

One of the chief indications of this trend was the appearance of Matsudaira Sadanobu in the high councils of the Tokugawa.

On the first day of the twelfth month of 1785 (Temmei 5. 12. 1) the following order was issued by the Shogun: [17] "It has been ordered that henceforth when Matsudaira attends official duties he will take his place in the Antechamber. . . It is further stated that this is in accord with the requests of Hōren'in-ni.[18] This appointment is not to become a precedent for his house."

This order held deep significance for Tanuma's political future. Sadanobu, it will be remembered, was not an outsider to the inner Tokugawa circle. Seventh son of Tayasu Munetake, the senior member of the Three Lords, he had been in position first to head the Tayasu house and later to be named heir to the Shogun Ieharu. Both times, candidates chosen by Tanuma Okitsugu had preceded him. Whether Tanuma was aware of the enmity which Sadanobu held for him is not known. Sadanobu himself seems not to have concealed it from his close associates, and at a later date even confessed to have contemplated assassinating Tanuma for the good of the country.[19]

In 1783 at the age of twenty-five, Sadanobu was named head of the Matsudaira house enfeoffed at Shirakawa in Mutsu (110,000 koku). The times in which he took over were desperate; the whole domain was on the verge of bankruptcy, while floods and unseasonal frosts had devastated the lands. Sadanobu immediately embarked on a strenuous retrenchment program and began by curtailing his own living expenses as an example to the rest of his officers and the people. To bring relief to the suffering people, he imported foodstuffs from Edo. Fields were rehabilitated, waterworks repaired, the peasants instructed in better methods of agriculture as well as in their social responsibilities. In the course of a few years, Sadanobu was being praised as one of the model administrators of his day; his fief had begun to pull itself through the disastrous years of Temmei.[20] We can imagine, therefore, what Sadanobu's opinion must have been of the state of affairs within the shogunate. Sadanobu himself notes the chagrin with which he watched what he believed to be a hopeless mismanagement by Tanuma and his associates.[21]

Now Sadanobu was raised to a position in the Antechamber, a privilege which gave him full contact with the Senior Councilors and with the formation of Tokugawa policy. A great deal has been written about the possible interpretation of this appointment. Why was it, for instance, that Tanuma, still supreme in the Shogun's confidence, would have permitted such a move? Was he ignorant of Sadanobu's real character, or was his ability to control shogunal affairs already weakening? So far no evidence has been found to answer these questions.

There is also the question of whether the appointment was a conscious political move undertaken by the opposition, or whether the reason stated in the Shogun's order is to be taken at face value. Again there is no evidence to show that Sadanobu was actually placed in the Antechamber with the idea that he should work for Tanuma's fall, nor does it appear that in 1785 there was any intention on the part of any group behind the scenes that Sadanobu should take over the direction of Tokugawa affairs once Tanuma had been eliminated. We know from Sadanobu's own words, however, that immediately upon his appointment to the Antechamber he began to consult with like-minded members of the Senior Council and that he soon entered into confidence with a number of them.[22] At the same time, his family connections made it possible for him to act as an intermediary between the Collaterals and the Senior Councilors. He was able to open the way for the assertion of new influences in the Tokugawa councils.

Scarcely a month elapsed between Sadanobu's new appointment and an event which is believed by some to be the first indication of a new temper in the Edo administration. This was the dismissal of the Fushimi Magistrate, Kobori Masakata. Kobori was one of Tanuma's close associates and in his early years as Magistrate had performed his duties with distinction. However, as time went by, he became more and more exacting and arbitrary in his administration and increasingly profligate in his personal life. Finally word of his irresponsible conduct reached Edo. This apparently gave an opportunity to those within the shogunate who favored a house-cleaning to bring pressure to bear on Tanuma. Masakata was dismissed from office (Temmei 5. 12. 27) and, as Tsuji has expressed it, the first leaf of what was to be Tanuma's autumn had fallen.[23]

3. THE DEATH OF THE SHOGUN IEHARU

In the eighth month of 1786, the Shogun Ieharu took to his bed and was unable to attend the usual court assembly. This was the first time since becoming Shogun that he had missed such a function, and it was immediately known that his illness was serious.[24] Tanuma was obviously greatly concerned. He hastily called in two trusted town physicians, Hyūga Tōan and Wakabayashi Keijun, to treat the Shogun. On the nineteenth day of the eighth month these two men were appointed Attendant Physicians with incomes of 200 hyō. They replaced the court physician Ōyagi Den'an Morimi, who up to this time had been treating the Shogun's illness.[25] From this point on two distinct stories emerge, the official version of the Shogun's death and the version as it appears in the majority of nonofficial sources.[26] The official story which follows will give a background for the more dramatic and probably more authentic popular account.

According to the *Tokugawa jikki*,[27] on the twentieth day of the eighth month, the two new physicians provided by Tanuma were discarded, and the Shogun was again placed under the treatment of Ōyagi. From about this time the members of the Three Houses and Three Lords went daily to the Central Citadel, while Tanuma, on account of illness, kept to his residence. On the twenty-fourth, the floating loan scheme was countermanded, and the Imbanuma project and the gold-mining operations in Yamato were abandoned. On the twenty-sixth the physician attending the Shogun reported that, while during the previous days the illness had eased somewhat, another turn for the worse had taken place. The following day Tanuma Okitsugu's resignation was accepted. This resignation had previously been tendered by Tanuma on grounds of ill health. At the same time the Chamberlain, Inaba Masaakira, was relieved of office, and the 3000-koku fief recently given him by the Shogun was taken from him. On the twenty-eighth, the newly appointed shogunal physicians, Hyūga and Wakabayashi, were stripped of their rank and salary. On the sixth day of the ninth month, a report went out that the Shogun's illness was critical. Daimyo and officials assembled at court to inquire after the Shogun's health. His death was announced on the ninth.

Thus the annals record the passing of the Tenth Shogun. The official version would have us believe, however, that before his death he had finally become aware of Tanuma's evil influence and had had the courage to root it out.[28] The old Shogun had broken Tanuma's power, and the new Shogun was in the hands of another group.

But let us turn to one of the private accounts of what took place behind the scenes at the time of Ieharu's death. The most reliable

seems to be that contained in Kanzawa Tokō's *Okinagusa*. Going
back to the twentieth day of the eighth month, Kanzawa states that
of the two physicians pushed forward by Tanuma, Hyūga declined
to treat the Shogun. Wakabayashi, however, advanced and presented
a potion. The Shogun drank it and shortly thereafter took a turn for
the worse and died. Immediately rumors began to fly through the
castle. It was declared that the Shogun should never have been put
under the care of a town physician. The women of the Great Interior
and the various officials on hand at the time called in the Shogun's
medical corps. They examined the medicine which Wakabayashi had
prepared and reported that it was extremely coarse and unfit for
presentation to the Shogun.

From here on it was but a short step to the rumor that the Shogun
had been poisoned.[29] Tanuma, upon hearing of these developments,
immediately rushed to the castle. But he was met by a Chief of the
Attendants and informed that there were other persons ahead of
him and that he must wait his turn before entering into the shogunal
apartments. Tanuma was about to push the man aside and enter by
force when one of the Attendants came forward and said, "It is the
Shogun's wish. You are not to enter." Tanuma was forced to retire.

Meanwhile the women's apartments were in commotion as talk
spread of the poisoning of the Shogun. Everywhere Tanuma's name
was slandered. Mizuno Tadatomo made his way to the Great Interior and talked to the women, saying that though it was regrettable
that unfit medicine had been administered, any talk of poisoning was
not only utterly false but was dangerous for the future of the country.
He managed to quiet the rumors, but Tanuma himself was obliged
to return to his residence.

In the nearly twenty days which separated the Shogun's death
and its public announcement, Tanuma's political opposition worked
fast. The heads of the Three Houses met together and mapped out
the drastic steps which in the course of the next few days eliminated
the power of Tanuma and his party. The Senior Councilors, who
were in secret session at the same time, sent Tanuma an order sug-
gesting that he tender his resignation.[30] On the twenty-seventh, the
following order was handed to Tanuma:

To Tanuma Tonomo-no-kami
   According to your request, you are hereby relieved of your office and
   attached to the Hall of the Geese.

Signed (as representative of the Senior Councilors) by Nishio Oki-no-kami
Ditto, Matsudaira Tōjirō
The above was decided in the *hame-no-ma*[31] by Kamon-no-kami[32] and
the assembled Senior Councilors. This order has been communicated by
Dewa-no-kami.[33]

Thus by the time of the public announcement of the Shogun's death
the entire alignment of political influence within the shogunate had
been altered, and Tanuma had been cut away from his sources of
power. The opposition had made clever use of the dead Shogun's
name to effect a seizure of control.

Tanuma's final elimination was now only a matter of time. How
this was brought about may perhaps best be grasped by a chronological listing of the events which transpired during the next two years.

Temmei 6 (1786) 8th and 9th months: Nearly all of Tanuma's elaborately contrived family connections collapsed. The first to break with
Tanuma was Mizuno Tadatomo, who gave back the son he adopted
from Tanuma. Matsudaira Yasufusa, whose son had married one of
Tanuma's granddaughters, severed his ties with Tanuma even though
the girl had long since died.[34]
6. intercalary 10. 5: Tanuma was deprived of 20,000-koku income, his
Osaka storehouses, and his official mansion in Edo. He was given two
days to vacate the latter.[35]
On the same day: the Superintendent of Finance, Matsumoto Hidemochi,
was relieved of office.
6. 11. 15: Akai Tadaakira was expelled from the post of Superintendent
of Finance.[36]
Temmei 7. (1787) 6. 19: Matsudaira Sadanobu was named chief of the
Senior Councilors.[37]
7. 10. 2: Tanuma's remaining 37,000-koku income was confiscated, and he
was imprisoned in his lower mansion. His castle at Sagara was ordered
demolished. His grandson, and heir, was given a fief of 10,000-koku in
Mutsu and Echigo.[38]
7. 11. 26: The Ginseng Monopoly was abolished.
7. 12. 5: Akai and Matsumoto were convicted of crime and further punished.[39]
7. 12. 9: An order prohibited the erection of houses on open land throughout
the city of Edo. This had been one of Tanuma's ways of making money,
and it was now opposed because it increased the fire hazard in the
city.[40]
Temmei 8. (1788) 3. 4: Matsudaira Sadanobu was named Regent.[41]
8. 5. 29: The minting of *nishu* silver was discontinued. Shortly thereafter
the *shi-mon* coin was abandoned.
8. 7. 24: Tanuma Okitsugu died. Although his funeral was kept a secret,

it is stated that the townspeople heard of it and gathered to throw stones at his remains as they were taken through the streets on the way to their final resting place.[42]

The fall of Tanuma Okitsugu was thus complete. A new conservative group had come to power. Under the leadership of Matsudaira Sadanobu the so-called Kansei Reform (*Kansei no kaikaku*) was begun. There is, in fact, no better way to appreciate what Tanuma had stood for than to contrast his policies with the main features of Sadanobu's reform. Some comparisons have already been made. We have seen the results of Sadanobu's complete negation of all of Tanuma's policies, good or bad, and his thoroughgoing elimination from office of all Tanuma sympathizers. Having thus cleared the way, Sadanobu went on to effect a program of drastic retrenchment. He began by issuing a series of frugality regulations and sumptuary laws which flooded the whole of Tokugawa society from daimyo to peasant with pious exhortations. In particular, he singled out such items as prostitution, bribery, expensive clothing, elaborate hair styles, and lewd popular literature for condemnation. In his determination to repair the damage which he believed to have been inflicted on the Tokugawa system, Sadanobu placed special emphasis on reinforcing the seclusion policy and bolstering the lax intellectual standards of his predecessor's age. He reversed the policy of expanded trade at Nagasaki, abandoned plans for the economic development of Ezo, and dealt severely with Hayashi Shihei, whose tracts on the Russian menace had inflamed the people. To strengthen the official Shu Shi school of Confucianism, he filled the staff of the Tokugawa College with vigorous but narrow-minded men and invoked the infamous suppression of heresies, which sought to restrict all unorthodox schools of Confucian thought and to check the spread of Dutch studies. The Kansei Reform was a recognized success in many fields. Matsudaira Sadanobu could claim a balanced treasury and a heightened morale among the Tokugawa vassals. Feudal authority had regained some of its lost prestige. But Sadanobu's methods were basically of a negative nature. They rested on government restriction and on the self-discipline of the Japanese people. The increased tensions which they created could not be endured for long. In the face of Japan's rapidly changing foreign and internal conditions, these restrictive efforts were of little avail. After 1893 the Kansei Reform too became a memory. Yet for his self-righteous attempt to turn back the development of Japanese society, Sadanobu won the plaudits of his own and later generations, while by contrast Tanuma went down in history as a corrupting influence.

In retrospect one cannot help feeling a certain pity for a man whom fate has treated so badly. Certainly Tanuma cannot be blamed for all the innumerable ills which beset the country during his years of power. His arrival upon the political scene was at a most inauspicious moment, when the smaller periodic cycle of troubles was accentuated by the larger down-sweep of general Tokugawa decline. Tanuma himself affected no sudden drop in this curve. On the contrary, Tanuma brought to the shogunate certain qualities which were most rare for the Tokugawa period. The liberal atmosphere which he fostered, the spirit of enterprise and inquiry which he inspired, were valuable gifts for an age too much under the shadow of the past. In the period which bears his name are discernible the origins of many of the movements which in later years were to make possible Japan's spectacular adjustment to the modern world.

It is gratifying, therefore, to find that, in the remaining years of the Tokugawa period, there were those who realized that not all of what Tanuma had stood for had been evil and who had the courage to break the pattern of condemnation to express their approval of his policies. Such a man was Uezaki Kuhachirō, who had been lavish in his praise of Sadanobu but who eventually, in the depths of disillusionment over the short-sightedness of the Kansei Reform, called for a return to the freedom of Tanuma's days.[43] Such also was Naitō Chūmei, who in the troubled decades of the 1830's and 1840's voiced the sentiment that only an imaginative forward-looking policy such as Tanuma might have conceived could save the country.[44] Nor was it long before the great mass of the common people, harassed by Sadanobu's harsh reforms, acknowledged the error of their judgment. For Tanuma, despite his shortcomings, had given them the freedom they most desired. It is among such people that there appeared one of the most touching monuments of appreciation to Tanuma, an ephemeral but deep-felt poem which circulated in the streets of Edo.

The fish [the people] unable to live in the pure water of the white river [Matsudaira Sadanobu] [45]
Yearn for the muddiness of the field pond [Tanuma].[46]

Notes

Notes*

CHAPTER I. INTRODUCTION

1. See Nishida Naojirō's brilliant treatment of this theme in his *Nihon bunkashi josetsu* (Tokyo, 1932), pp. 526 ff.

2. For a full discussion of what the Japanese have termed "the re-feudalization of Japanese society" see Nakamura Kichiji, *Nihon hōkensei saihensei shi* (Tokyo, 1939). An excellent short summary of the subject is contained in Inobe Shigeo, *et al.*, *Nihon kinseishi* (Tokyo, 1935) [Heibonsha, *Sekai rekishi taikai*, vol. 13B], pp. 5–18.

3. The daimyo was a feudal lord ruling an area with a nominal yearly rice production of 10,000 *koku* (5.1 American bushels) or more. The domain over which he had jurisdiction was called a *han*, sometimes translated "fief" or "clan." Neither translation, however, does justice to the original Japanese concept. In this study I have avoided using the term "clan" entirely. Han I have rendered as "domain," and, for feudal holdings of less than han size, I have used the term "fief."

4. Literally "generalissimo." The title is an abbreviation of *sei-i-tai-shōgun* (barbarian-quelling-generalissimo). Given by the emperor to his chef commander in the field, it was first used as a political title in 1192 by Minamoto Yoritomo. Thereafter, until 1867, it became the office through which the "military dictators" ruled Japan.

5. During the Tokugawa period, three broad social classes were distinguished. These were the warrior (*bushi* or *samurai*), the peasant (*nōmin*), and the bourgeoisie (*chōnin*). In a strict sense the chōnin were comprised of artisans (*kōnin*) and merchants (*shōnin*). The warriors were of various degrees of aristocratic rank. Peasants and bourgeoisie were classed as commoners (*heimin*). Court nobles (*kuge*) and priests (*sōni*) represented minor subclasses, the nobles on a plane above and the priests slightly below that of samurai.

6. The resulting cult of bushido is well known to Western readers. An excellent treatment of the development of bushido as a rationalization of the samurai's position of social leadership is given by Tani Yoshihiko, "Yamaga Sokō no rekishiteki hihanteki kōsatsu," *RK* 3.1 (1936). A more generalized account will be found in Shirazawa Kiyoto, *Edo jidai zenki* (Tokyo, 1922) [Daitōkaku, *Nihon bunka shi*, vol. 10], pp. 54 ff.

7. Kurita Motoji, *Edo jidai shi* (Tokyo, 1935) [Kokushi Kōza Kankōkai, *Kokushi kōza*, vol. 8], pp. 85 ff. Also Nishida, pp. 589–590.

8. For a lucid survey of Tokugawa economic growth see Abe Makoto, "Keizai to shakai" in Inobe, *et al.*, pp. 19–142.

9. E. H. Norman, *Japan's Emergence as a Modern State* (New York, 1940), pp. 50 ff. One of the more common results of this alliance were the han and shogunal monopolies. These are briefly described by Abe Makoto, pp. 123–142.

10. The Meiji Restoration (*Meiji ishin*, 1867–68) refers to the political

* Characters for bibliographical citations are given below in the Bibliographical List.

movement which overthrew the Tokugawa shogunate and signalized the recognition of the Emperor as the *de facto* as well as *de jure* ruler of the nation. Historians have generally looked upon the period from about 1854 to 1877, or even 1890, as the transitional Restoration period.

11. Nishida, pp. 584 ff.

12. The Kokugaku (lit. national learning) movement began during the late seventeenth century as a return to the study of ancient Japanese historical and literary works. It eventually brought about a revival of interest in the native doctrine of Shinto. Increasingly theistic and nationalistic as time went on, the movement became strongly anti-Buddhist and anti-Confucianist and played a conspicuous part in building an intellectual foundation for the Meiji Restoration. A recent survey of Kokugaku is to be found in Yamamoto Masahide and Watanabe Shu, *Kokugaku ron* (Tokyo, 1939) [Mikasa Shobō, *Nihon rekishi zensho*, vol. 19]. An excellent short account of Tokugawa intellectual movements is contained in Horst Hammitsch, "Kokugaku und Kangaku," *Monumenta Nipponica* 2. 1 (1939). 1–23.

13. See Edwin O. Reischauer, *Japan Past and Present* (New York, 1946), pp. 105–106, for a brief mention of the significance of the popular Shinto sects which sprang up during the late Tokugawa period.

14. A useful summary of these policies is contained in Nakamura Kōya, "Edo kōki jidai bunka no tokushitsu" [Seibundō Shinkōsha, *Nihon bunkashi taikei*, vol. 10, *Edo kōki bunka* (Tokyo, 1939), pp. 2–21], pp. 18–19.

15. Kitajima Masamoto, *Nihon kinseishi* (Tokyo, 1939) [Mikasa Shobō, *Nihon rekishi zensho*, vol. 6], p. 250.

16. Nakamura Kōya, pp. 8–9.

17. Yūzankaku-henshūkyoku, *Isetsu Nihonshi* (Tokyo, 1931–1933; 25 vols.), vol. 8, p. 130.

18. Kurita Motoji, *Edo jidai shi, ge* (Tokyo, 1929) [Yūzankaku, *Dai Nihon shi kōza*, vol. 8], pp. 185–191.

19. *Ibid.*, p. 198.

20. See in particular the treatment by James Murdoch, *A History of Japan* (Kobe, 1910; Kobe, 1903; London, 1926; 3 vols.), vol. 3, chap. 10.

21. The pioneer study of Tanuma and his policies, a work still to be superseded, is Tsuji Zennosuke, *Tanuma jidai* (Tokyo, 1915) [Nihon Gakujutsu Fukyūkai, *Rekishi kōza*, vol. 1].

CHAPTER II. THE TOKUGAWA ADMINISTRATIVE SYSTEM

1. Western literature on Tokugawa Japan contains a number of generalized accounts of the Edo bureaucracy, in particular those by Murdoch, 3. 1–26; F. Brinkley, *A History of the Japanese People* (London, 1915), pp. 632–637; John H. Wigmore, "Materials for the Study of Private Law in Old Japan," *TASJ* 20, Supplement, Introduction 20–35; Maurice Courant, "Les clans japonais sous les Tokugawa," *Annales du Musée Guimet, Bibliothèque de Vulgarisation* 15 (1904), 1–82. These accounts, however, are not sufficiently exact or detailed to meet the needs of the present study. The following description of the Tokugawa bureaucracy is derived chiefly from two authoritative Japanese works: Matsudaira Tarō, *Edo jidai seido no kenkyū* (Tokyo, 1919), and Jingū Shichō, *Koji ruien* (Tokyo, 1914 and 1936; 60 vols.). Pertinent sections in the latter

work are to be found in the *Kan'i bu* (1936 ed., vols. 16, 17) and in the *Hōroku bu* (1936 ed., vol. 18).

2. Literally, "tent government." Originally the term for the military head-quarters of the Shogun, it was extended to refer to the Shogun's government as a whole.

3. The number of daimyo fluctuated between 292 in the early Tokugawa period and 275 for the late Tokugawa. The majority of daimyo domains were comparatively small, between 10,000 and 30,000 koku. The Collaterals and a few of the Outside Lords, however, held sizable domains, the largest being those of Maeda (1,022,000 koku in 1722) and Shimazu (770,000 koku in 1722). As time went on, koku assessments gave increasingly less indication of a particular daimyo's real economic status. Some daimyo, through the reclamation of land, or, as in the case of the Shimazu, through the development of trade, were able to augment considerably their real tax intake. And conversely, in many instances domains actually deteriorated. In the late Tokugawa period, therefore, the koku assessment was used primarily as a means of determining the daimyo's place in the feudal hierarchy and not as an absolute measure of his wealth.

4. Some confusion exists as to whether the title kamon was a generic one including the Three Houses and the Three Lords or whether it referred only to the remainder of the Collaterals. A more common term referring to the Collaterals was *shimpan*. I have followed the *Koji ruien* in the use of kamon.

5. The Three Lords were not daimyo. They did not possess domains but were domiciled in the vicinity of Edo Castle and were supported by rice stipends of 100,000 koku each. Moreover their house officials were considered members of the bakufu and came under the jurisdiction of the Shogun's Senior Councilors.

6. Other members of the Collaterals included the House of Echizen (*Echizen-ke*), the House of Aizu (*Aizu-ke*), and various branches of the Three Houses. The surname Matsudaira was also held by a large number of more remote relatives of the Tokugawa, not considered Collaterals. Also eighteen unrelated daimyo families, both Outside Lords and Hereditary Vassals, were given the special privilege of using the name.

7. This was true of all daimyo except those on duty as bakufu officials. These were designated as being "retained at the capital" (*jōfu*). The sankinkōtai system developed out of an earlier practice of giving hostages to the Shogun as a pledge of loyalty. Daimyo were obliged, therefore, to leave important members of their families, sometimes also important retainers, in Edo when they returned to their domains.

8. Referred to also as *honjō*.

9. The system of court ranks used at this time had been established in A.D. 701. There were in all thirty classifications held by courtiers and officials. These were ranged into nine ranks by number, number one being the highest. Ranks were further divided into senior (*shō*) and junior (*ju*) branches which in certain instances were subdivided further into upper (*jō*) and lower (*ge*) grades. In the hierarchy of ranks a sharp dividing line was drawn below the Junior Fifth Rank Lower Grade (*jugoi-ge*). Those above this line were classed as courtiers (*tenjōbito*); those below it were commoners. Hence to attain this rank was equivalent to rising to the status of nobility. During the Tokugawa period the bulk of the feudal aristocracy were of this minimum noble rank.

10. The most commonly used were the titles of provincial governorships. See J. H. Gubbins, "The Feudal System in Japan under the Tokugawa Sho-

guns," *TASJ* 15. 2 (1887). 138–141. But Gubbins' explanation of the origin of such titles is not always accurate.

11. Naturally the size of the hyō varied considerably both by location and time, so that this ratio of hyō to koku seldom existed in practice. It should also be noted that while feudal incomes were calculated in terms of rice, in actual payment, money replaced a certain per cent of the rice.

12. This chart is indebted in large part to the more complete breakdown of the Tokugawa bureaucracy contained in the Tōkyō Teikoku Daigaku Shiryō Hensansho, *Tokushi biyō* (Tokyo, rev. ed., 1942) [Hereafter cited *Tokushi biyō*.], pp. 540–543. In choosing English equivalents the attempt has been made to give, where possible, some indication of the function of each office. Honorifics have been dropped throughout. The figures in parentheses after the English equivalents indicate the number of individuals generally chosen for the post. It should be noted that when an Heir Apparent was in residence in the Western Citadel, he was provided with a small staff of Councilors, Chamberlains, Guards, Pages, and other attendants necessary for the conduct of his affairs.

CHAPTER III. TANUMA OKITSUGU, FAVORITE OF THE TENTH SHOGUN

1. There are four chief groups of Tokugawa genealogical compilations. (1) The most complete set of genealogies is to be found in the two monumental collections produced for the bakufu under the editorship of Hotta Masaatsu. The first of these, the *Kansei chōshū shokafu*, begun in 1799 and completed in 1812, runs to 1530 chapters and contains the genealogies of all daimyo (with the exception of the Collaterals) and most of the shogunal officials. Fortunately this work is available in two modern printed editions (Tokyo, 1917, 1922; 9 vols.). [Citations which follow will be from the 1917 edition.] The second, the *Kanjō roku*, was completed in 1835 and consists of 235 chapters of genealogies of lesser Tokugawa vassals omitted in the larger work. It was never published. (2) Two less pretentious genealogical collections limited to the daimyo houses of the Tokugawa period are Arai Hakuseki's *Hankampu*, completed in 1701, and its continuation, *Zoku-hankampu*, published in 1806 by Kondō Yoshizaemon, *et al.* These works have been printed in several editions, the most accessible being in vols. 1 and 2 of Hakuseki's collected works, ed. Kokusho Kankōkai, *Arai Hakuseki zenshū* (Tokyo, 1905–1907; 6 vols.). [Citations will be from this edition.] (3) The various *Bukan*, or yearly directories to the daimyo and Tokugawa officials, also contain genealogical information. A large number of these have been brought together by Hashimoto Hiroshi in his *Dai bukan* (Tokyo, 1935–1936; 13 vols.). [Pages are numbered internally for each *Bukan*.] (4) A final important biographical source is Iida Tadahiko's *Dai Nihon yashi* (completed 1853). This work adheres to the Chinese model of historiography and is therefore essentially a series of biographies. It exists in modern printed edition (Tokyo, Zuihitsu Taisei Kankōkai, 3rd ed., 1930; 6 vols.).

2. The bakufu registers, or diaries, exist only in manuscript, but they have been extensively reworked into the *Tokugawa jikki*, completed in 1849 under the editorship of Hayashi Kō. [References which follow will be to the edition contained in Kuroita Katsumi, *Shintei-zōhō kokushi taikei*, vols. 38–47 (1929–1935).]

3. The following section on Tanuma's official career, unless otherwise indicated, is derived from the account given in the Hotta, 7. 397–399.

4. A perusal of Hotta's *Kansei chōshū shokafu* shows that the majority of the Tokugawa warrior aristocrats traced their family lines back to branches of the Minamoto (Genji), Taira (Heike), or Fujiwara houses. A few lines, such as the Sugawara, the Kusunoki, and the Abe, figure in a minor capacity.

5. At a later date the house of origin was changed to Seiwa Genji by an adoptive heir who traced his descent from that line. The Tanuma genealogy is included under the Seiwa Genji in both Hotta and the various *Bukan*.

6. The present Tanuma is located approximately five miles northwest of the modern Sano. Cf. Yoshida Tōgo, *Dai Nihon chimei jiten* (Tokyo, 1922–23, rev. ed.; 6 vols.), p. 3407.

7. This post was classed at 500 koku and carried with it a salary of 300 hyō. Pages generally received a court title and the Junior Fifth Rank Lower Grade. Jingū Shichō, 17. 50 ff.

8. This date would be December 30, 1724 according to the Gregorian calendar. See William Bramsen, "Japanese Chronological Tables," *TASJ* 37. 3 (1910). 117. In the following pages no attempt has been made to convert lunar days and months to Gregorian equivalents. The practice which has been adopted is to indicate the year in the Western system. Following this the full Japanese lunar date is set in parentheses.

9. This title, *Tonomo-no-kami*, was, of course, purely honorary and involved no duties nor any association whatsoever with the imperial court.

10. The duties of this post were to supervise the activities of the hundred or more Attendants (*ko'nando*) and to act as intermediary between the Shogun and his outer officials. For this reason the office possessed a certain amount of influence. It was classed at 1500 koku but did not command a salary. Jingū Shichō, 17. 73 ff. and Matsudaira, pp. 361–364.

11. Hayashi, 46. 299, 301, 303.

12. A great deal of confusion is to be found in reading the names of members of the Tanuma family. The given names invariably include the same first character which may be read as either "oki" or "moto." Okitsugu's name is there-fore frequently read Mototsugu. For the purposes of this study, the pronunci-ations appearing in Hotta have been taken as standard.

13. In describing this portion of Tanuma's life Murdoch, 3. 379, states: "In the old Shogun's time (i.e., Yoshimune's) he held an officer's commission in the *Koshōgumi*, but does not seem to have been regarded with any very marked degree of favor. Under Ieshige he found means of ingratiating himself . . ." The implication here is that Tanuma began his career as a member of the Inner Guard (*koshōgumi*) attached to Yoshimune, that the morally upright Yoshimune showed him no favoritism, and that it was only after the weak-willed Ieshige succeeded to the shoguncy that Tanuma was able to use his wiles to gain advancement.

In actuality, however, Tanuma was from the start of his career "under Ieshige," as Page (*koshō*) rather than as Inner Guard. It should also be remem-bered that he was still very young and that service with the Heir Apparent was not likely to bring as rapid promotion as that in the Central Citadel. Once Ieshige became Shogun, however, Tanuma's rise was extremely rapid.

14. *Koshōgumiban-gashira-gaku.* Tanuma was undoubtedly assigned the status of Rank Equivalent because his basic income was considerably below the standard for the office and because his previous service and training had been among the Pages, not the Inner Guard. The captaincy of the guard was classed at

4000 koku. It was customary to grant captains on active duty a stipend equivalent to half their basic income. Jingū Shichō, 17. 317, 365, 384–385.

15. The Chamberlains were classed at 5000 koku. They were divided into three watches which attended the Shogun in rotation. Tanuma, however, was given the special duty of *yōtoritsugi*, which required his daily attendance as intermediary between the Shogun and the Business Office. Jingū Shichō, 16. 824.

16. This appointment appears to have been quite unusual, since only Grand Chamberlains were regularly assigned to the Supreme Court of Justice. Jingū Shichō, 16. 1168 ff.

17. Murdoch's statement, 3. 380, that "a few months later he was transferred to a new fief of 20,000 koku" may possibly be a repetition of the error in Iida, p. 2781. Tanuma did not reach 20,000 koku until twelve years later. It is true that the Sagara fief was later classed at 20,000 koku, but during the time of Tanuma's predecessor it was listed at only 10,000 koku. Hashimoto, 5. Hōreki 5. 7. By some strange error the *Tokushi biyō*, p. 478, in its table of daimyo for the year 1813, lists the Sagara fief at 30,000 koku under the name of Tanuma Okitsugu. Tanuma was deprived of his Sagara holdings in 1787, and his heir was reduced to 10,000 koku. The Tanuma family eventually returned to Sagara but never rose above 10,000 koku.

The town of Sagara, later to be the site of Tanuma's castle, was located in the district of Saibara on the waters of Suruga bay. In the *Bukan* it was listed as 55 *ri* (ca. 134 miles) distant from Edo and was reached by branching off the Tōkaidō at Kakegawa.

18. Honda was enfeoffed at Sagara in 1749. He later held the post of Superintendent of Temples and Shrines and eventually rose to become Junior Councilor. At this point he fell into disgrace and was deprived of his office in 1759. Shortly thereafter his domain was confiscated. Hotta, 4. 645–646. Also Oda Akinobu, *Haizetsuroku* (completed 1814) [modern edition in Kondō Heijo, *Kaitei shiseki shūran*, vol. 11 (1901)].

19. This residence, traditionally occupied by the retired Shogun, had been destroyed by fire in 1747.

20. Literally "seasonal garments." The garments were not made up, but consisted of material from which clothing could later be sewn. The giving of jifuku was one of the most common forms of commendation used by the Tokugawa Shogun. Material varied, as would be expected, according to season.

21. Hayashi, 46. 765.

22. *Ibid.*, 47. 826. I have found no evidence to support Murdoch's statement, *History of Japan* 3. 379, that Ōoka Tadayoshi, son of Ieshige's chief favorite, was instrumental in placing Tanuma "near the person of Ieharu," despite the fact that a certain intimacy must have existed between these two men. Tadayoshi's second wife was an adopted daughter of Okitsugu. Hotta, 6. 531–532.

23. Hayashi, 47. 48–58.

24. *Ibid.*, 47. 184–185.

25. This post, the highest of the "inner offices," was usually limited to a single appointment at one time. There were exceptions, however, in particular during the time of Tsunayoshi (1680–1709) when five Grand Chamberlains existed at one time. Jingū Shichō, 16. 817 ff. Murdoch's constant reference to the "Sobayōnin" in the plural would seem to indicate that he lumped the Chamberlains and the Grand Chamberlain together. This has led him into the unfortunate

position of having to use the term "chief of the Sobayōnin," a title for which there was no equivalent in Japanese.

26. This gave Tanuma the status of Lord of a Castle.

27. When listed in the *Bukan*, such appointees by family association had their father's name listed beside their own.

28. Several technical terms were used to indicate this official classification. The post of Senior Councilor (*rōjū*) was referred to sometimes as *shukurō* or *kahan*, the concept of "rank equivalent," by the adjectives *kaku* or *nami*, or the verb *junzuru*. Jingū Shichō, 16. 731 and Hayashi, 46. 311 (Meiwa 6. 8. 18). The status of rank equivalent to that of Senior Councilor (*rōjū-gaku*) was an infrequent assignment, and was generally given to officials coming up through the "inner" ranks whose holdings were insufficient for that of Senior Councilor. Matsudaira, 723.

29. Tanuma now held 25,000 koku. After the mid-Tokugawa period this was apparently the minimum acceptable holding for those appointed to the post of Senior Councilor. Jingū Shichō, 16. 745.

30. It was customary after the Kan'ei era (1624–1643) for Senior Councilors to be given the honorary court title of Court Chamberlain. Matsudaira, 236.

31. Hayashi, 47. 311 (Meiwa 6. 8. 18). According to Matsudaira, 726, Tanuma did not have the authority to sit in on the conferences in the Business Office, nor did he at this time carry the authority of Senior Councilor of the Month (*getsuban-kahan*).

32. Hayashi, 47. 311 (Meiwa 6. 8. 23).

33. This honor, which was attendant upon becoming a full Senior Councilor, was apparently a special dispensation for Tanuma at this time. Matsudaira, 726, implies incorrectly that Mizuno Tadatomo was (in 1781) the first to be so honored while still a rōjū-gaku. See Matsudaira, pp. 289 ff., for a discussion of the paraphernalia of the daimyo train.

34. Hayashi, 47. 379. The *Bukan* for 1773 lists his official title as Senior Councilor with concurrent duties in the Interior. Hashimoto, 6. An'ei 2. 16. There is no indication that Tanuma gave up his duties of attendance upon the Shogun until his final downfall in 1786. Whether this meant that he retained the actual title of Grand Chamberlain is not clear. *Tokushi biyō*, p. 505, fails to list a terminal date for Tanuma's duty as Grand Chamberlain. However, Mizuno Tadatomo, who combined the two important posts under identical conditions (see Hayashi, 47. 674), is listed as having given up the office of Grand Chamberlain when he became Senior Councilor.

35. The ryō was a monetary unit for gold coins. One ryō gold was equal to 60 *momme* (10 oz. av.) silver. It was made equal to one *yen* in 1871.

36. The previous additions had all been in line with his official advancements. This grant was termed an added favor (*kaon*). Hayashi, 47. 542.

37. In the districts of Saibara, Suruga, Shita, and Masutsu.

38. The gift of a horse was a signal mark of honor.

39. Hayashi, 47. 627 (An'ei 9. 4. 15). Okitsugu returned after 23 days' absence (9. 4. 29). *Ibid.*, 47. 628.

40. The other members of the commission were the Junior Councilor Sakai Iwami-no-kami Tadayasu and the Keeper of Edo Castle Yoda Buzen-no-kami Masatsugu. *Ibid.*, 47. 657.

41. Born in 1773, he was eight years old at this time. He became Shogun in his thirteenth year.

42. The Hitotsubashi House was the second of the Three Lords.

43. Not younger brother, as Murdoch asserts, *History of Japan*, 3. 402. Tanuma's brother Okinobu died in the Hitotsubashi service in 1773 (An'ei 2. 12. 19).

44. Hayashi, 47. 663.

45. It was customary for the heir of a Senior Councilor to enjoy his father's ceremonial privileges. Matsudaira, 293.

46. In the official hierarchy, as it appears in the *Bukan* of this period, the Masters of Shogunal Ceremony ranked next to the Junior Councilors. Appointments were generally made from daimyo rank. Jingū Shichō, 16. 834.

47. Junior Councilors were generally chosen from among castleless Hereditary Vassals. The post did not carry a salary, since only those with sufficient feudal incomes were appointed. But in cases such as this, where Mototomo was not yet head of his house, a special salary of 5000 hyō was given. *Ibid.*, 16. 769. Mototomo appears not to have been given full powers as Junior Councilor. He was not to stand monthly duty but to present himself only when special duties required his attendance. Hayashi, 47. 731–732. It was considered quite irregular for father and son to hold high bakufu positions simultaneously. So also was it unusual to appoint to the post of Junior Councilor a man who had not yet advanced to the headship of his house. Kanzawa Tokō, *Okinagusa* (completed *ca.* 1790 in 200 *kan*) [References are in *Nihon zuihitsu taisei*, series 3, vols. 11–13 (1931)], 12. 473.

48. This brought the total value of his holdings up to 57,000 koku.

49. Matsudaira Sadanobu was given a seat in the Antechamber in 1785.

50. This was his Upper Residence (*kami-yashiki*), located at Kandabashi-no-uchi only three *chō* (*ca.* 357 yards) from the main entrance to the Central Citadel. The mansion was formerly the residence of the leading Senior Councilor, Akimoto Suketomo. Kanzawa, 12. 472. The *Bukan* for the year 1773, Hashimoto, 6. An'ei 2. 16, records Tanuma as possessing three residences: the upper already referred to, a middle at Kakigarachō, and a lower at Kobikichō-bara. A second lower residence appears in the *Bukan* for 1783, Temmei 3. 9, located at Komagome-maki-no-nae-koborichō.

51. His Osaka *kura-yashiki*, built for the purpose of storing and disposing of the rice from his domain.

52. It is interesting to note that the Tanuma family managed a partial recovery under the succeeding Shogun. This was accomplished by Okitsugu's second son, Okimasa, who had previously been adopted by Mizuno Tadatomo. Okimasa was ejected from the Mizuno family at the time of Okitsugu's disgrace. He eventually (*ca.* 1804) became head of the Tanuma family and occupied the post of Junior Councilor, after 1822, and Grand Chamberlain, from 1825 to 1834. Under him the Tanuma family returned to Sagara, but their domain was kept at 10,000 koku.

53. For useful indices to this type of material see Koizumi Yasujirō, *Nihon shiseki nempyō* (Tokyo, 1904), Hirose Satoshi, *Nihon sōshō sakuin* (Tokyo, 1930), and Ōta Tamesaburo, *Nihon zuihitsu sakuin* (Tokyo, 1925 and 1932; 2 vols.).

54. An exception to this statement may be found in the appointment of his son, Mototomo, to the post of Junior Councilor in the face of Tokugawa custom that father and son should not hold high bakufu office simultaneously.

55. He was the favorite of the Shogun Tsunayoshi, whose service he

entered while Tsunayoshi was still daimyo of Tatebayashi. He eventually received the important Kōfu domain and the special surname Matsudaira, together with one of the characters of Tsunayoshi's name. Heibonsha, *Shinsen dai jimmei jiten* (Tokyo, 1937–1941; 9 vols.), 6. 304.

56. Oda Akinobu (Matazō), *On'ei roku* (3 kan, completed *ca.* 1818) [Kondō Heijo, *Kaitei shiseki shūran*, vol. 11 (1901)].

57. Of these, eight were given to Tanuma.

58. Hotta, 2. 846, also Oda, *Haizetsu roku*, 89–90. The Mizuno family previously was enfeoffed at Matsumoto castle in Shinano (70,000 koku).

59. He was Yoshimune's brilliant Edo City Magistrate whose years of honest administration and impartial justice became legendary among the Edo citizens.

60. Considerable confusion exists over the details of this story. The *Temmeido Tanuma seisui rin'e no ki* [Quoted in Jingū Shichō, 46. 417–418] refers to the shrine at Sano in Kataoka-gun in Kōzuke as being already named Tanuma Daimyōjin. But it says that Tanuma took possession of it and severed its connection with the Sano family. Tsuji, 33–35, drawing his information from the *Sano Tanuma shimatsu*, says that a Sano Daimyōjin was located in the Sano fief, which occupied the two villages of Nishioka and Takai in the Anraku district of Kōzuke, and that Tanuma not only forced a change of names but confiscated the surrounding property as well. Titsingh, *Illustrations of Japan* (London, 1822), pp. 102–103, makes no mention of the shrine. His version of the story, the geography of which is quite confused, is that Tanuma, while building his castle at Sagara, was in need of more space and, through the Shogun's interference, obtained possession of the neighboring Sano estate. This matter of the estates is repeated by Murdoch, 3. 403, who places the Sano fief along the Tōkaidō in Suruga. Unfortunately the Sano in question was not the one Murdoch saw from the Tōkaidō railroad line but one many miles away in the province of Kōzuke (the modern Gumma-ken). I have found no Japanese sources to corroborate either Titsingh's or Murdoch's version.

61. See *Zoku sannō gaiki* (completed after 1787 in 3 kan by an unidentified author using the pen name Wakamushi), kan 3, p. 8. [Page citations are from the author's manuscript copy.]

62. Several years after his fall, one of his former vassals, who had found employment as a menial in Kyoto, told of the extreme solicitude with which Tanuma treated his vassals. Even his humblest retainers were offered the warmth of sake on cold days. This man said that, at the time of the breakup of Tanuma's household, each of the 270 dismissed retainers was given a fund to start him off. Kanzawa, 12. 501–502; Mikami Sanji, *Edo jidai shi* (Tokyo, 1944; 2 vols.), 2. 310. This casts a somewhat different light on the character of the man whom Murdoch, 3. 380, describes as being "insufferably haughty and outrageously insolent" toward those whom he had no occasion to fear.

63. Matsuura Kiyo, *Kasshi yawa* (completed between 1821 and 1841 in 280 kan) [*Nihon zuihitsu taisei*, series 3, vols. 7–8 (1930)], 8. 447.

64. Kitajima, *Nihon kinseishi*, p. 254, and Tokutomi Iichirō, *Tanuma jidai* (Tokyo, 1936) [*Kinsei Nihon kokuminshi*, vol. 23], pp. 3–4.

65. Wakamushi, 3. 29 and 47; Tsuji, 24–5; Hayashi 47. 827 and 835.

66. There is no evidence to confirm Murdoch's statement, 3. 379, that Ōoka Tadayoshi was his chief rival for the ear of the Shogun. Tadayoshi, though the son of the previous Shogun's favorite, Ōoka Tadamitsu, never rose above

Master of Shogunal Ceremony, which post he reached in 1760. In 1772 (An'ei 1. 10. 29) he retired from office. He died in 1782, not, as Murdoch states, a few years after Ieharu's accession. Hotta, 6. 531–532. The father, Tadamitsu, died in the same year that Ieharu became Shogun, and this undoubtedly weakened the son's chances in the new Shogun's administration.

67. Ukon-shōgen, head of the Ochi branch of the Matsudaira. He was enfeoffed at Tatebayashi castle in Kōzuke (54,000 koku).

68. Tajima-no-kami, lord of Kawagoe castle in Musashi (60,000 koku).

69. Repeated by Murdoch, 3. 370.

70. Wakamushi, 3. 15–16.

71. Given him in 1769 in the province of Izu. This brought his total income up to 61,000 koku. Oda, *On'ei roku*, 715.

72. Wakamushi, 3. 19–20.

73. *Ibid.*, 3. 8–9. Murdoch, 3. 380, places this incident in 1767. According to Wakamushi, the date should be 1764, and this is borne out by the notices in the *Tokugawa jikki*, Hayashi, 47. 143 and 195. Five months after his resignation he was appointed Senior Councilor attached to the Heir Apparent. His retirement from active life came in 1767, at which time his domain was transferred to Yamagata castle in Dewa. Kondō Yoshizaemon, 567–568. Kanzawa, 12. 501, suggests that this change of fief was also the result of Akimoto's fall from favor.

74. Wakamushi, 3. 8–9.

75. It was even rumored that Tanuma attempted to hasten the death of this man by urging him to take part in several strenuous hunting expeditions. *Ibid.*, 3. 22. But Takemoto seems to have lived to ripe age notwithstanding.

76. Ukyō-dayū, Lord of Takasaki castle in Shimōsa (72,000 koku).

77. Wakamushi, 3. 27.

78. Suō-no-kami, Lord of Hamada castle in Iwami (50,000 koku). This branch of the Matsudaira family is listed under Matsui in Hotta, *Kansei Chōshū shokafu*.

79. Wakamushi, 3. 27–28.

80. Kamon-no-kami, Lord of Hikone castle in Ōmi (30,000 koku). This family was one of the houses which had the hereditary privilege of occupying the post of Great Councilor.

81. Wakamushi, 3. 38–39.

82. Takase Umetani, *Edo jidai ranjakki* (Tokyo, 1921) [Waseda Daigaku Shuppambu, *Kokumin no Nihonshi*, vol. 11], pp. 223 ff.

83. For one example of this, see the correspondence between Date Shigemura, Daimyo of Sendai, and the Lady Takatake of the Great Interior, published in the *Date-ke monjo* [Tōkyō Daigaku Shiryō Hensansho, *Dai Nihon komonjo, Iewake Monjo*, 3 (Tokyo, 1912, 10 vols.)], vol. 8, pp. 113 ff.

84. Wakamushi, 3. 17.

85. *Ibid.*, 3. 55–56; also Mikami Sanji, *Shirakawa Rakuō Kō to Tokugawa jidai (Nihon bunka meicho sen* edition, Tokyo, 1940), pp. 58–59. As would be expected, Matsudaira Sadanobu gave their petition short shrift. Tsuji quotes several other manuscript sources commenting on Tanuma's strong position in the Great Interior. Tsuji, 6.

86. Cf. Tatsui Matsunosuke, "Tanuma Okitsugu imbō," *Chūō shidan* 7. 1 (1933). 217–220.

87. In particular, Tanuma passed over the Shogun's own brother Shimizu Shigeyoshi, then thirty-six years old, and also the brilliant scion of the senior

house of the Three Lords, Matsudaira (Tayasu) Sadanobu, then in his twenty-third year. Sadanobu, as direct grandson of the Shogun Yoshimune, had prior claim on the shogunate over Ienari, who was a great-grandson. Previous to this, Sadanobu had been given yet another setback when the succession in the Tayasu house passed over him and was given to the sixth son of Hitotsubashi Harunari. The hand of Tanuma could be seen in both of these choices. Sadanobu's enmity toward Tanuma undoubtedly had its beginning in these early incidents. Wakamushi, 3. 32–33; Mikami, *Shirakawa*, 11–12.

88. The new Heir Apparent, the future Shogun Ienari, was placed in the Western Citadel under the attendance of Okitsugu's nephew. The latter had previously been a Councilor of the Hitotsubashi house, and it was through him that Tanuma exerted his influence. Wakamushi, 3. 32–33, states that Okitsugu even planned to have himself made Great Councilor after the death of Ieharu. It was his hope that the Hitotsubashi family would support him in this move.

89. Takase, 221.

90. Hayashi, 47. 675.

91. Takase, 222.

92. Tatsui, 217, discredits the account but repeats it as an example of what the people of the time believed Tanuma capable of.

93. Takase, 220–222. See also Takekoshi Yosaburo, *Nihon Keizaishi* (Tokyo, fourth ed., 1928; 6 vols.), vol. 5, p. 342.

94. *Date-ke monjo*, 8. 88, 91, 93–94, 116–119.

95. *Ibid.*, 75–76. Two technical points were involved in this matter. The Date and Shimazu houses by tradition occupied equal status at the Shogun's court. In 1764 Shimazu Shigehide had been promoted to Middle Commander. Date Shigemura was too young to receive this rank at the time, but Tanuma managed to have this objection set aside.

96. Daimyo of Tanaka in Suruga. He reached the post of Master of Court Ceremony. His adoptive heir was the second son of the Senior Councilor Makino Sadanaga. Kondō Yoshizaemon, 502.

97. Daimyo of Kakegawa in Tōtomi (45,000 koku). He became Master of Shogunal Ceremonies in 1770 and Junior Councilor for the Heir Apparent in 1781. His own heir was the 9th son of Ii Naoyuki. Kondō Yoshizaemon, 270.

98. Daimyo of Susano in Ise (15,000 koku).

99. Daimyo of Ayabe in Tamba (19,500 koku).

100. Hotta, 2. 846–847.

101. Hayashi, 47. 675. Mizuno took over this special duty from Matsudaira Terutaka. It was customary for one of the Senior Councilors to specialize in financial matters. Such a one was referred to as the *katte gata*. It appears, however, that other Senior Councilors continued to handle certain aspects of the bakufu finances. Mizuno's appointment, therefore, is quite unusual and deserves to be quoted in full:

"Mizuno Dewa-no-kami Tadatomo has just been appointed to superintend national finances. Henceforth all matters of finance, whether or not they were formerly referred to other Senior Councilors in charge of finance, will be brought to him alone. Problems referred from the provincial officers and matters of national expenditure, which were referred to the assembled Senior Council, shall now be handled by Tadatomo alone. Tadatomo's signature will be sufficient for all matters." Hayashi, 47. 675–676.

Mizuno seems to have had a special capacity for practical management of financial and construction work, and he frequently was brought up for commendation in this respect. If this appointment of Mizuno was part of Tanuma's attempt to gain control of bakufu financial administration, however, he appears to have overstepped himself. One month later the order was reversed as follows: "In reference to the above order to send all matters of national finance referred from the provinces to Mizuno Dewa-no-kami Tadatomo alone, this will be amended. Communications are to be addressed jointly to Tadatomo and the other Senior Councilors." Hayashi, 47. 677.

102. Echizen-no-kami. Hotta, 4. 198, also Kanzawa, 13. 495.

103. A 3000-koku post carrying a salary of 700 hyō and 300 gold ryō. Jingū Shichō, 16. 1027.

104. Echizen-no-kami. Hotta, 7. 292.

105. The post was listed at 500 koku and carried an annual rice stipend of 300 hyō. Jingū Shichō, 16. 1985.

106. Izu-no-kami. Hotta, 2. 942, also Kanzawa, 13. 473.

107. Echizen-no-kami. Hotta, 3. 404–405.

108. Tango-no-kami. Dates not included in Hotta, 3. 404–405.

109. A 1000-koku post with a 1000-hyō salary. Jingū Shichō, 17. 704–706.

110. The class and salary were identical with those of the Uraga Magistrate. Jingū Shichō, 17. 681–684.

111. Titsingh, 183–184.

112. Matsuura, 7. 31–32.

113. It should be noted that, as Senior Councilor, Tanuma was under orders to be the recipient of periodic gifts from the daimyo. See, for instance, the Tokugawa order of 1769 (Meiwa 6. 8. 19) which, along with the notice of Okitsugu's promotion to the Senior Council, restates the order that on such occasions the daimyo, from the Three Houses on down, were to pay their respects to the Senior Councilors and make appropriate presents. Hayashi, 47. 311.

114. A story, which appears in Wakamushi, 3. 37–38, will illustrate this point. It is said that two men, Makino Sadanaga and Torii Tadamoto, were both desirous of becoming Senior Councilors. Makino underlined his desire with a generous gift, while Torii refused to do so. As a result Makino received the appointment in 1784.

115. From the *Edo kemmon roku* quoted in Tokutomi, *Tanuma*, 20.

116. A listing of Tanuma's wealth, which was circulated at the time of his fall, though undoubtedly of small historical value, is nevertheless interesting enough to be included here. It is quoted without clear reference by Tsuji, 19–20.

Kantō rice	120,000 hyō	at Edo
Kinai rice	250,000 "	at Shimanouchi, Osaka
Ōshu rice	1,420,000 "	at Konaminato
Nankai rice	5,850,000 "	at Sagara
Hokkoku rice	303,000 "	at Nagasaki
Other rice	8,828,000 " plus	
Lamp oil	2,800,000 barrels	in various locations
Cash from sale of	70,080,000 " oil	in his residences at Sagara and Edo

City residences 270

117. Kitamura, 110.

118. Kanzawa, 13. 497.

CHAPTER IV. FILLING THE TOKUGAWA COFFERS

1. Tanuma's familiarity with his underlings was matched by his willingness to include men of low status in his household. His two chief retainers, Inoue Iori and Miura Shōji, were both from peasant stock. Inoue was employed as a wholesale merchant before his entrance into the service of the Tanuma house. Kanzawa, 13. 497.

2. Matsuura, 7. 869, uses the term "unlettered" (*fubun*) to characterize Tanuma.

3. Yoshida Tōgo, *Tōjo Nihonshi* (Tokyo, 1913; 11 vols.) 5. 263–264.

4. Hiraga Gennai's association with Tanuma is treated in detail in Chapter V.

5. Nomura Kanetarō, *Tokugawa jidai keizai shisō* (Tokyo, 1939), pp. 4 ff.

6. A convenient history of the development of Confucianism in Japan is to be found in Joseph John Spae, *Itō Jinsai, A Philosopher, Educator and Sinologist of the Tokugawa Period* (Peiping, 1948), pp. 11 ff.

7. See J. K. Fairbank, *The United States and China* (Cambridge: Harvard University Press, 1948), pp. 59–73, and Tsuda Sōkichi, *Shina shisō to Nihon* (Tokyo, 1938), pp. 5–30.

8. Honjō Eijirō, "Kinsei Nihon keizai shisō," *Keizaishi kenkyū* 19. 3 (1938). 292. For an expression of this view see *The Doctrine of the Mean* (chap. xxx 7, 11): ". . . the sovereign may not neglect the cultivation of his own character. . . Knowing how to cultivate his own character, he knows how to govern other men. Knowing how to govern other men, he knows how to govern the empire with all its States and families."

9. Cf. *The Great Learning* (chap. 10, 19): "Let the producers be many and the consumers few. Let there be activity in the production, and economy in the expenditure. Then the wealth will always be sufficient." Matsudaira Sadanobu expressed the same idea in his *Shiji seiyō*: "Wealth comes from the people. When consumption is great, wealth is insufficient, and the tax burden is increased. This in turn impoverishes the people. Thus their strength is exhausted, and the whole basis (of the state) is shaken." Quoted in Kanzawa, 12. 728.

10. Cf. Yamagata Bantō, *Yume no shiro* (preface dated 1802). The following excerpt quoted in Takimoto Seiichi, *Nihon hōken keizaishi* (Tokyo, 1930), p. 370, is an extreme statement of this view: "Encourage agriculture, and shun commerce, for while the peasants are the foundation of the nation we can do without the artisans or merchants."

11. Referred to as *jōsho, hōji,* or *kengi*. Some outstanding examples of this type of writing during the mid-Tokugawa period are Ogyū Sorai's *Seidan*, Motoori Norinaga's *Hihon tamakushige*, Nakai Chikuzan's *Sōbōkigen*, and the *jōsho* by Getaya Jimbei, Uezaki Kuhachirō, and Yamashita Kōnai. An earlier work of this nature, Kumazawa Banzan's *Daigaku wakumon*, has been translated. Cf. Galen M. Fisher, "Daigaku Wakumon. A Discussion of Public Questions in the Light of Great Learning," *TASJ* Ser. 2. 16 (1938). 259–356.

12. The conservative view was expressed in the phrase *kikoku senkin* (prize the cereals despise money), Honjō, "Kinsei shisō," 294.

13. Dazai was not particularly anti-traditional in his other ideas, but his realistic approach marked him off from the general run of Confucian scholars. He was another who believed that material well-being came before insistence on

virtuous conduct. Honjō Eijirō, *Nihon keizaishi jiten* (Tokyo, 1940; 3 vols.), pp. 1010–1011. Also Nomura, *Tokugawa shisō*, 33.

14. Kaibo spent a great deal of his life traveling in Central and Eastern Japan. Much of his writing was done with the problems of merchants and peasants in mind. Honjō, *Nihon keizaishi jiten*, 215–216; Nomura, *Tokugawa shisō*, 34.

15. The degree of Western influence traceable in this line of thinking is worthy of closer investigation. Take for instance this passage from Kaibo Seiryū: "On hearing that the Dutch king engages in business we burst into laughter. But do not I myself sell some things and buy others? It is a universal principle that goods are bought and sold. No one laughs at this." Quoted in Nomura, *Tokugawa shisō*, 34.

16. In particular, note the discussion of *han* industries by Abe Makoto, 131 ff. During the second quarter of the nineteenth century many of the progressive domains had succeeded in recovering their financial strength by engaging in monopoly enterprises. The Tsuwano domain, for instance, obtained nearly 60 per cent of its total revenue from its paper industry.

17. For a discussion of the financial decline of the shogunate see the article by Sawada Shō, "Financial Difficulties of the Edo Bakufu," translated into English by Hugh Borton, *HJAS* 1, 3 and 4 (1936). 308–326.

18. Tanuma's most positive supporter was the Dutch factor, Isaac Titsingh. See *Illustrations of Japan*, 182–184. Subsequent Japanese writers have drawn heavily on these pages.

19. Cf. Watanabe Eisaburō, "Edo jidai tochi kaikon jigyō ni arawarata chōnin no seiryoku," *RC* 64. 4 (1935). 384; 507. The land itself either went entirely to the reclaimer or was split with the government on a half-and-half basis. See also Honjō, *Nihon keizaishi jiten*, pp. 838–869. The "10 per cent system" came into effect in 1723.

20. The koku assessment of a domain by late Tokugawa days was seldom an accurate indication of the actual productivity of its land. One of the notorious practices of the Tanuma period appears to have been the exchanging of unproductive fiefs for ones of identical assessment but greater actual revenue. For this reason it was important to be on good terms with the Superintendent of Finance, since it was he who worked out the fief transfers. An indication of the discrepancy existing between nominal and actual incomes is seen in the 10,000-koku domain granted to Tanuma's heir in 1787. This domain in actuality yielded only 4–5000 koku. Tsuji, 241–242.

21. According to widely circulated but undoubtedly inexact figures which are the only data obtainable on the total cultivated area in Tokugawa Japan, agricultural land had nearly doubled in area from the time of Hideyoshi (1589–1595) to that of Yoshimune: from 1,500,000 to 2,977,180 *chō* (2.45 acres). Rice production rose from 18,000,000 koku to 25,910,674 koku over the same interval. Cf. Watanabe, 386.

22. A surplus of rice together with Yoshimune's reformed currency, which shrank the quantity and improved the quality of the circulating medium, combined to depress the price of rice to an all-time low of 8.3 hyō for 1 ryō. Sawada, 318.

23. Watanabe, 504, cites examples of mass protests for the purpose of forcing the authorities to revoke the reclamation licenses of land exploiters.

24. Honjō, *Nihon keizaishi jiten*, 869.

25. Watanabe, 496. See also Ikeda Shirō, "Kinsei hōken shakai ni okeru chōnin ukeoi shinden no ichi kōsatsu," [Shibata Minoru, *Nihon bunkashi kenkyū* (Kyoto, 1944)], pp. 251–294.

26. Cf. Abe Makoto, 48.

27. Watanabe, 498.

28. Kaibo Seiryū was especially outspoken on the subject of obtaining profit from new fields. Reclamation would pay off, he felt, only if it did not force the authorities into debt and if the work did not harm already existing fields. Nomura, *Tokugawa shisō*, 61–62.

29. *Ibid.*, 63–64. All indications lead to the conclusion that by the mid-eighteenth century the Japanese had expanded their cultivated land to the limit of the technology then available. Further reclamation was most difficult and required extensive capital resources.

30. Hayashi, 47. 550; Jingū Shichō, 21. 1187.

31. I have been unable to consult the chief source on the Imbanuma project, which according to Tsuji, 188, is Oda Matayuki, *Imbanuma kei'i ki* (Tokyo, 1883; 3 vols.), a thorough study of the history and the modern possibilities of carrying through the scheme which had attracted so much controversy.

32. Tokutomi, *Tanuma*, 423. Work on Teganuma likewise ended in failure in 1728 when storms destroyed the nearly completed embankments.

33. It was estimated that a strip approximately 240 yards by 7.3 miles would result.

34. This would make it possible for transport boats from the north to avoid the long and dangerous voyage around the Bōshū Peninsula.

35. Two estimates of the possible cost were made, one of 30,000 ryō, and the other of 60,000 ryō. Upon completion, the financial backers were to receive 80 per cent of the new fields, the remaining 20 per cent going to the local inhabitants. Tsuji, 187.

36. Matsumoto was placed in charge of reclamation projects as early as 1775, before he became Superintendent. Jingū Shichō, 21. 1186–1187.

37. Since the levels of Imbanuma and the Tone river were so close, the draining of the lake incurred the danger of a possible backflow from the Tone. For this reason a dam and watergate were necessary at the far end of the lake. It was the collapse of this dam which eventually caused the project to fail. Tokutomi, *Tanuma*, 425.

38. Hayashi, 47. 809.

39. See Abe Masami, "Shōnai han Imbanuma sosui kaisaku temmatsu,"*RC* 68 (1936). 2; 3; 4, for a discussion of another attempt in 1843 under Mizuno Tadakuni, when the combined resources of five daimyo were conscripted. Mizuno had no more success than Tanuma. For an English summary of Abe's article, see Edwin Reischauer, "Bibliography," *HJAS* 2. 1 (1937). 130–131. Since World War II the Japanese government has undertaken the project with greater assurances of success.

40. Wakamushi, 3. 45.

41. Tsuji, 189.

42. See Sadanobu's memorial to the Shogun Ienari, probably written in late 1786. Tsuji, 224 ff.

43. The authorities realized that, unless Ezo were more thoroughly colonized, Japan had a poor claim to the island and a weak defense against the Russians. Inobe Shigeo, *Ishin zenshi no kenkyū* (Tokyo, 1935), p. 87.

44. It was estimated that 1/10 of the entire area, or 1,166,400 chō (*ca.* 2,858,000 acres), was arable, sufficient to produce 5,832,000 koku of rice. The chief documentary source for this project is the *Ezo-chi ikken.* While I have been unable to consult this work, ample selections from it have been quoted in Inobe and Tokutomi, *Tanuma.*

45. The standard expression of this opinion appears in the early Meiji work by Naitō Chisō, "Tokugawa uji kahei no koto" [Kokugakuin, *Kokushi ronsō* (Tokyo, 1903)], pp. 458–520. It has been repeated in such works as Takizawa Matsuyo, *The Penetration of Money Economy in Japan and its Effects Upon Social and Political Institutions* (New York, 1927), p. 44.

46. Takekoshi, *Keizaishi*, 5. 385 ff., entitles his chapter on these policies "The Great Meiwa and An'ei Currency Reform." He considers the program a landmark in the history of Japanese currency.

47. The most useful of these is Kusama Naokata, *Sanka zui*, [Takimoto Seiichi, *Nihon keizai taiten*, vols. 39–40 (1929–1930)]. The most voluminous is the Ōkura-shō, *Dai Nihon kahei shi* (Tokyo, 1876–1883; 46 vols.) (Edition used, Tokyo, 1925–26; 8 vols.). In English see Neil Gordon Munro, *Coins of Japan* (Yokohama, 1904).

48. For instance Katsu Yasufusa, *Suijin roku* (Tokyo, 1890; 12 vols.) or Ōkura-sho, *Nihon zaisei keizai shiryō* (Tokyo, 1922–23; 10 vols.).

49. I refer to the extensive modern collections of Tokugawa writings published by Honjō, Takimoto, and others, the most complete being Takimoto's great *Nihon keizai taiten*, cited above.

50. For a traditional account of Tokugawa currency and finance see Takizawa, 30 ff.

51. Silver actually circulated by lump up to the year 1765. The term "silver coin" as used by Takizawa, 40–41, does not apply until this date.

52. The unit of gold coin was the ryō, its subdivisions being the *bu* (¼ ryō) and the *shu* (¼ bu). Silver was measured in momme, a unit of weight. Ten momme of silver were equal to one silver bu. One thousand momme of silver were a kan. Copper coins (*zeni*) were minted in one *mon* pieces. One thousand mon were equivalent to one kan of copper. The ratio of 1 gold ryō to 60 momme silver was that of 1 to 10.

53. Nomura Kanetarō, "Tokugawa kahei seido no honshitsu ni tsuite," *Shigaku* 17. 3 (1937). 341 ff.

54. *Ibid.*, 351–352; 368–369. Nomura points out that while the growth of paper money and bills of exchange are generally taken as signs of monetary progress in Japan, they were actually the products of an advanced economy working on a feudalistic currency base and thus must not be too closely compared to the similar developments in Europe.

55. Kokushō Iwao, "Tokugawa jidai no kahei seido," *Shakai kagaku* 2. 7 (1926). 299.

56. This profit was termed *deme*. Cf. Honjō, *Nihon keizaishi jiten*, 263.

57. For the avowed objectives of the Tanuma program, see Hayashi 47. 593 (An'ei 8. 2. 30).

58. *Ibid.*, 47. 198.

59. Kusama, 39. 588–589; Jingū Shichō, 26. 238–239.

60. Hayashi, 47. 267–268 (Meiwa 4. 12. 18).

61. Tsuji, 175.

62. Kurita, *Edo jidai shi*, 229.

63. Takekoshi, *Keizaishi*, 5. 385.
64. Hayashi, 47. 395.
65. This term has a long history, both in China and Japan, as a euphemism for silver. The *Er-ya* definition is repeated in all standard modern dictionaries. It will also be recalled that the shu was a unit of gold currency rather than silver.
66. The 1-ryō gold piece was called a koban.
67. Hayashi, 47. 415. After 1774 all payments to the government were required to be made at least 50 per cent in nanryō.
68. Hayashi, 47. 446.
69. Kusama, 39. 290.
70. Takimoto, *Nihon keizai taiten*, 23. 147–156.
71. *Ibid.*, 23. 315–543.
72. See Nomura Kanetaro's excellent article on this problem, "Nanryō nishu gin no ryūtsū ni tsuite," *Mitagakkai zasshi* 14. 3 (1947). 147–159.
73. Nomura, "Nanryō," pp. 154 ff.
74. Nomura, "Tokugawa kahei," 357.
75. Takekoshi, *Keizaishi*, 5. 395.
76. *Ibid.*, 5. 396. Also Jingū Shichō, 26. 143.
77. Hayashi, 47. 596 (An'ei 5. 6. 18).
78. *Ibid.*, 47. 313 (Meiwa 6. 9. 12).
79. Lord Date of Sendai received permission in 1784, Hayashi 47. 760. The shape of the coins was square, and circulation was legally limited to the Sendai domain. But it would appear that these coins leaked out to Tokugawa lands and helped depress the value of central government coins. Mikami, *Edo jidai shi*, 2. 321.
80. Hayashi 47. 279. A total of 157,425,360 pieces of this coin is said to have been issued up to 1788. Jingū Shichō, 26. 148; Tsuji, 176.
81. This is mentioned in the Getaya memorial quoted by Tsuji, 179, as well as in Kitamura, 131. But the wave pattern does not appear to have been Kawai's crest. Perhaps the association between this pattern and Kawai's name came from the character *kawa* (river) which was the first element of Kawai's surname.
82. Takekoshi, *Keizaishi*, 5. 395.
83. Hayashi, 47. 447.
84. Takekoshi, *Keizaishi*, 5. 396.
85. The shogunate budget was cut in 1757 and 1764. In 1770 a five-year plan of retrenchment and frugality was enunciated. Mikami, *Edo jidai shi*, 2. 313; Hayashi, 47. 354.
86. See Satō Jizaemon, *Kahei hiroku* (complete *ca.* 1845) [Takimoto Seiichi, *Nihon keizai taiten*, vol. 45], 168–170, for figures on the government profit made on coinage during the years 1833–1843.
87. Cf. Yoshida Tōgo, "Edo jidai no kōzan-gyō ni tsuite," *SZ* 27. 10 (1916) 1074–1075.
88. Hayashi, 47. 113.
89. Yoshida, "Kōzan," 1076.
90. *Ibid.*, 1077.
91. Hayashi 47. 224.
92. *Ibid.*, 47. 224–225.
93. Yoshida, "Kōzan," 1077. After Tanuma's fall, the forced step-up of production was called off, and Japan's copper output fell rapidly. Her mines did

not succeed in improving production until the introduction of modern technological advances after 1854.

94. Hayashi, 47. 248.

95. Tsuji, 192, gives as an example of these wildcat ventures, the attempt to mine copper out of Kombuzan in Yoshino. So much money was squandered in the process that the Daigo Sampōin temple protested to Tanuma and had the affair called off. An attempt to get gold out of Kongōzan in Yamato was one of the first of Tanuma's schemes to be discontinued by Matsudaira Sadanobu. Hayashi, 47. 809.

96. Cf. Irita Seizō, "Hiraga Gennai to kagaku," in Tōkyō Kagaku Hakubutsukan, *Edo jidai no kagaku* (Tokyo, second ed. 1938), pp. 18–24. During the Tanuma period, the silver mines on Sado nearly doubled their output. Honjō, *Nihon keizai jiten*, 653.

97. Tsuji, 193–194.

98. Hayashi, 47. 636–637.

99. *Ibid.*, 47. 757.

100. Jingū Shichō, 16. 1129.

101. Hayashi, 47. 547; 707.

102. *Ibid.*, 47. 135, 140. He held the post of Keeper of Edo Castle from 1765 to his death. Thus his influence in matters of financial policy was limited to the period before Kawai's appearance. Isshiki was undoubtedly on intimate terms with the Tanuma faction, since his eldest son married a daughter of Tanuma's Superintendent of Finance, Akai Tadaakira. Hotta, 1. 490.

103. His literary name was Ransui. He became an Attendant Physician in 1763.

104. Before the time of Yoshimune, all ginseng used in Japan came from Korea and China. The resultant high price put the product out of reach of the general populace. Therefore the Shogun had seeds imported from Korea and planted in the Kantō area. The fruits of his efforts were just now becoming evident, as several places in the Kantō began to grow ginseng which was said to equal that imported from Korea. Hayashi, 47. 174.

105. The government had for some time been disturbed by the poor quality of Chinese ginseng. A warning was sent out in 1764, and it is said that some 30,000 ryō worth of Canton ginseng was destroyed at Nagasaki. Hayashi 47. 154; Tsuji, 196.

106. While the overall results were beneficial, the money-making motive seems to have been pushed to excess. In 1771 the shogunate cautioned the salesmen of the 28 firms to discontinue the practice of forced sales to local apothecaries. Hayashi, 47. 373.

107. Or perhaps even earlier, in 1735; see Honjō, *Nihon keizaishi jiten*, 1579.

108. Hayashi, 47. 258–259.

109. *Ibid.*, 47. 702.

110. *Ibid.*, 47. 282.

111. *Ibid.*, 47. 699; Tsuji, 197.

112. Hayashi, 47. 760.

113. Cf. Yamamoto Saburō, "Tokugawa Bakufu shuzōmai tōsei," *RK* 8. 9 (1938). 45–46. Breweries were kept under close government control, and each manufacturer was confined to a certain quota of rice. Restrictions on sake brewing were effected by cutting these quotas by a uniform percentage.

114. Tsuji, 198. Honjō, *Nihon keizaishi jiten,* 1808, incorrectly places the origin of the coal monopolization program in 1804.

115. Hayashi, 47. 476.

116. Tsuji, 199.

117. Hayashi, 47. 214; 244; 340; 362; 743.

118. Kurita, *Edo jidai shi,* 154.

119. Hayashi, 47. 206.

120. Yoshida, *Tōjo Nihonshi,* 5. 264–265.

121. Hayashi, 47. 783.

122. *Ibid.*

123. Such inspection services were not uncommon. In 1773, government inspection of silkworms was made compulsory. Mikami, *Edo jidai shi,* 2. 318.

124. Located in Kōzuke province. It was the castle of Matsudaira Terutaka, chief of the Senior Councilors at the time. He appears to have had a hand in setting up the silk tax program. It was his inability to control the mob which caused the abandonment of the project. Hayashi, 47. 671.

125. Descriptions of this episode are extremely numerous and differ somewhat in details. I have taken the account as it appears in Hayashi, 47. 670–671. For other accounts in English see Hugh Borton, "Peasant Uprisings in Japan of the Tokugawa Period," *TASJ* 2. 16 (1938), pp. 57–59; Sawada, 320; Takekoshi Yosoburo, *The Economic Aspects of the History of the Civilization of Japan* (New York, 1930; 3 vols.), 3. 140.

126. Shogunal loans, called *ondai,* were a regular feature of the Tokugawa system, Tanuma himself having received such a loan to aid in the reconstruction of his official mansion. But the years of frequent natural calamity, which marked the latter half of Ieharu's shoguncy put an inordinate strain on the Tokugawa treasury. In 1783 the government found it necessary to institute a seven-year frugality program during which daimyo loans could not be made. Hayashi, 47. 736.

127. Wakamushi, 3. 41–42.

128. *Ibid.*

129. Murdoch, in telling this story, *History of Japan,* 3. 401, has confused the details of the 1785 and 1786 orders. He places the incidents all in 1786.

130. Hayashi, 47. 803–804. An English translation of this order appears in Takekoshi, *Economic Aspects,* 3. 141.

131. Hayashi, 47. 809.

132. The lack of accurate budgetary information makes it extremely difficult to determine the exact government intake from its monopolies and commercial taxes. An undocumented chart of shogunal revenues and expenditures in rice and money prepared by Takekoshi indicates, however, that, while the rice income generally fell below expenditures during these years, the income in money was sufficient to leave a surplus. Takekoshi, *Keizaishi,* 3. 736–739.

133. Yano Jin'ichi, *Nagasaki shishi, tsūkō bōeki hen, Toyō shokoku bu* (Nagasaki, 1938), 272, 287.

134. Kimiya Yasuhiko, *Nisshi kōtsū shi* (Tokyo, 1927; 2 vols.), 1. 487–498.

135. *Ibid.,* 1. 497. The kin is equivalent to 1.32 lb.

136. *Ibid.,* 1. 498–502.

137. For a discussion of varying Tokugawa theories on the merits of foreign trade, see Honjō, "Japan's Overseas Trade in the Closing Days of the Tokugawa Shogunate," *Kyoto University Economic Review,* 14. 2 (1939). 1–31. The school

of realists, represented at the turn of the century by such men as Hayashi Shihei and Honda Toshiaki, was vigorous in its demand that Japan enrich herself through foreign trade.

138. Kurita, *Edo jidai shi*, 230. After the expiration of the first twenty-year period in 1782, the agreement was renewed for another twenty years at 330 kan worth of additional trade. This agreement was broken off by Matsudaira Sadanobu in 1790.

139. Cf. Uchida Ginzō, "Tokugawa jidai toku ni sono chūsei igo ni okeru gaikoku kin-gin no yu'nyū," [*Nihon keizaishi no kenkyū* (Tokyo, 1921, 2 vols.)]. Uchida estimates that up to 1790 this agreement accounted for the import of over 351 kan of gold and 8853 kan of silver. Kurita, *Edo jidai shi*, 230.

140. The following paragraphs are drawn largely from Numata Jirō, "Nisshin bōeki ni okeru ichi mondai. Tawaramono no yushutsu ni tsuite," *RC* 68 (1936). 5. 1–14; 6. 25–46. For an English summary of this article see Edwin Reischauer, "Bibliography," pp. 126–127.

141. Hayashi, 47. 145, 195.

142. *Ibid.*, 47. 768–769.

143. It is estimated that up to 1830, gold imports amounted to over 1419 kan and silver more than 13,538 kan. Kurita, *Edo jidai shi*, 230–231. Furthermore, Tanuma's policy had greatly increased the Tokugawa tax receipts from the Nagasaki trade. This tax, which in 1714 amounted to 50,000 ryō yearly, had shrunk to 15,000 ryō by 1746. Tanuma succeeded in raising the figure to 20,000 ryō by 1785. Honjō, *Nihon keizaishi jiten*, 1218.

144. From 1790 to 1808 the Nagasaki trade authorities were exempted from sending any tax to Edo. *Ibid.*

CHAPTER V. — THE DUTCH AND THE RUSSIANS

1. Inobe, *Ishin zenshi*, pp. 29 ff., gives a summarization of the various pro-seclusion arguments of Kumazawa Banzan, Yamaga Sokō, Arai Hakuseki, Muira Baien, and others.

2. Pioneers in this respect were Dazai Shundai and Satō Nobusue, father of the famous Nobuhiro. Cf. Ueno Kikuji, "Edojidai no kaikoku shisō ni tsuite," *RC* 34. 4 (1919). 309–319.

3. For Arai Hakuseki's thoughts on Western civilization see Inobe, *Ishin zenshi*, 55 ff.

4. The Sidotti incident is described by Murdoch, 2. 304 ff. Jean-Baptiste Sidotti (1668–1715) was an Italian priest. He left Europe for the Far East in 1703. After a few years in the Philippines he determined to carry his message to Japan. Braving the seclusion edict, he landed on an island off Kagoshima in 1708. He was immediately captured.

5. Inobe, *Ishin zenshi*, 58–60.

6. Cf. Shimmura Izuru, "Yōgaku" [Seibundō Shinkōsha, *Nihon bunkashi taikei*, vol. 10, *Edo kōki bunka* (Tokyo, 1939)], 164–165. Also Saitō Agu, "Tokugawa Yoshimune to seiyō bunka," *SZ* 47. 11 (1936). 1376–1377. See the article by Shio Sakanishi, "Prohibition of Import of Certain Chinese Books and the Policy of the Edo Government," *JOAS* 57, 3 (1937). 290–303, for a discussion of the earlier prohibition policy.

7. Tsuji, 294–295.

8. Pertinent sections of Thunberg's voluminous *Voyages de C. P. Thunberg*

au Japon . . . (4 vols., Paris, 1796) have been brought together in Richard Hildreth, *Japan as It Was and Is* (Boston, 1855), pp. 387–423.

9. A full treatment of Titsingh's stay in Japan is given by Shimmura Izuru in his article "Temmei jidai no kaigai chishiki," *SZ* 26. 10; 27. 2. This article was later reprinted in Shimmura's *Zoku Namban kōki* (Tokyo, 1925). It also forms the basis for Charles Boxer's chapter on Titsingh in his *Jan Compagnie in Japan 1600–1817* (The Hague, 1936).

10. The following biographical information comes largely from Heibonsha, *Shinsen dai jimmei jiten* 3. 290.

11. Titsingh, 182.

12. Murdoch, 3. 551.

13. The work was in thirty kan. Cf. Samura Hachirō, *Kokusho kaidai* (Tokyo, 1926, third ed.; 2 vols.), 1. 1147.

14. Called the *Meiji-kan.* Among other projects, the college worked on a special calendar for the Satsuma domain.

15. Abe Makoto, 131.

16. Daimyo of Fukuchiyama in Tamba (32,000 koku). He is usually referred to as Samon. Hotta, 3. 152–153.

17. Titsingh, 182.

18. Published in 1789 in 17 kan. Samura, 2. 1283–1284.

19. Published in 1777 in 1 kan. Samura, 1. 1162.

20. Shimmura, "Yōgaku," 174–175.

21. *Ibid.*

22. Murdoch, 3. 548.

23. Takase, 327–329.

24. Wada Tatsuo, "Bijutsu," [Seibundō Shinkōsha, *Nihon bunkashi taikei*, vol. 10, *Edo kōki bunka* (Tokyo, 1939)], 254–256.

25. The following details of Hiraga's life are taken for the most part from Nagata Gonjirō, *Tokugawa sambyakunen shi* (Tokyo, 1903–1906, vols. 2, 3, vol. 1 never published), 3. 296–376. Hiraga's biography is by Mizutani Futō.

26. Jingū Shichō, 5. 417–418.

27. Tanuma Mototomo.

28. Tanuma Okitsugu.

29. Titsingh's spelling for Shogun. The obvious error of stating that Tanuma was uncle to the Shogun is a curious commentary on the great power wielded by Tanuma at this time.

30. The Nagasaki Magistrate, Kuze Hirotami.

31. Titsingh, 182–184.

32. For some reason Tadatsune is not included in Hotta, *Kansei chōshū shokafu.* The meager data on his official career comes from the *Sho goyaku daidai ki* (contained in Jingū Shichō, 16. 780).

33. Murdoch, 3. 505.

34. Shimmura, "Temmei jidai," 27. 2. 158–159.

35. Cf. Itō Tazaburō, "Yogaku no ichi kōsatsu," *Shakai keizaishigaku* 7. 3 (1937). 268–270.

36. For a scholarly study of early Japanese relations with Russia see Tabohashi Kiyoshi, *Kindai Nihon gaikoku kankei shi* (Tokyo, 1933), pp. 1–93.

37. Tabohashi gives a lengthy treatment of this romantic character, 97–143.

38. Cf. V. V. Barthold, *La Découverte de l'Asie* (Paris, 1947), 229–230.

39. The Japanese were warned of Russian designs by both A. W. Feith in 1772 and Titsingh in 1781. Kurita, *Edo jidai shi*, 233.

40. Kudō was not the first to write of the importance of Japan's northern frontiers. Inobe, *Ishin zenshi*, pp. 47–51, lists a succession of writers from the Mito and Sendai domains who called for the development of Ezo for both economic and strategic reasons. Kudō, however, offered the first well-informed discussion of the problem.

41. Ueno, 311.

42. This was a misconception which dated from Arai Hakuseki's pioneer description of Ezo, entitled *Ezo shi* (preface dated 1720) [Kokusho Kankōkai, *Arai Hakuseki zenshū*, vol. 3].

43. Kudō Heisuke's willingness to have precious metals exported from Ezo derived from his belief that the island was actually not Japanese territory. Both Hakuseki's gazetteer and the *Dai Nihon shi* of Mito refer to Ezo as a foreign country. Inobe, *Ishin zenshi*, 74.

44. Tabohashi, 145.

45. Inobe, *Ishin zenshi*, 82.

46. *Ibid.*, 83–86.

47. Tsuji, 307–308, is extremely puzzled over Matsumoto's failure to advocate trade with the Russians and suspects that some hidden motive was involved. He thinks perhaps Matsumoto was influenced by the Matsumae daimyo or the merchants who were making profits from illegal trade with the Russians.

48. Matsudaira Sadanobu did not necessarily shut his eyes to the foreign problem. He himself made a thorough study of Western countries and at one time even favored opening a port in Ezo to Russian trade. The program he actually put into practice, however, was basically conservative.

CHAPTER VI. POLITICAL DECLINE AND SOCIAL UNREST

1. Cf. Murdoch, 3. 377.

2. On the occasion of Ieyasu's 150th anniversary. Most of the high shogunal officials were sent to Nikkō for these services. Hayashi, 47. 148.

3. This event took up almost the entire activity of the shogunate for three months during the spring of 1776 (An'ei 5. 3–6). An entire chapter of the *Tokugawa jikki* is devoted to the description of the progress alone. Hayashi, 47. 496–516. The affair entailed immense expenditures both by the Tokugawa and by the daimyo. To the Tokugawa Shogun, however, the progress to Nikkō held great significance. It was essentially an act of spiritual renewal and dedication at Ieyasu's tomb and was undertaken once by each Shogun. Discontinued for lack of funds after the time of the Fourth Shogun, Ietsuna, it was revived, surprisingly enough, by the frugal Yoshimune. Ieshige had been too weak to take the trip, but Ieharu insisted on going through with the ceremony. It was his deep conviction that the country would benefit by its observance. The project was three times given up because of insufficient funds but at the Shogun's insistence was carried out in 1776. Hayashi, 47. 820.

4. Moriyama Takamori, *Shizu no odamaki* (Preface dated 1802) [Printed edition in Iwamoto, *Enseki jisshū*, vol. 1], p. 220.

5. Hayashi 47. 246.

6. *Ibid.*, 47. 455.

7. *Ibid.*, 47. 170. It should be noted that the dress of the bushi class was

prescribed as rigidly as our present-day military uniforms and hence was not to be considered a matter of personal taste.

8. 1476–1559. He was the second head of the Kano school, and his work was perhaps the most highly regarded of all Kano painters.

9. The part of the room set apart for decorations of flowers and works of art.

10. Takase, 296–297.

11. *Ibid.*, 297.

12. Tsuji, 16.

13. A penetrating study of the merchant mentality as it developed under the pressure of social and political oppression has been made by Yamamoto Katsu-tarō, *Genroku jidai no keizaigakuteki kenkyū* (Tokyo, 1925), pp. 10 ff.

14. Takase, 303.

15. *Ibid.*, 305–306. The new hair styles were made possible by the develop-ment of two new conveniences, the umbrella, which replaced the shade hat, and the availability of professional hairdressers. For illustrations of these new styles see Ema Tsutomu, "Fūzoku to seikatsu," [Seibundō Shinkōsho, *Nihon bunkashi taikei*, vol. 10, *Edo kōki bunka* (Tokyo, 1939)], pp. 302 ff.

16. An outer garment worn over the kimono.

17. The sash or wide cloth belt worn with kimono.

18. Ema, 312. Ema believes that food and entertainment revealed the true measure of bourgeois luxury, since in matters of clothing government surveillance was too strict to allow the merchants to express themselves freely.

19. This was in part due to the many devastating fires of the period, on account of which the government drew up more stringent building laws. Tile roofs became compulsory in the major cities, and attempts were made to keep down excessive overcrowding.

20. Ema, 311–314.

21. Tsuji, 98.

22. Takano Tatsuyuki, "Bungaku oyobi ongaku" [Seibundō Shinkōsha, *Nihon bungakushi taikei*, vol. 10, *Edo kōki bunka* (Tokyo, 1939)], p. 215.

23. Quoted by Inobe Shigeo, "Edo bakufu seiji (3)" (Tokyo, 1934) [Kuroita Katsumi, ed., *Iwanami kōza: Nihon rekishi*, case 8], p. 8.

24. Hayashi, 47. 735.

25. *Ibid.*, 47. 160.

26. *Ibid.*, 47. 232.

27. *Ibid.*, 47. 248, 261.

28. *Ibid.*, 47. 374.

29. *Ibid.*, 47. 419.

30. *Ibid.*, 47. 200.

31. Murdoch, 3. 382; also Tsuji, 84–91.

32. Kurita, *Edo jidai shi*, 151. The event was lampooned in a popular song in which a geisha is made to inquire, "Which four-thousand-koku lord shall I sleep with (tonight)?"

33. Hayashi, 47. 95.

34. *Ibid.*, 47. 77.

35. *Ibid.*, 47. 357.

36. *Ibid.*, 47. 400.

37. *Ibid.*, 47. 609.

38. Kanzawa, 12. 503.

39. Hayashi, 47. 705. This reduction in rank obliged Sakakibara to cut down

on his staff, his retainers, his military outlay, and in many other ways curtail his expenses.

40. Kurita, *Edo jidai shi*, 151.

41. A variety of popular ballad sung to the accompaniment of the shamisen, later combined with puppets into a form of drama.

42. Kurita, *Edo jidai shi*, 153.

43. His *Ichiwa ichigen*, a collection of anecdotes and comments on the social and official world of his day, is one of the chief sources on the life of the Tanuma period.

44. Lit. "insane songs," a type of comic poetry of 31 syllables. It became popular in Edo during the mid-Tokugawa period.

45. Witty short stories which generally depicted the life of the gay quarters.

46. Ōta Nampo, *Kanesoki* (completed 1810) [*Nihon zuihitsu taisei*, series 1, vol. 3], 746–747.

47. Hayashi, 47. 330, 720, 758.

48. *Ibid.*, 47. 266, 377.

49. *Ibid.*, 47. 197.

50. *Ibid.*, 47. 757. This land was put into the name of local peasants so that it would not be detected by the government authorities. Naturally the relationship of the samurai to land held in this way differed considerably from that to the fief. Though such land paid its feudal tax, its ownership was non-feudal in nature.

51. *Ibid.*, 47. 626.

52. *Ibid.*, 47. 206.

53. See *Tanuma Tonomo-no-kami nite ōse wataserare no mune*, a spurious document which circulated after Tanuma's death and which lists "26 crimes" committed by Tanuma. The work is included in Tsuji, pp. 242–254. Crimes 10, 11, 12, and 13 mention specifically the unauthorized favors Tanuma granted the merchants.

54. Ogawa Kendo, *Chirizuka dan* (compiled in 8 kan after 1814) [Iwamoto, *Enseki jisshū*, vol. 1].

55. Kanzawa, 13. 116.

56. It is said that Sano Masakoto squandered some 620 ryō on fruitless presents to the younger Tanuma in hopes of promotion.

57. See his memorial to the Shogun, Ienari, quoted by Tsuji, 224 ff.

58. *Ibid.*, 60–61.

59. Hayashi, 47. 556.

60. *Ibid.*, 47. 85.

61. Murdoch's statement, 3. 372–375, that no peasant uprisings occurred in Tokugawa domains during Yoshimune's time was obviously written before the works of Kokushō Iwao or Kurita Motoji were made available. Numerous uprisings have come to light during Yoshimune's shoguncy; some of the worst of these were in the shogunal domains. In 1734 the shogunate was obliged to order its local officials to call upon neighboring daimyo for military aid in suppressing peasant disturbances. Kurita, *Edo jidai shi, ge*, 194–195.

62. Kitajima Masamoto has made this amply clear in his article, "Tokugawa bakufu ryō no shoyakunin no shikyoku ni tsuite," *RK* 6. 7 (1937). The following conclusions for the most part follow his study.

63. Hayashi, 47. 339.

64. Kitajima, "Tokugawa bakufu," 779.

65. An exhaustive study which lists all recorded natural calamities since the

beginning of Japanese history has been made by Okashima Minoru, *Nihon saii shi* (Tokyo, 1894).

66. See Kurita Motoji's study of the coincidence of political decline and natural calamity "Edo jidai ni okeru tensai to seiji to no kankei," *Chūō shidan*, 8. 1 (1924). 49–61.

67. At Odawara, in the province of Sagami, water was rationed to one *shō* (3.2 pints) per person per day during the summer of 1770. Tsuji, 117.

68. Hayashi, 47. 308. This was without doubt the well-known Lexell's Comet.

69. The details come from Saitō Kōsei, *Bukō nempyō* (completed 1878) [Printed editions, Tokyo, Kokusho Kankōkai, 1911; *Edo sōsho*, 1917]. See the passages quoted in Tsuji, 117–119; Tokutomi, 472–476, and Okashima, 101–102. The *Tokugawa jikki*, Hayashi, 47. 382, gives a more moderate description and estimates the width at half this figure.

70. The following are some of the categories: Senior Councilors, 10,000 ryō; Junior Councilors, 5000 ryō; 1000-koku Bannermen, 50 ryō. Hayashi, 47. 384, 385–386.

71. *Ibid.*, 47. 393–394; Tsuji, 121.

72. The pun was made between the words Meiwa *ku* (Meiwa 9) and the word *meiwaku* (misfortune, annoyance).

73. Hayashi, 47. 400.

74. Tsuji, 122.

75. Hayashi, 47. 433, 448–449, 551.

76. *Ibid.*, 47. 551.

77. Tsuji, 123. No doubt this figure, as well as many of the others cited below, is exaggerated.

78. Hayashi, 47. 631.

79. This is the figure given in the *Tokugawa jikki*, Hayashi 47. 726, which at this point appears to be relying on Sugita Gempaku's *Nochimi gusa*. There are numerous other accounts of this eruption both in Japanese and English. See Titsingh, 97–100; Takekoshi, *Economic Aspects*, 3. 132; Tsuji, 123–125; and Tokutomi, *Tanuma*, 475–478.

80. It is hard to believe, however, that the distant province of Suruga was included among the areas buried "feet deep under ashes" as Murdoch states, 3. 396.

81. Takekoshi, *Economic Aspects*, 3. 132, says that it was not until the peasants of the devastated area had risen up in revolt that the government "agreed" to aid in reclaiming their lands. This was on the ninth day of the eleventh month. But previously in the eighth month a Comptroller of Finance had already been sent to the stricken areas to supervise reclamation work.

82. Hayashi, 47. 731, 733.

83. Takase, 269. An estimated 1,200,000 persons starved to death. The accuracy of such an estimate is highly doubtful.

84. Hayashi, 47. 805–806. Again the shogunate set up a sliding scale program of relief loans to the Bannermen and Housemen, while rice was rushed into the city from areas untouched by the flood. *Ibid.*, 47. 807.

85. Tsuji, 117.

86. Hayashi, 47. 401, 537.

87. One contemporary estimate of the population of Edo in 1791 went as high as 2,600,000 inhabitants. Mozume Takami, 3. 985–988. But a modern

scholar believes that Edo never had more than one million inhabitants. Kōda Shigetomo, *Edo to Osaka* (Tokyo, revised ed., 1942), pp. 17–19.

88. Murdoch, 3. 384–392; Kurita, *Edo jidai shi,* 240 ff.

89. The results of Mori Kahei's studies on the famine conditions in northern Japan during the Temmei period, though dealing primarily with lands outside of Tokugawa control, may be applied to the whole of this region. His conclusions are that after eight years of near or actual famine, neither the authorities nor the people had any reserves to meet the great famine of 1783. According to him, the government officials did all that was in their power to aid the people, but the catastrophe was too widespread for effectual relief. Mori Kahei, "Kyū Nambu ni okeru Temmei-do no kikin," *Shakai keizaishigaku* 2. 1 (1932). 61–86.

90. See the excerpt from the diary of the court noble Nonomiya Sadaharu, quoted by Tsuji, 120, in which he blames the calamities of his generation on the governing officials.

91. In particular, Kokushō Iwao's *Hyakushō ikki no kenkyū* (Tokyo, 1928). In English see Hugh Borton, "Peasant Uprisings in Japan of the Tokugawa Period," *TASJ,* Series 2, vol. 14 (1938).

92. Borton, 47–48.

93. Tsuji, 135–141.

94. Borton, 49–53.

95. *Ibid.,* 53–54.

96. Tsuji, 150–151.

97. See the chart in Honjō Eijirō, *Tokugawa bakufu beika chōsetsu* (Kyoto, 1924), 407–415.

98. Tsuji, 151–157.

99. Kurita, *Edo jidai shi,* 248 ff.

100. Takekoshi, *Economic Aspects* 3. 140, goes to the extreme of blaming all of these peasant disturbances on the exactions of Yoshimune's administration, but a great deal of research into the background of the uprisings and the motives of the peasant participants must yet be made before the true responsibility can be determined.

101. Mori, 84–85.

102. Kurita, *Edo jidai shi,* 251. Deputies did not have military forces at their immediate disposal.

103. Hayashi, 47. 299.

104. *Ibid.,* 47. 328.

105. See the shogunal order of 1767 (Meiwa 4. 10. 12) which decried the practice of infanticide and urged the local officials to suppress it.

106. See Hayashi, 47. 544, for a Tokugawa order warning the local officials to keep a strict census of the peasants and to prevent the escape of manpower from the fields. It states that many fields were being neglected at this time.

107. The contemporary commentator, Uezaki Kuhachirō, in his *Sensaku zasshū* (completed 1801) [modern text in Takimoto, *Nihon keizai taiten,* vol. 20], 534–535, describes at length the decline in manpower and production of the Kantō area.

108. See Sasaki Gazan, "Edo jidai rampaiki ni okeru bungaku shisō," *Chūō shidan,* 7 (1923), 3. 477 ff.

109. Note especially the humorous, 17-syllable, *senryū* poetry, much of which satirized the government or commented on the degeneracy of the samurai. Kurita has included a number of these in his chapter on the Edo scene, *Edo*

jidai shi, ge, 148–156. See also Kuramoto Hatsuo, "Kaikyū bungaku to shite no senryū gaikan," *Bungaku* 17. 5 (1949). 318–326.

110. These became particularly numerous during times of social unrest. Tsuji has quoted a large number of them in his *Tanuma jidai.*

111. In two parts, the first written in 1763, the second in 1768. A modern printed edition is included in the Yūhōdō Library. *Yūhōdō bunkō,* ser. 2, vol. 49, *Hiraga Gennai shū* (Tokyo, 1915).

112. The poem read as follows: "Yononaka wa ka (mosquito; this) hodo urusaki mono nashi, bumbu (buzz-buzz; literary and military arts) to iite yo mo nerarezu." It had the double meaning: "In this world there is nothing so irritating as mosquitoes (this, i.e., the officials). They go around saying buzz-buzz (literary and military arts) until we cannot sleep at night." The first article of the chief code of the Tokugawa, the *Buke sho hatto* reads: "Let the literary and military arts, archery and horsemanship, be your chief interest."

113. Tsuji, 161–175.

114. *Ibid.,* 176–178.

115. *Ibid.,* 17–21.

116. A number of these songs were transcribed and translated by Titsingh, pp. 149–157.

117. These two incidents have been extensively, but rather uncritically, treated by Yoshisaburō Kuno in his *Japanese Expansion on the Asiatic Continent* (Berkeley, 1937, 1940; 2 vols.), vol. 2, pp. 143–183.

118. Kurita, *Edo jidai shi, ge,* 204–209.

119. Samura, 2. 2009.

120. Kuno, 2. 168–175.

121. Hayashi, 47. 256.

CHAPTER VII. THE TRIUMPH OF REACTION

1. Kurita, "Edo jidai ni okeru tensai to seiji to no kankei," p. 60.

2. These are most clearly set forth in the *kōjōsho* (oral confession) made to the authorities by Sano himself and copied into the anonymous *Eichū ninjō ki* [Kokusho Kankōkai, *Shin enseki jisshū,* vol. 2], 467–468.

3. A notice of this event is contained in the *Tokugawa jikki,* Hayashi, 47. 734–735. Four officers were commended with jifuku for their markmanship, but Sano was not among them.

4. Titsingh, 100–106.

5. There are numerous detailed accounts of this episode recording everything from the size and depth of Tanuma's wounds and the names of the swords involved to the exact seating arrangement in the rooms through which Tanuma passed. I have used the account in the *Tokugawa jikki,* Hayashi, 47. 746, the *Eichū ninjō ki,* and Kanzawa 12. 472–485.

6. His words were "You remember, don't you?" (*Oboe ga aru darō?*).

7. Matsuura, 8. 2–3, reports that at the time a rumor was current that even Tadasato could have put a stop to the affair earlier but stayed behind Sano until he had gotten in some fatal blows.

8. An official memorandum which came out after the event expressed the suspicion that the other members of Sano's guard group must have known or suspected Sano's intentions. It ordered all officials henceforth to report any suspicious conduct among their colleagues. Hayashi, 47, 747.

9. One of these, interestingly enough, was Kuze, the former Nagasaki Magistrate of whom Titsingh reported such liberal views. Why Kuze did nothing to protect Tanuma is difficult to understand. But it will be recalled that he was one of the few members of the Tanuma faction to retain his position in Sadanobu's administration. Those who are familiar with the course of political assassination in modern Japan will realize that it required no preconceived plot to cause the majorty of the onlooking officials to refrain from interfering in what they may well have considered the workings of the hand of fate.

10. Cf. Honjō, *Beika chōsetsu*, 407–415.

11. Iwase Kyōzan, *Kumo no itomaki* (written 1806) [Kokusho Kankōkai, *Hyakka setsurin*, vol. 1], 1206.

12. Fujimura Saku, *Nihon bungaku daijiten* (Tokyo, 1932–1935; 7 vols.), 6. 485.

13. Lit. "yellow book." A type of popular short story which came out in illustrated form, originally with yellow covers.

14. Tsuji, 54–58.

15. *Eichū ninjō ki*, 468–469.

16. Various other writings ridiculing the elder Tanuma on account of his son's assassination are quoted in Tsuji, 45 ff. Titsingh records some popular songs in his "Fragments of Japanese Poetry," included in his *Illustrations of Japan*, 149-167. Also, for a collection of *rakushu* on Tanuma, some of which deal with the Sano episode, see the *Tanuma kyōsho* [Kokusho Kankōkai, *Retsukō shimpi roku* (Tokyo, 1914)].

17. Hayashi, 47. 786.

18. Hōren'in was Sadanobu's adoptive mother. Born of the Konoe family of the court nobility, she became the legitimate wife of Tayasu Munetake, Sadanobu's father. Sadanobu was born of a secondary consort but was later adopted by Hōren'in as her own. The title *ni* indicates that at this time she had become a lay nun.

19. See Sadanobu's *Memorial*, Tsuji, 233.

20. Mikami, *Shirakawa*, 28–41.

21. Sadanobu's *Memorial*, Tsuji, 226–237.

22. *Ibid.*, 234.

23. Tsuji, 220–223.

24. Hayashi, 47. 808.

25. *Ibid.*, 47. 808.

26. Wakamushi, 3. 48 ff.; Kanzawa, 12. 495 ff.

27. Hayashi, 47. 808–809.

28. See Wakamushi, 3. 47, where it is stated that the Shogun had been unaware of the deplorable condition of the nation and that he learned of it only on his deathbed. The Shogun is said to have rallied sufficiently to call Tanuma to task for his maladministration and to order his main policies countermanded.

29. One version states that the accusation was first made by Ochio-no-kata, who is said to have personally opposed Tanuma's entrance into the castle interior by drawing her dagger. Cf. Takekoshi, *Economic Aspects* 3. 142. Another version states that one of the ladies in waiting happened to be a divorced wife of the physician Wakabayashi and that she started the rumor. Kanzawa, 12. 495.

30. Tanuma was, of course, not present in these meetings, but it is most likely that Matsudaira Sadanobu was on hand. The request for resignation is said to have been sent Tanuma on the twenty-fifth. Wakamushi, 3. 48.

31. A room of the Central Castle located between the Business Office and the Shogun's audience hall.

32. The Great Councilor, Ii Naoyuki.

33. Dewa-no-kami was, of course, Mizuno Tadatomo. It will be recalled that he was mentioned before in the scene in the women's apartments. It is clear from these two incidents that Mizuno was no longer the trusted Tanuma partisan that he had once been. His position on the inside of the door which was closed to Tanuma was to do the latter little good, for apparently Mizuno at this time was busy saving his own political future. He was the first to disassociate himself from Tanuma, by cutting his family connections with him. The dismissal of the Chamberlain Inaba Masaskira may indicate that he alone of the inner group stood behind Tanuma. This Inaba was neither a Grand Chamberlain nor a brother of Tanuma, as Murdoch asserts, 3. 405.

34. Iida, 2781–2782.

35. Kanzawa, 12. 497.

36. *Zoku Tokugawa jikki* (Unfinished MS. edited by Kuroita Katsumi, *Shintei zōhō kokushi taikei*, vols. 48–52), 48. 8.

37. *Ibid.*, 48. 35.

38. Kanzawa, 12. 498–499.

39. *Zoku Tokugawa jikki*, 48. 52.

40. *Ibid.*, 48. 53.

41. *Ibid.*, 48. 62.

42. Kanzawa, 12. 504.

43. Uezaki expressed these sentiments in his memorial to the Tokugawa authorities, *Sensaku zasshū*, 509–524.

44. See the quotation from Naito's *Naian roku* in Yūzankaku, *Isetsu Nihon shi*, vol. 8, p. 132.

45. Matsudaira Sadanobu is often referred to as Shirakawa Kō (Lord of Shirakawa). The name Shirakawa (lit. white river) is taken from the castle town of that name which acted as Sadanobu's domain headquarters.

46. The literal translation of Tanuma is field pond.

Bibliographical List

Character List

Index

ABBREVIATIONS OF TITLES OF PERIODICALS

HJAS   Harvard Journal of Asiatic Studies (Cambridge, Mass.)

JAOS   Journal of the American Oriental Society (Baltimore, Md.)

RC   Rekishi Chiri (Tokyo)

RK   Rekishigaku Kenkyū (Tokyo)

SZ   Shigaku Zasshi (Tokyo)

TASJ   Transactions of the Asiatic Society of Japan (Tokyo)

BIBLIOGRAPHICAL LIST

of Works Cited in the Text and Notes

ABE MAKOTO, "Keizai to shakai," in Inobe, et al., Nihon kinseishi, pp. 19-142. 阿部眞琴, 經濟と社會

ABE MASAMI, "Shōnai han Imbanuma sosui kaisaku temmatsu," RC 68 (1936). 2. 77-90; 3. 69-78; 4. 67-80. 阿部正巳, 莊内藩印旛沼疏水開鑿顚末

ARAI HAKUSEKI, Ezo shi (preface dated 1720) [Kokusho Kankōkai, Arai Hakuseki zenshu, vol. 3]. 新井白石, 蝦夷志

--- Hankampu (completed 1701) [Kokusho Kankōkai, Arai Hakuseki zenshū, vol. 1 (1905)]. 藩翰譜

--- Seiyō kibun (written 1715) [Kokusho Kankōkai, Arai Hakuseki zenshū, vol. 4]. 西洋紀聞

BARTHOLD, V. V., La Découverte de l'Asie (Paris, 1947).

BORTON, HUGH, "Peasant Uprisings in Japan of the Tokugawa Period," TASJ Series 2. 16 (1938)

BOXER, CHARLES, Jan Compagnie in Japan 1600-1817 (The Hague, 1936).

BRAMSEN, WILLIAM, "Japanese Chronological Tables," TASJ 37. 3 (1910). 1-131.

BRINKLEY, F., A History of the Japanese People (London, 1915).

COURANT, MAURICE, "Les clans japonais sous les Tokugawa," Annales du Musée Guimet, Bibliothèque de Vulgarisation 15 (1904). 1-82.

Date-ke monjo [Tōkyō Daigaku Shiryō Hensansho, Dai Nihon komonjo, Iewaki monjo, Series 3 (Tokyo, 1912, 10 vols.)]. 伊達家文書, 東京大學史料編纂所, 大日本古文書,家別文書

Edo kemmon roku [MS. quoted in Tokutomi, Tanuma, p. 20]. 江戸見聞錄

Eichū ninjō ki [Kokushō Kankōkai, Shin enseki jisshū, vol. 2 (1912)]. 螢中又傷記

EMA TSUTOMU, "Fūzoku to seikatsu" [Seibundō Shinkōsha, Nihon bunkashi taikei, vol. 10, Edo kōki bunka (Tokyo, 1939), pp. 300-317]. 江馬務, 風俗と生活

FAIRBANK, J. K., The United States and China (Cambridge: Harvard University Press, 1948).

FISHER, GALEN M., "Daigaku Wakumon. A discussion of Public Questions in the Light of the Great Learning," TASJ Series 2. 16 (1938). 259-356.

FUJIMURA SAKU, Zōhō kaitei Nihon bungaku daijiten (Tokyo, 1932-1934, 7 vols.). 藤村 作, 增補改訂 日本文學大辭典

GETAYA JIMBEI, Jōsho (written 1787) [Takimoto, Nihon keizai taiten, vol. 23, pp. 147-156; also Tsuji, pp. 178-184]. 下駄屋甚兵衞, 上書

GUBBINS, J. H., "The Feudal System in Japan under the Tokugawa Shoguns," TASJ 15.2 (1887). 131-142.

HAMMITSCH, HORST, "Kokugaku und Kangaku," Monumenta Nipponica 2.1 (1939). 1-23.

HASHIMOTO HIROSHI, Dai bukan (Tokyo, 1935-1936, 13 vols.) [Pages numbered internally for each Bukan]. 橋本 博, 大武鑑

HAYASHI KŌ, ed., Tokugawa jikki (completed 1849) [Kuroita Katsumi, ed., Shintei-zōhō kokushi taikei, vols. 38-47 (1929-1935)]. 林 衞, 德川實紀

HEIBONSHA, Shinsen dai jimmei jiten (Tokyo, 1937-1941, 9 vols.). 平凡社, 新撰大人名辭典

HILDRETH, RICHARD, Japan as It Was and Is (Boston, 1855).

HIRAGA GENNAI, Nenashigusa. (1763 and 1768) [Yūhōdō, Yūhōdō bunko, Series 2, vol. 49, Hiraga Gennai shū (Tokyo, 1915)]. 平賀源内, 根なし草

HIROSE SATOSHI, Nihon sōshō sakuin (Tokyo, 1930). 廣瀬敏, 日本叢書索引

HONJO EIJIRO, "Japan's Overseas Trade in the Closing Days of the Tokugawa Shogunate," Kyoto University Economic Review 14.2 (1939). 1-31.

HONJŌ EIJIRŌ, "Kinsei Nihon keizai shisō," Keizaishi kenkyū 19.3 (1938). 291-308. 本庄榮治郎, 近世日本經濟思想, 經濟史研究

--- Nihon keizaishi jiten (Tokyo, 1940, 3 vols.). 日本經濟史辭典

--- Tokugawa bakufu beika chōsetsu (Kyoto, 1924). 德川幕府の米價調節

HOTTA MASAATSU, Kanjō roku (completed 1835, unpublished). 堀田正敦, 干城錄

--- Kansei chōshū shokafu (completed 1812, modern editions, Tokyo, 1917 and 1922, 9 vols.) [Citations from the 1917 edition]. 寬政重修諸家譜

IIDA TADAHIKO, Dai Nihon yashi (completed 1853, modern edition, Tokyo, Zuihitsu Taisei Kankōkai, 3rd ed., 1930, 6 vols.). 飯田忠彦, 大日本野史

IKEDA SHIRŌ, "Kinsei hōken shakai ni okeru chōnin ukeoi shinden no ichi kōsatsu," in Shibata Minoru, Nihon bunkashi kenkyū (Kyoto, 1944). 池田史郎, 近世封建社會に於ける町人請負新田の一考察, 柴田實, 日本文化史研究

INOBE SHIGEO, Edo bakufu seiji (3) (Tokyo, 1934) [Kuroita Katsumi, ed., Iwanami kōza: Nihon rekishi, case 8].
井野邊茂雄，江戸幕府政治

--- Ishin zenshi no kenkyū (Tokyo, 1935). 維新前史の研究

INOBE SHIGEO, et al., Nihon kinseishi (Tokyo, 1935) [Heibonsha, Sekai rekishi taikei, vol. 13B].
井野邊茂雄，日本近世史，平凡社，世界歷史大系

IRITA SEIZŌ, "Hiraga Gennai to kagaku," in Tōkyō Kagaku Hakubutsukan, Edo jidai no kagaku (Tokyo, 2nd ed., 1938).
入田整三，平賀源內と化學，東京化學博物館，江戶時代の化學

ITŌ TAZABURŌ, "Yōgaku no ichi kōsatsu," Shakai keizaishigaku, 7.3 (1937). 251-270. 伊東多三郎，洋學の一考察，社會經濟史學

IWAMOTO DARUMAYA KATTOSHI, Enseki jisshū (compiled 1863) (Kokusho Kankōkai edition, Tokyo, 1907-1908, 3 vols.).
岩本達磨屋活東子，燕石十種

IWASE KYŌZAN, Kumo no itomaki (written 1806) [Yoshikawa Kōbunkan, Hyakka setsurin, vol. 1, pp. 1188-1215].
岩瀨京山，蜘蛛の絲卷

JINGŪ SHICHŌ, Koji ruien (Tokyo, 1896-1914, 51 vols.; 1936, 60 vols.). Chi bu, vols. 3-5; Kan'i bu, vols. 4-17; Hōroku bu, vol. 18; Seiji bu, vols. 19-22; Senka bu, vol. 26; Seimei bu, vol. 47.
神宮司廳，古事類苑

KANZAWA TOKŌ, Okinagusa (completed ca. 1790 in 200 kan) [Nihon zuihitsu taisei, Series 3, vols. 11-13 (1931)]. 神澤杜口，翁草

KATSU YASUFUSA, Suijin roku (Tokyo, 1890, 12 vols.).
勝安房，吹塵錄

KIMIYA YASUHIKO, Nisshi kōtsu shi (Tokyo, 1927, 2 vols.).
木宮泰彥，日支交通史

KITAJIMA MASAMOTO, Nihon kinseishi (Tokyo, 1939) [Mikasa Shobō, Nihon rekishi zenshō, vol. 6].
北島正元，日本近世史，三笠書房，日本歷史全書

--- "Tokugawa bakufu ryō no shoyakunin no shikyoku ni tsuite," RK 6.7 (1937). 德川幕府領の諸役人の私曲に就いて

KITAMURA KASHIRO, Satsuki-ame zōshi (written ca. 1868) [Kokusho Kankōkai, Shin enseki jisshū, vol. 2 (1912)].
喜多村香城，五月雨草紙

KŌDA SHIGETOMO, Edo to Ōsaka (Tokyo, rev. ed., 1942).
幸田成友，江戶と大阪

KOIZUMI YASUJIRŌ, Nihon shiseki nempyō (Tokyo, 1904).
小泉安次郎，日本史籍年表

KOKUSHŌ IWAO, Hyakushō ikki no kenkyū (Tokyo, 1928).
黑正巖，百姓一揆の研究

--- "Tokugawa jidai no kahei seido," Shakai kagaku, 2.7 (1926).
徳川時代の貨幣制度, 社會科學

KOKUSHO KANKŌKAI, Arai Hakuseki zenshū (Tokyo, 1905-1907,
6 vols.). 國書刊行會, 新井白石全集

--- Shin enseki jisshū (Tokyo, 1912-1913, 5 vols.). 新燕石十種

KONDŌ HEIJO, Kaitei shiseki shūran (Tokyo, 1900-1903, 33 vols.).
近藤瓶城, 改定史籍集覽

KONDO YOSHIZAEMON, et al., Zoku-hankampu (completed 1806)
[Kokusho Kankōkai, Arai Hakuseki zenshū, vol. 2 (1905)].
近藤吉左衛門, 續藩翰譜

KUMAZAWA BANZAN, Daigaku wakumon (written ca. 1655) [Takimoto,
Nihon keizai taiten, vol. 3, pp. 109-166]. 熊澤蕃山, 大學或問

KUNO, YOSHISABURO, Japanese Expansion on the Asiatic Continent
(Berkeley, 1937-1940, 2 vols.).

KURAMOTO HATSUO, "Kaikyū bungaku to shite no senryū gaikan,"
Bungaku 17.5 (1949). 318-326.
倉本初夫, 階級文學としての川柳概觀, 文學

KURITA MOTOJI, "Edo jidai ni okeru tensai to seiji to no kankei,"
Chuo shidan 8.1 (1924). 49-61.
栗田元次, 江戸時代に於ける天災と政治との關係, 中央史壇

--- Edo jidai shi (Tokyo, 1935) [Kokushi Kōza Kankōkai, Kokushi
kōza, vol. 8]. 江戸時代史, 國史講座刊行會 國史講座

--- Edo jidai shi, ge (Tokyo, 1929) [Yūzankaku, Dai Nihon shi kōza,
vol. 8]. 江戸時代史, 下, 雄山閣, 大日本史講座

KUROITA KATSUMI, ed., Iwanami kōza: Nihon rekishi (Tokyo, 1933-
1935, 18 cases). 黒板勝美, 岩波講座, 日本歷史

--- Shintei-zōhō kokushi taikei (Tokyo,. 1929-). 新訂増補國史大系

KUSAMA NAOKATA, Sanka zui (completed 1815) [Takimoto, Nihon
keizai taiten, vols. 39-40 (1929-1930)]. 草間直方, 三貨圖

MATSUDAIRA SADANOBU, Shiji seiyō [Contained in Kanzawa,
Okinagusa, 12.721-729]. 松平定信, 資治清要

MATSUDAIRA TARŌ, Edo jidai seido no kenkyū (Tokyo, 1919).
松平太郎, 江戸時代制度の研究

MATSUURA KIYO, Kasshi yawa (completed between 1821 and 1841 in
280 kan) [Nihon zuihitsu taisei, Series 3, vols. 7-8 (1930)].
松浦清, 甲子夜話

MIKAMI SANJI, Edo jidai shi (Tokyo, 1944, 2 vols.).
三上參次, 江戸時代史

--- Shirakawa Rakuō Kō to Tokugawa jidai (Nihon bunka meicho sen edition, Tokyo, 1940). 白河樂翁公と德川時代, 日本文化名著選

MONRO, NEIL GORDON, Coins of Japan (Yokohama, 1904).

MORI KAHEI, "Kyū Nambu ni okeru Temmei-do no kikin," Shakai keizaishigaku 2.1 (1932). 61-86. 森嘉兵衞, 舊南部に於ける天明度の飢饉, 社會經濟史學

MORIYAMA TAKAMORI, Shizu no odamaki (preface dated 1802) [Iwamoto, Enseki jisshū (Tokyo, 1907-1908, 3 vols.), vol. 1, pp. 201-236]. 森山孝盛, 賤のをだ巻

MOTOORI NORINAGA, Hihon tamakushige (written 1787) [Motoori Norinaga zenshū (Tokyo, 1901-1903, 7 vols.), vol. 6, pp. 22-60]. 本居宣長, 秘本玉くしげ, 本居宣長全集

MOZUME TAKAMI, Kōbunkō (Tokyo, 1916-1918, 20 vols.). 物集高見, 廣文庫

MURDOCH, JAMES, A History of Japan (Kobe, 1903; Kobe, 1910; London, 1926, 3 vols.).

NAGATA GONJIRŌ, Tokugawa sambyakunen shi (Tokyo, 1903-1906, vols. 2, 3, vol. 1 never published). 長田權次郎, 德川三百年史

NAITŌ CHISO, "Tokugawa uji kahei no koto," Kokushi ronsō (Tokyo, 1903). 內藤耻叟, 德川氏貨幣の事, 國史論叢

NAKAMURA KICHIJI, Nihon hōkensei saihensei shi (Tokyo, 1939). 中村吉治, 日本封建制再編成史

NAKAMURA KŌYA, "Edo kōki jidai bunka no tokushitsu" [Seibundō Shinkōsha, Nihon bunkashi taikei, vol. 10, Edo kōki bunka (Tokyo, 1939), pp. 2-21]. 中村孝也, 江戶後期時代文化の特質

NAKAI CHIKUZAN, Sōbōkigen (written 1789) [Takimoto, Nihon keizai taiten, vol. 23, pp. 315-543]. 中井竹山, 草茅危言

Nihon zuihitsu taisei (Tokyo, 1927-1931, 41 vols.). 日本隨筆大成

NISHIDA NAOJIRŌ, Nihon bunkashi josetsu (Tokyo, 1932). 西田直次郎, 日本文化史序説

NOMURA KANETARŌ, "Nanryō nishu gin no ryūtsū ni tsuite," Mitagakkai zasshi 14.3 (1947). 147-159. 野村兼太郎, 南鐐二朱銀の流通について, 三田學會雜誌

--- Tokugawa jidai keizai shisō (Tokyo, 1939). 德川時代經濟思想

--- "Tokugawa kahei seido no honshitsu ni tsuite," Shigaku, 17.3 (1937). 341 ff. 德川貨幣制度の本質について, 史學

NORMAN, E. H., Japan's Emergence as a Modern State (New York, 1940).

NUMATA JIRŌ, "Nisshin bōeki ni okeru ichi mondai. Tawaramono no yushutsu ni tsuite," RC 68 (1936). 5.1-14; 6.25-46.
沼田次郎, 日清貿易に於ける一問題, 俵物の輸出に就いて

ODA AKINOBU (MATAZŌ), On'ei roku (3 kan. completed ca. 1818) [Kondō Heijo, Kaitei shiseki shūran, vol. 11 (1901)].
小田彰信 (又藏), 恩榮録

--- Haizetsuroku (completed 1814) [Kondō Heijo, Kaitei shiseki shūran, vol. 11 (1901)]. 廢絶録

ODA MATAYUKI, Imbanuma kei'i ki (Tokyo, 1883, 2 vols.).
織田完之, 印旛沼經緯記

OGAWA KENDŌ, Chirizuka dan (compiled in 8 kan after 1814) [Iwamoto, Enseki jisshū, vol. 1, pp. 237-279]. 小川顯道, 塵塚談

OGYŪ SORAI, Seidan (written 1707 in 4 kan) [Takimoto, Nihon keizai taiten, vol. 9. pp. 3-194]. 荻生祖徠, 政談

OKASHIMA MINORU, Nihon saii shi (Tokyo, 1894).
小鹿島果, 日本災異史

ŌKURA-SHŌ, Dai Nihon kahei shi (Tokyo, 1876-1883, 46 vols.; 1925-1926, 8 vols.) [Citations from 1925-1926 editions].
大藏省, 大日本貨幣史

--- Nihon zaisei shiryō (Tokyo, 1922-1923, 10 vols.). 日本財政史料

ŌTA NAMPO, Ichiwa ichigen (written 1820) [Takimoto, Nihon keizai taiten, vol. 52]. 太田南畝, 一話一言

--- Kanesoki (completed 1810) [Nihon zuihitsu taisei, Series 1, vol. 3 (1927), pp. 727-757]. 金曾木

ŌTA TAMESABURŌ, Nihon zuihitsu sakuin (Tokyo, 1925 and 1932, 2 vols.). 太田爲三郎, 日本隨筆索引

REISCHAUER, EDWIN O., "Bibliography," HJAS 2.1 (1937). 15-134.

--- Japan Past and Present (New York, 1946).

SAITŌ AGU, "Tokugawa Yoshimune to seiyō bunka," SZ 47.11 (1936). 1356-1377. 齋藤阿具, 德川吉宗と西洋文化

SAITŌ KŌSEI, Bukō nempyō (completed 1878) (Tokyo, Kokusho Kankōkai ed., 1911; Edo sōsho ed., 1917).
齋藤幸成, 武江年表, 江戸叢書

SAKANISHI, SHIO, "Prohibition of Import of Certain Chinese Books and the Policy of the Edo Government," JAOS 57.3 (1937). 290-303.

SAMURA HACHIRŌ, Kokusho kaidai (Tokyo, 3rd ed., 1926, 2 vols.).
佐村八郎, 國書解題

Sano Tanuma shimatsu (MS. quoted in Tsuji, pp. 33-35).
佐野田沼始末

SASAKI GAZAN, "Edo jidai rampaiki ni okeru bungaku shisō," Chūō shidan 7. 3 (1925). 477-483.
佐々木臥山，江戸時代爛麗期に於ける文學思想，中央史壇

SATŌ JIZAEMON, Kahei hiroku (completed ca. 1845) [Takimoto, Nihon, keizai taiten, vol. 45, pp. 147-171].
佐藤治左衛門，貨幣秘錄

SAWADA SHO, "Financial Difficulties of the Edo Bakufu," translated into English by Hugh Borton, HJAS 1 (1936). 308-326.

SEIBUNDO SHINKOSHA, Nihon bunkashi taikei (Tokyo, 1937-1941, 12 vols.). 誠文堂新光社， 日本文化史大系

SHIMMURA IZURU, "Temmei jidai no kaigai chishiki," SZ 26. 10 (1916). 1228-1255; 27. 2 (1917). 155-180.
新村出， 天明時代の海外知識

--- "Yōgaku" [Seibundō Shinkōsha, Nihon bunkashi taikei, vol. 10, Edo kōki bunka (Tokyo, 1939)], pp. 164-175. 洋學

--- Zoku namban kōki (Tokyo, 1925). 續南蠻後紀

SHIRAZAWA KIYOTO, Edo jidai zenki (Tokyo, 1922) [Daitōkaku, Nihon bunka shi, vol. 10]. 白澤清人，江戸時代前期，大鐙閣，日本文化史

Sho goyaku daidai ki [Jingū Shichō, Koji ruien, 16. 780].
諸御役代々記

SPAE, JOSEPH JOHN, Ito Jinsai, A Philosopher, Educator and Sinologist of the Tokugawa Period (Peiping, 1948).

SUGITA GEMPAKU, Nochimi gusa (completed ca. 1787) [Iwamoto, Enseki jisshū, vol. 1 (1907)]. 杉田玄白，後見草

TABOHASHI KIYOSHI, Kindai Nihon gaikoku kankei shi (Tokyo, 1933).
田保橋潔， 近代日本外國関係史

TAKANO TATSUYUKI, "Bungaku oyobi ongaku" [Seibundō Shinkōsha, Nihon bunkashi taikei, vol. 10, Edo kōki bunka (Tokyo, 1939), pp. 198-225]. 高野辰之，文學及び音樂

TAKASE UMETANI, Edo jidai ranjakki (Tokyo, 1921) [Waseda Daigaku Shuppambu, Kokumin no Nihonshi, vol. 11].
高須梅 ， 江戸時代爛熟期，早稻田大學出版部，國民の日本史

TAKEKOSHI YOSABURŌ, Nihon keizaishi (Tokyo, 4th ed., 1928, 6 vols.). 竹越與三郎， 日本經濟史

--- The Economic Aspects of the History of the Civilization of Japan (New York, 1930, 3 vols.).

TAKIMOTO SEIICHI, Nihon hōken keizaishi (Tokyo, 1930).
瀧本誠一， 日本封建經濟史

--- Nihon Keizai taiten (Tokyo, 1928-1930, 54 vols.).
日本經濟大典

TAKIZAWA, MATSUYO, The Penetration of Money Economy in Japan and Its Effects upon Social and Political Institutions (New York, 1927).

TANI YOSHIHIKO, "Yamaga Sokō no rekishiteki hihanteki kōsatsu," RK 3.1 (1936). 谷義彦, 山鹿素行の歴史的批判的考察

Tanuma kyōsho [Kokusho Kankōkai, Retsukō shimpi roku (Tokyo, 1914)]. 田沼狂書, 國書刊行會,

Tanuma Tonomo-no-kami nite ōse wataserare no mune (a spurious document circulated ca. 1787 purporting to be the official judgment against Tanuma). [Quoted in Tsuji, pp. 242-254.] 田沼主殿頭にて被仰渡趣

TATSUI MATSUNOSUKE, "Tanuma Okitsugu imbō," Chūō shidan 7.1 (1933). 217-220. 龍居松之助, 田沼意次陰謀, 中央史壇

Temmei-do Tanuma seisui rin'e no ki (MS. quoted in Jingū Shichō, Koji ruien, 46.417-418. 天明度田沼盛衰輪廻記

THUNBERG, C. P., Voyages de C. P. Thunberg, au Japon (Paris, 1796, 4 vols.).

TITSINGH, ISAAC, Illustrations of Japan (London, 1822).

TOKUTOMI, IICHIRŌ, Kinsei Nihon Kokuminshi (Tokyo, 1934-1936, 50 vols.). 德富猪一郎, 近世日本國民史

--- Tanuma jidai (Tokyo, 1936) [Tokutomi, Kinsei Nihon Kokuminshi, vol. 23]. 田沼時代

Tōkyō Teikoku Daigaku Shiryō Hensansho, Tokushi biyō (Tokyo, rev. ed., 1942). [Cited Tokushi biyō.] 東京帝國大學史料編纂所, 讀史備要

TSUDA SŌKICHI, Shina shisō to Nihon (Tokyo, 1938). 津田左右吉, 支那思想と日本

TSUJI ZENNOSUKE, Tanuma jidai (Tokyo, 1915). [Nihon Gakujutsu Fukyūkai, Rekishi kōza, vol. 1.] 辻善之助, 田沼時代, 日本學術普及會, 歷史講座

UCHIDA GINZŌ, "Tokugawa jidai toku ni sono chūsei igo ni okeru gaikoku kin gin no yu'nyū," Nihon keizaishi no kenkyū (Tokyo, 1921, 2 vols.). 內田銀藏, 德川時代特に其中世以後に於ける外國金銀の輸入, 日本經濟史の研究

UENO KIKUJI, "Edo jidai no kaikoku shisō ni tsuite," RC 34.4 (1919). 309-316. 上野菊爾, 江户時代の開國思想に就いて

UEZAKI KUHACHIRŌ, Jōsho (written 1787) [Takimoto, Nihon keizai taiten, vol. 20, pp. 487-501]. 植崎九八郎, 上書

--- Sensaku zasshū (completed 1801) [Takimoto, Nihon keizai taiten, vol. 20, pp. 505-639]. 僭策雜收

WADA TATSUŌ, "Bijutsu" [Seibundō Shinkōsha, Nihon bunkashi taikei, vol. 10, Edo kōki bunka (Tokyo, 1939), pp. 226-287].
和田辰雄, 美術

WAKAMUSHI (pen name), Zoku sannō gaiki (completed after 1787 in three kan). [Citations from MS. in author's possession.]
若無子, 續三王外記

WATANABE EISABURŌ, "Edo jidai tochi kaikon jigyō ni arawareta chōnin no seiryoku," RC 64.4 (1935). 373-386; 4.493-508.
渡部英三郎, 江戸時代土地開墾事業に現はれた町人の勢力

WIGMORE, JOHN H., "Materials for the Study of Private Law in Old Japan," TASJ 20, Supplement (1892). 1-203, i-xli, 1-138, 1-426, i-xvii, 1-112.

YAMAGATA BANTŌ, Yume no shiro (preface dated 1802, 12 kan.) [Takimoto, Nihon keizai taiten, vol. 37 (1936)].
山片蟠桃, 夢之代

YAMAMOTO KATSUTARŌ, Genroku jidai no keizaigakuteki kenkyū (Tokyo, 1925). 山本勝太郎, 元禄時代の經濟學的研究

YAMAMOTO MASAHIDE and WATANABE SHU, Kokugaku ron (Tokyo, 1939) [Mikasa Shobō, Nihon rekishi zensho, vol. 19].
山本正秀, 渡邊秀, 國學論, 三笠書房, 日本歴史全書

YAMAMOTO SABURŌ, " Tokugawa bakufu shuzōmai tōsei," RK 8.9 (1938). 山本三郎, 德川幕府酒造米統制

YAMASHITA KŌNAI, Jōsho (written 1726) [Takimoto, Nihon keizai taiten, vol. 11, pp. 273-308]. 山下幸内, 上書

YANO JIN'ICHI, Nagasaki shishi, tsūkō bōeki hen, Tōyō shokoku bu (Nagaaaki, 1938). 矢野仁一, 長崎市史, 通交貿易編, 東洋諸國部

YOSHIDA TŌGO, Dai Nihon chimei jiten (Tokyo, 1922-1923, rev. ed., 6 vols.). 吉田東伍, 大日本地名辭典

--- "Edo jidai no kōzan-gyō ni tsuite," SZ 27.10 (1916), 1049-1094.
江戸時代の鑛山業に就いて

--- Tōjo Nihonshi (Tokyo, 1913, 11 vols.). 倒叙日本史

YOSHIKAWA KŌBUNKAN, Hyakka setsurin (Tokyo, 1905-1906, 6 vols.).
吉川弘文館, 百家説林

YŪZANKAKU-HENSHŪKYOKU, Isetsu Nihonshi (Tokyo, 1931-1933, 25 vols.). 雄山閣編輯局, 異説日本史

Zoku Tokugawa Jikki (unfinished manuscript edited by Kuroita Katsumi, Shintei zōhō kokushi taikei, vols. 48-52). 續德川實紀

CHARACTER LIST OF JAPANESE NAMES, TERMS, AND PHRASES

Abe　阿部

Aikō　愛甲

Aizu-ke　會津家

Akaezo fūsetsu kō　赤蝦夷風説考

Akai Tadaakira　赤井忠晶

Akimoto Suketomo　秋元涼朝

Akimoto Takatomo　秋元高知

Akita　秋田

An'ei　安永

Ani　阿仁

Annaka　安中

Anraku　甘樂

Arai Hakuseki　新井白石

Asama　淺間

Ashigara　足柄

Ashikaga　足利

Ashikaga Naritoshi　足利成俊

Aso　安積

Atsumi　渥美

Awabi　鮑

Ayabe　綾部

Bakufu　幕府

Bu　分

Bukan　武鑑

Buke shohatto　武家諸法度

Bumbu　文武

Bunka-Bunsei　文化文政

Bushi　武士

Bushidō　武士道

Chigyō　知行

Chō　町

Chōnin　町人

Chōsho Shōzaemon　調所笑左衛門

Chūjō　中將

Chūnagon　中納言

Daigo Sampōin　醍醐三寶院

Daijin　大臣

Daikan　代官

Daimyō　大名

Dainagon　大納言

Dai Nihon shi　大日本史

Danzaemon　彈左衛門

Date　伊達

Date Shigemura　伊達重村

Dazai Shundai　太宰春臺

Deme　出目

Dewa-no-kami　出羽守

Dochaku ron　土著論

Doi　土井

Dōza　銅座

Echigo　越後

Echigoya　越後屋

Echizen-ke　越前家

Echizen-no-kami　越前守

Edojō　江戸城

Edo machi-bugyō
　江戸町奉行

Enkyō　延享

Er-ya　爾雅

Eta　穢多

Etoru　擇捉

Ezo　蝦夷

Ezo-chi ikken　蝦夷地一件

Fubun　不文

Fuchi　扶持

Fudai　譜代

Fudasashi　札差

Fujii Umon　藤井右門

Fujiwara　藤原

Fukuchiyama　福智山

Fushimi-bugyō　伏見奉行

Fushin-bugyō　普請奉行

Fushin-yaku　普請役

Gan-no-ma　雁間

Geisha　藝者

Gembun　元文

Genji　源氏

Genroku　元祿

Getaya Jimbei　下駄屋甚兵衛

Getsuban-kahan　月番加判

Ginza　銀座

Go-momme gin　五匁銀

Gumma-ken　郡馬縣

Gundai　郡代

Hamada　濱田

Hame-no-ma　羽目間

Han　藩

Haori　羽織

Hasegawa Shingorō
　長谷川新五郎
Hatamoto　旗下

Hayashi (Rin) Shihei　林子平

Heike　平家

Heimin　平民

Hideyoshi　秀吉

Hijikata Katsutoshi　土方雄年

Hikone　彦根

Hine　日根

Hinin　非人

Hirado　平戸

Hiraga Gennai　平賀源内

Hitotsubashi　一橋

Hitotsubashi Harunari
　一橋治齊
Hitotsubashi Ienari　一橋家齊

Hitotsubashi-karō　一橋家老

Hōi　寶飼

Hōji　封事

Hommaru　本丸

Hondaka　本高

Honda Tadanaka　本多忠央

Honden　本田

Honjō　本城

Hōreki　寶曆

Hōren'in-ni　寶蓮院尼

Hosa　輔佐

187

Hosakawa Shigekata 細川重賢

Hotta 堀田

Hotta Masatoshi 堀田正俊

Hyakushō ikki 百姓一揆

Hyō 俵

Hyōjōsho 評定所

Hyūga Toan 日向陶菴

Ieharu 家治

Iemitsu 家光

Iemoto 家基

Ienari 家齊

Ieshige 家重

Ieyasu 家康

Ii 井伊

Ii Naoaki 井伊直朗

Ii Naoyuki 井伊直幸

Ikeda Kihachirō Tokiyasu 池田喜八郎秀康

Imbanuma 印旛(幡)沼

Ina Hanzaemon Tadasuke 伊奈半左衛門忠宥

Inaba Masaakira 稲葉正明

Inabikari tagoto-no-tsuki 稻光田毎月

Inoue Iori 井上伊織

Iriko 煎海鼠

Ise 伊勢

Ishi 醫師

Isshiki Masahiro 一色政沆

Itakura Katsukiyo 板倉勝清

Iwami 石見

Izu 伊豆

Izu-no-kami 伊豆守

Izumi 和泉

Jidai sewa nichō tsutsumi 時代世話ニ挺鼓

Jifuku 時衣

Jijū 侍從

Jisha-bugyō 寺社奉行

Jō 上

Jōfu 定府

Jōruri 浄瑠璃

Jōsho 上書

Jōshu 城主

Jōshu-gaku 城主格

Ju 從

Jūemon Yoshifusa 次右衛門義房

Jugoi-ge 從五位下

Jūhachi daitsū 十八大通

Ju'nii 從二位

Junzuru 准ずる

Jusammi 從三位

Jusha 儒者

Jūshichi-ka-jō 十七箇條

Jushii-ge 從四位下

Jushii-jō 從四位上

Kabuki 歌舞伎

Kabu nakama 株仲間

Kagoshima 鹿兒島

Kahan 加判

Kahan-no-retsu 加判の列

188

Kai 甲斐

Kaibo Seiryō 海保青陵

Kaikoku bōeki ron 開國貿易論

Kaisho 會所

Kaitai shinsho 解體新書

Kakegawa 掛川

Kakigara chō かきがら丁

Kami-yashiki 上屋敷

Kamon 家門

Kamon-no-kami 掃部頭

Kan 貫

Kanda 神田

Kandabashi-no-uchi
神田橋之内

Kane-bugyō 金奉行

Kan'ei 寬永

Kan'en 寬延

Kanjō-bugyō 勘定奉行

Kanjō-gimmiyaku 勘定吟味役

Kano Motonobu 狩野元信

Kansei no kaikaku 寬政の改革

Kantō 關東

Kantō gundai 關東郡代

Kanzawa Tokō 神澤杜口

Kaon 加恩

Kataoka-gun 片岡郡

Katori 杳取

Katsuragawa Hoshū 桂川甫周

Kattegata 勝手方

Kawa 川

Kawachi 河內

Kawagoe 川越

Kawai Hisataka 川井久敬

Kazusa 上總

Keizai 經濟

Kemigawa 檢見川

Ken 間

Kengi 建議

Kenin 家人

Kibyōshi 黃表紙

Kii 紀伊

Kikoku senkin 貴穀賤金

Kiku-no-ma 菊間

Kin 斤

Kinza 金座

Kinzan-bugyō 金山奉行

Kirimai 切米

Kitō 城東

Koban 小判

Kobikichō-bara 木挽丁原

Kobori Masakata 小堀政方

Kobushin-bugyō 小普請奉行

Kōfu 甲府

Kōjōsho 口上書

Kōke 高家

Kōken 後見

Kokka keiei ron 國家經營論

Koku 石

Kokudaka 石高

Kokugaku	國學	Kuzu Hirotami	久世廣民
Komagome-maki-no-nae-koborichō こま込植苗木ほり丁		Kyōhō	享保
		Kyōka	狂歌
Kombu	昆布	Kyōto machi-bugyō	京都町奉行
Kombuzan	金峯山	Kyōto shoshidai	京都所司代
Ko'nando	小納戸	Maeda	前田
Ko'nando-tōdori	小納戸頭取	Maeno Ranka	前野蘭化
Kongōzan	金剛山	Makino Narisada	牧野成貞
Kōnin	工人	Makino Sadanaga	牧野貞長
Konoe	近衞	Manjū Hime	萬壽姫
Kōryō	口糧	Masutsu	益津
Koshōgumiban-gashira 小姓組番頭		Matsudaira	松平
Koshōgumiban-gashira-gaku 小姓組番頭格		Matsudaira Sadanobu	松平定信
Koshō-tōdori	小姓頭取	Matsudaira Settsu-no-kami Tadatsune 松平攝津守忠恒	
Kōzuke	上野		
Kuboyama	久保山	Matsudaira Tadasato	松平忠郷
Kuchiki Masatsuna 朽木昌綱		Matsudaira Takemoto	松平武元
Kudō Heisuke	工藤平助	Matsudaira Terutaka	松平輝高
Kuge	公家	Matsudaira Tōjirō	松平藤治郎
Kujikata	公事方	Matsudaira Yasufuku	松平康福
Kuki Takasada	九鬼隆貞	Matsudaira Yorimasa	松平賴恭
Kumazawa Banzan	熊澤蕃山	Matsumae	松前
Kumiai	組合	Matsumoto	松本
Kunimochi	國持	Matsumoto Hidemochi	松本秀持
Kunimochi-nami	國持並	Matsuura Kiyo	松浦清
Kura-bugyō	藏奉行	Meiji Ishin	明治維新
Kura-yashiki	藏屋敷	Meiwa	明和
Kuroda	黑田	Meiwaku	迷惑
Kusunoki	楠	Metsuke	目附

Mikami Mino-no-kami 三上美濃守

Mikawa 三河

Minamoto 源

Minamoto Yoritomo 源頼朝

Mito 水戸

Mitsui 三井

Miura Baien 三浦梅園

Mi wo wasuretaru furimai 身を忘れたる振舞

Mizuno Tadatomo 水野忠友

Mizutani Futō 水谷不倒

Momme 匁

Mon 文

Moriyama Takamori 森山孝盛

Mototomo 意知

Motoyuki 意行

Mujō 無城

Mura 邑

Murata Shunkai (Harumi) 村田春海

Musashi 武蔵

Musha 武射

Mutsu 陸奥

Myōban-kaisho 明礬會所

Myōga 冥加

Nagasaki-bugyō 長崎奉行

Naitō Chūmei 內藤忠明

Nakagawa Junnan 中川淳庵

Nakai Chikuzan 中井竹山

Nakama 仲間

Nakatsu 中津

Nami 並

Nando-gashira 納戸頭

Nanryō nishu 南鐐二朱

Naritoshi 成俊

Negata 額田

Nenashigusa 根南志貝佐

Nengō 年號

Ni 尼

Nijūshi-gumi 二十四組

Nikkō 日光

Ninjinza 人蔘座

Ni-no-maru 二丸

Nishio Oki-no-kami 西尾隱岐守

Nishio Tadayuki 西尾忠移

Nishioka 西岡

Nō 能

Nobunaga 信長

Nōmin 農民

Nonomiya Sadaharu 野宮定晴

Ōban-gashira 大番頭

Obi 帶

Ōbiroma 大廣間

Oboe ga aru darō 覺えがあるだらう

Ochi 越智

Ochio-no-kata 於知保の方

Oda Nobukuni 織田信邦

Oda Nobushige 織田信重

Ōdai ichiran 王代一覽

191

Odawara 小田原	Ransui 藍水
Ogyū Sorai 荻生徂徠	Ri 里
Ōhara Hikoshirō 大原彦四郎	Rimmai 廩米
Okimasa 意正	Rin 厘
<u>Okinagusa</u> 翁草	Rōjū 老中
Okinobu 意誠	Rōjū-gaku 老中格
Oku 奥	Rōnin 浪人
Ōmetsuke 大目附	Rusui 留守居
Ōmi 近江	Ryō 兩
Omote 表	Ryūnōza 龍腦座
Ondai 恩貸	<u>Ryūshi shinron</u> 柳子新論
<u>On'ei roku</u> 恩榮錄	Sado 佐渡
Ōoka Tadamitsu 大岡忠光	Sagami 相模
Ōoka Tadasuke 大岡忠相	Sagara 相良
Ōoka Tadayoshi 大岡忠喜	Saibara 榛原
Ōoku 大奥	Saijō 西城
Ōrōka 大廊下	Sakakibara Masanaga
Ōsaka-jodai 大坂城代	榊原政永
Ōsaka machi-bugyō 大坂町奉行	Sakai 酒井
Ōsaki 大崎	Sakai Iwami-no-kuni Tadayasu
Ōsumi 大住	酒井石見守忠休
Otame shugi 御爲主義	Sakuji-bugyō 作事奉行
Ōta Nampo 大田南畝	Sakurajima 櫻島
Ōtsuki Gentaku 大槻玄澤	Samon 左門
Owari 尾張	Samurai 士
Ōyagi Den'an Morimi	Sangi 參議
大八木傳庵盛御	Sanke 三家
Rakushu 落首	Sankinkōtai 參勤交代
Rangaku 蘭學	Sankyō 三卿
<u>Rangaku kaitei</u> 蘭學階梯	Sano 佐野
Rangakusha 蘭學者	

Sano Daimyōjin	佐野大明神	Shimazu Shigehide	島津重豪
Sano Naritoshi	佐野成俊	Shimban-gashira	新番頭
Sano Shigetsuna	佐野重綱	Shimizu	清水
Sano Zenzaemon Masakoto	佐野善左衛門政言	Shimizu Shigeyoshi	清水重好
Santō Kyōden	山東京傳	Shimmura Izuru	新村出
Santoku-hō	三德法	Shimon sen	四文錢
Satake	佐竹	Shimpan	親藩
Satō Genrokurō	佐藤玄六郎	Shimōsa	下總
Satō Nobuhiro	佐藤信淵	Shinano	信濃
Satō Nobusue	佐藤信季	Shinchūza	眞鍮座
Satsuma-no-kami	薩摩守	Shinden	新田
Sei-i-tai-shōgun	征夷大將軍	Shirakawa	白河
Seikei zusetsu	成形圖説	Shirakawa Kō	白河公
Seiwa Genji	清和源氏	Shita	志太
Seiyō kibun	西洋紀聞	Shō	正
Seiyō sempu	西洋錢譜	Shōgun	將軍
Seki Shōsō	關松牎	Shoinban-gashira	書院番頭
Sekigahara	關原	Shō, juichii	正從一位
Sekitan-kaisho	石炭會所	Shō, ju'nii	正從二位
Sendai	仙臺	Shōnin	商人
Senryū	川柳	Shōnin muyō ron	商人無用論
Shamisen	三味線	Shōrinji	勝林寺
Sharebon	酒落本	Shōshō	少將
Shiba Kōkan	司馬江漢	Shu	朱
Shidoura	志度浦	Shukurō	宿老
Shigemura	重村	Shu Shi	朱子
Shigetsuna	重綱	Shuza	朱座
Shimabara	島原	Sobashū	側衆
Shimazu	島津	Sobayōnin	側用人

Sōbōkigen 草茅危言

Soki 匝瑳

Sōni 僧尼

Sōshaban 奏者番

Sugawara 菅原

Sugita Gempaku 杉田玄白

Sui 粋

Sukiya 數寄屋

Sumpu 駿府

Suō-no-kami 周防守

Suruga 駿河

Susuno 薦野

Tadasuke 忠相

Taira 平

Tairō 大老

Taisei yochi zusetsu 泰西輿地圖説

Tajima-no-kami 但馬守

Takada 高田

Takai 高井

Takamatsu 高松

Takasaki 高崎

Takatake たかたけ

Takaza 高座

Takenouchi Shikibu 竹内式部

Tamba 丹波

Tamari-no-ma 溜間

Tamura Gen'yū 田村元雄

Tanaka 田中

Tango-no-kami 丹後守

Tanuma 田沼

Tanuma Daimyōjin 田沼大明神

Tanuma Jūemon Yoshifusa 田沼次右衛門義房

Tanuma Mototomo 田沼意知

Tanuma Motoyuki 田沼意行

Tanuma Okimasa 田沼意正

Tanuma Okimune 田沼意政

Tanuma Okinobu 田沼意誠

Tanuma Okitsugu 田沼意次

Tashidaka 足高

Tashiro Shichiuemon Takachika 田代七右衛門高近

Tatebayashi 館林

Tawaramono 俵物

Tawaramono-yakusho 俵物役所

Tayasu 田安

Tayasu Munetake 田安宗武

Teganuma 手賀沼

Teikan-no-ma 帝鑑間

Temmei 天明

Tempo 天保

Tenjōbito 天上人

Tennōji-ya Tōhachirō 天王寺屋藤八郎

Tetsuza 鐡座

Tokonoma 床間

Tokugawa 徳川

Tokugawa Ieharu 徳川家治

Tokugawa Iemitsu 徳川家光

Tokugawa Iemoto 德川家基
Tokugawa Ienari 德川家齊
Tokugawa Ieshige 德川家重
Tokugawa Ieyasu 德川家康
Tokugawa Muneharu 德川宗治
Tokugawa Tsunayoshi 德川綱吉
Tokugawa Yoshimune 德川吉宗
Tokugawa Jikki 德川實紀
Tokuhonji 德本寺
Tokumi-donya 十組問屋
Tomaya Kubei 苫屋久兵衛
Tone 利根
Tonomo-no-kami 主殿守
Tonya 問屋
Torii Tadamoto 鳥居忠意
Tōtomi 遠江
Tozama 外樣
Tsubo 坪
Tsūjin 通人
Tsunayoshi 綱吉
Tsuwano 津和野
Uchikowashi 打毀
Ueda 上田
Ueno 上野
Uesugi Harunori 上杉治憲
Uezaki Kuhachirō 植崎九八郎
Ukon-shōgen 右近將監
Ukyō-dayū 右京大夫
Unjō 運上

Uraga-bugyō 浦賀奉行
Wakabayashi Keijun 若林敬順
Wakadoshiyori 若年寄
Wakayama 和歌山
Yakuhō 役俸
Yamagata 山形
Yamagata Daini 山縣大貳
Yamaga Sokō 山鹿素行
Yamaguchi Tetsugorō 山口鐵五郎
Yamashita Konai 山下幸内
Yamato 大和
Yamazaki Ansai 山崎安齋
Yanagi-no-ma 柳間
Yanagizawa Yoshiyasu 柳澤吉保
Yashiki 屋敷
Yōbeya 用部屋
Yoda Buzen-no-kami Masatsugu 依田豊前守政次
Yonaoshi Daimyōjin 世直大明神
Yoshimune 吉宗
Yoshino 吉野
Yoshiwara 吉原
Yōtoritsugi 用取次
Yuhitsu 右筆
Yūzūkin 融通金
Za 座
Zen-bugyō 膳奉行
Zeni 錢
Zeniza 錢座
Zoku sannō gaiki 續三王外記

Index

Abe house, 149 (n. 4)
Aikō, district, 36
Ainu, 104
Aizu house, 147 (n. 6)
Aizu-ke. *See* Aizu house
Akaezo fūsetsu kō. See Kūdo Heisuke, *Akaezo fūsetsu kō*
Akai Tadaakira, 53, 66, 118, 140, 156 (n. 107)
Akimoto Suketomo, 45–47, 152 (n. 50), 154 (n. 68, 73)
Akimoto Takatomo, 41
Akita district, 96; mines of, 75–76
Alaska, Russian exploration of, 100
Alternate attendance. *See* Daimyo, duties of, alternate attendance
Amur region, Russian penetration of, 100
An'ei. *See* Meiwa, ninth year of
Ani mine, 75–76
Anraku district, 153 (n. 60)
Antechamber, 24, 28; as advisors to Shogun, 27; Matsudaira Sadanobu elevated to, 136
Arai Hakuseki, 148 (n. 1), 164 (n. 1); attitude toward Sidotti, 88–89; foreign trade policies of, 83–84; *Seiyō kibun* of, 89
Architecture, domestic, 111, 167 (n. 19)
Art, growth of realism, 11; Haranobu school, 94; Kano school, 94, 167 (n. 8); Western influence on, 94
Artisans, 145 (n. 5)
Asama volcano, 121–122, 169 (n. 80, 81)
Ashikaga, 34
Ashigara district, 36
Aso district, 34
Atsumi district, 37
Attendants, 30; functions of, 31; number of, 149 (n. 10)
Attendant Confucianists, 29
Attendant Physicians, 29, 39, 138
Audience hall, of Shogun, 173 (n. 31)
Awabi. *See* Sea ears
Ayabe, Daimyo of, 155 (n. 99)

Bakufu (*see also* Tokugawa bureaucracy); defined, 21, 147 (n. 2); diaries, 148 (n. 2)
Bale goods, Ezo contractors of, 104; factory for, 85
Bales. *See* Hyō
Bannermen, 26, 27, 31, 107, 113, 114
Basic income, method of classifying lesser military houses, 26
Batavia, 98
Benyowsky, Count, 101
Bering, Vitus, expeditions of, 100
Bi-metalism. *See* Currency, attempted bimetalism
Bōshū peninsula, 159 (n. 34)
Bourgeoisie, defined, 145 (n. 5). *See also* Merchant class
Brass Monopoly, 77
Brass refineries, locations of, 77
Bu, defined, 160
Buddhism, 11; decline of, 12
Bukan, 148 (n. 1), 149 (n. 5)
Bunka-Bunsei era, 107
Bunsei era, 120
Bureau of Calendars, 93
Bushi. *See* Samurai
Bushido, 9, 145 (n. 6). *See also* Samurai, Confucian moral code of
Business office, 27–30, 47, 134, 173 (n. 31)

Cabinet. *See* Councilors
Camphor Monopoly, 78
Canton, 101
Captains of the Body Guard, 29
Captains of the Great Guards, 28
Captains of the Inner Guards, 29, 149 (n. 14)
Captains of the New Guards, 29
Cash, 71–73, 160 (n. 52); brass four-mon piece, 72–73, 161 (n. 80); exchange ratio of, 72, 73; minted by Gold and Silver Monopolies, 75; minting in iron and brass, 72, 73; one-mon piece, 72;

102; mines of, 102, 166 (n. 43); Russian contact with, 101, 166 (n. 48); trade with Manchuria, 104; trade with Russians, 104

Ezo, Daimyo of. *See* Matsumae

Factories, 74; Alum Factory, 78; Coal Factory, 79, 163 (n. 114) for bale goods export, 85

Feith, A. W., 166 (n. 39)

Fief, contrasted to other land holdings, 168 (n. 50); defined, 145 (n. 3); income measured in koku, 26; received by Bannermen, 26

Foreign trade, 77–78, 83–86; Cinnabar Monopoly, 77; curtailment by Arai Hakuseki, 84; export of copper, 83, 84; in bale goods, 85–86, Bale Goods Office, 86, government monopoly in, 85–86; products of, 83, 85; Tanuma's encouragement of, 18, 84–86; with China, 74, 75, 77, 78, 83, 84–85, 86; with Dutch, 75, 83, 84, 86, 97; with Russians, 19, 100–105

Formosa, 87

Fourth Shogun. *See* Tokugawa Ietsuna

French Revolution, 86

Fuchi. *See* Ration

Fudai. *See* Hereditary Vassals

Fudasashi. *See* Rice Brokers

Fujii Umon, 130

Fujiwara house, 34, 149 (n. 4)

Fukuchiyama, Daimyo of. *See* Kuchiki Masatsuna

Fushimi, 77

Fushin-bugyō. *See* Superintendents of Public Works

Fushinyaku. *See* Public Works Service

Gan-no-ma. *See* Hall of Geese

Ge. *See* Court ranks, lower grades

Geisha, 112; origin of, 111

Genealogical compilations, 148 (n. 1)

Genji house. *See* Minamoto house

Genroku era, 107, 110, 120

Getaya Jimbei, memorial of, 71

Getsuban-kahan. *See* Senior Councilor of the Month

Ginseng, domestic cultivation of, 84, 162 (n. 104); Chinese product, 162 (n. 105); sources of, 162 (n. 104)

Ginseng Monopoly, 78, 162 (n. 106); abolished, 140

Ginza. *See* Silver Monopoly

Gold, export of, 84; importation of, 86, 97, 164 (n. 143)

Gold Monopoly, 28, 75; ordered to strike iron cash, 72

Go-momme gin. *See* Momme, five-momme silver piece

Grand Chamberlains, 29; functions of, 30; number of, 150 (n. 25), on Supreme Court of Justice, 29; Tanuma appointed to post of, 37

Great Corridor, 24; as advisors to Shogun, 27, 28

Great Councilor, 28; figurehead nature of during Ieharu period, 47–48; function as regent, 27; tendency to become hereditary, 32

Great Counselor. *See* Court titles, Great Counselor

Great Hall, 24

Great Interior, 118, 132, 139; influence of, 48, 154 (n. 83); of Central Citadel, 27

Guards, functions of, 31

Guilds, government licensed, 74; privately organized, 74, 80; Ten Guilds of Edo, 80; Twenty-four Guilds of Osaka, 80; yearly tax on, 80

Gundai. *See* Superintendents of Finance, deputies

Hachijō island, 130

Hall of Emperors, 24

Hall of Geese, 24, 139

Hamada Castle, 154 (n. 78)

Hame-no-ma, 140, 173 (n. 31)

Han. *See* Domain

Haori, 111, defined, 167 (n. 16)

Harima-no-kami. *See* Tanuma Mototomo

Harunobu school. *See* Art, Harunobu school

Hasegawa Shingorō, 66

Hatamoto. *See* Bannermen

Hayashi Shihei, 102, 103, 141, 164 (n. 137)

Heike house. *See* Taira house

Heimin. *See* Commoners

Heir apparent, residence of (*see* Western Citadel); staff of, 148 (n. 12)

Hereditary Vassals, 23, 24, 25, 31, 32

Hida, chronic dissatisfaction in Tokugawa lands of, 125

Hijikata Katsutoshi, 50, 51, 109, 155 (n. 98)

Hikone Castle, 154 (n. 80)

Hine district, 38

Hinin. *See* Pariah class

Hirado, village of, 65, 66

Hirado, Daimyo of. *See* Matsuura Kiyo

Hiraga Gennai, 94, 96, 115; association

with Tanuma, 57–58, 95–97; interest in mining techniques, 76–77; writings of, 96, 128
Hitotsubashi Harunari, 38, 155 (n. 87)
Hitotsubashi house, 23, 51, 152 (n. 42), 152 (n. 43)
Hitotsubashi Ienari. *See* Tokugawa Ienaru
Hitotsubashi-Councilor, 38
Hitotsubashi-karō. *See* Councilors for the Three Lords
Hoi district, 37
Hōji. *See* Memorials
Hokkaido. *See* Ezo
Hommaru. *See* Central Citadel
Honda Tadanaka, 36, 150 (n. 18)
Honda Toshiaki, 164 (n. 137)
Hondaka. *See* Basic income
Honden, defined, 64
Honjō. *See* Central Citadel
Hōreki affair, 128–129
Hōren'in-ni, 136, 172 (n. 18)
Hosa, 28
Hosokawa Shigekata, 124
Hotta Masatoshi, 41
Housemen, 26, 27, 31, 52, 107
Hyakushō ikki. *See* Peasant uprisings
Hyō, as measure of income, 26, 148 (n. 11)
Hyōjōsho. *See* Supreme Court of Justice
Hyūga Tōan, 138

Ieharu. *See* Tokugawa Ieharu
Iemoto. *See* Tokugawa Iemoto
Ietsuna. *See* Tokugawa Ietsuna
Ieyasu. *See* Tokugawa Ieyasu
Ii Naoaki, 50, 155 (n. 97)
Ii Naoyuki, 47, 140, 154 (n. 80), 155 (n. 97), 173 (n. 32)
Ikeda Kihachirō Tokiyasu, 119
Imba district, 65
Imbanuma lake, 65
Imbanuma project. *See* Land reclamation, Imbanuma project
Imperial court, 31; center of political opposition to Tokugawa, 8, 16–17; role in growth of nationalism, 12
Ina Hanzaemon Tadasuke, 125
Inaba Masaakira, 52, 156 (n. 102)
Inabikari tagoto-no-tsuki, 135
Income, temporary augmentation of, 32
India, 87
Infanticide, 127, 170 (n. 105)
Inner Guard, Tanuma's alleged service in, 149 (n. 13)
Inoue Iori, 157 (n. 1)

Inspectors, 29
Inspectors General, 28, 29
Interior, of Central Citadel, 27
Iriko. *See* Sea slugs
Iron Monopoly, 77
Ishi. *See* Attendant Physicians
Itakura Katsukiyo, 45
Itorup, 104
Iwami province, 154 (n. 78)
Izu province, 154 (n. 71)
Izumi province, 38
Izu-no-kami. *See* Matsumoto Hidemochi

Japan, 16th c. anti-feudal elements of, 4; cultivated area of, 158 (n. 21); opening of, 1, 19; Westernization of, 1–2, 8–9
Jesuits, 11
Jifuku, 38, 171 (n. 3); received by Tanuma, 36
Jijū. *See* Court titles, Court Chamberlains
Jisha-bugyō. *See* Superintendents of Temples and Shrines
Jō. *See* Court ranks, upper grades
Jōfu, 147 (n. 7)
Jōruri, 115; defined, 168 (n. 41)
Jōsho. *See* Memorials
Jōshu. *See* Lord of a Castle
Jōshugaku. *See* Rank Equivalent to Lord of a Castle
Ju. *See* Court ranks, junior branch
Jugoi-ge. *See* Court ranks, Junior Fifth Lower Grade
Jūhachi daitsū. *See* Dandies, group of eighteen
Ju'nii. *See* Court ranks, Junior Second Rank
Junior Councilors, 29, 134; duties of, 27; income qualifications of, 32, 152 (n. 47); tendency to become hereditary, 32
Jusammi. *See* Court ranks, Junior Third Rank
Jusha. *See* Attendant Confucianists
Jūshichi-ka-jō. *See* Seventeen Articles
Jushii-ge. *See* Court ranks, Junior Fourth Rank Lower Grade
Jushii-jō. *See* Court ranks, Junior Fourth Rank Upper Grade

Kabu nakama. *See* Guilds, government licensed
Kabuki theater, 115; during Tanuma period, 111
Kagoshima, 121; botanical gardens at, 92; Sidotti lands at, 164 (n. 4)

Index

Tango-no-kami. *See* Kuze Hirotami
Tanuma Daimyōjin, 42, 153 (n. 60)
Tanuma Mototomo, 38, 51, 53, 97, 132,
168 (n. 56); advancement thwarted by
Matsudaira Takemoto, 46; as Junior
Councilor, 38, 39, 133, 152 (n. 47, 54);
as Master of Shogunal Ceremony, 39;
assassinated, 39, 42–43, 98, 128, 133–
134, 171 (n. 6, 7); assigned to Chrysanthemum Room, 37; assigned to Hall
of Geese, 38; attitude toward Western
learning, 95; ranks and titles, 38, 39
Tanuma Motoyuki, 35
Tanuma Okimasa, 152 (n. 52)
Tanuma Okimune, 38, 51
Tanuma Okinobu, 51
Tanuma Okitsugu, appointments of, 47–
48, 50–53; association with Hiraga
Gennai, 95–97; biographical materials
on, 34, 148 (n. 12); career analyzed,
40–56; compared to Yanagizawa Yoshiyasu, 41; corruption in office, 54–56,
117, 118; court rank and titles of, 25,
35, 37; credit policies of, 81–82; death
of, 40, 140–141; decline and fall of,
39–40, 135, 138, 139–141, 150 (n. 17),
172 (n. 30); early life of, 35, 149 (n.
13); economic policies of, 18–19, 62–
63, 74, 75–79; Edo residences of, 37–38,
39, 54, 55, 140, 152 (n. 50); evaluation
of, 14, 18, 19–20, 57, 106–107, 142;
family of, 34–35, 41–43, 149 (n. 5);
fiefs and land holdings of, 36, 38, 40,
150 (n. 17); financial policies of, 68,
69–74; foreign trade policies of, 18–19,
84–86, 97, 99–100, 103–105; genealogical falsification by, 42, 96; income of,
36, 37, 38, 39, 149 (n. 14), 150 (n. 17),
151 (n. 29), 152 (n. 48); intellectual
influences on, 57–58, 90, 95; land reclamation projects of, 65–67, 159 (n. 32,
33, 36, 43, 44); opponents of, 18, 50,
56, 131, 132; political influence of, 37–
39, 53–54; relations with Great Interior,
48–49, 118, 154 (n. 85); retainers of,
157 (n. 1); rise of, 35–38, 40–41, 43,
45–50, 149 (n. 13), 149–150 (n. 14),
150 (n. 22), 151 (n. 26, 34, 38); satirized, 128; tastes of, 108, 115; tax policies of, 80–81, 83; treatment of his
vassals, 153 (n. 62); use of nepotism,
50–51; variations in given name of, 149
(n. 12); wealth of, 55–56, 156 (n. 116)
Tanuma period, attitude toward Occident,
89–90; Chinese political theory, 58–60;
defection within ruling class, 128–130;
fashions of, 110–111, 167 (n. 15, 16,
17); growing power of merchant class,

116–117, 128; historical evaluation of,
13–14, 17–20; lax behavior of, 115–116;
luxury of, 107–111; moral decay of,
111–117; natural calamities during, 119–
124, 169 (n. 79, 83), 170 (n. 89); official corruption, 117–119; social life of,
108, 109, 111, 167 (n. 18); trend towards economic realism, 58, 61–63
Tanuma Shigetsuna, 34
Tanuma Tonomo-no-kami. *See* Tanuma
Okitsugu
Tanuma, town of, 34, 149 (n. 6)
Tashidaka. *See* Income
Tashiro Shichiuemon Takachika, 35
Tatebayashi Castle, 154 (n. 67)
Tawaramono. *See* Foreign trade, bale
goods
Tawaromono-yakusho. *See* Foreign Trade,
bale goods, Bale Goods Office
Taxes, lack of uniformity of, 80; on com-
mercial enterprises, 79, 80; on land, 5,
15; on silk, 81, 163 (n. 124); opposi-
tion to, 80–81; rice tax, 5, 80, 126, 127
Tayasu house, 23, 136
Tayasu Munetake, 136, 172 (n. 18)
Tayasu-Karō, 28
Teganuma lake, 65, 66
Teikan-no-ma. *See* Hall of Emperors
Temmei period, 110, 115
Tempō era, 120
Tenancy, growth of, 64
Tenjōbito. *See* Court ranks, courtiers
Tennōji-ya Tōhachirō, 66
Tenth Shogun. *See* Tokugawa Ieharu
Terutaka. *See* Matsudaira Terutaka
Tetsuza. *See* Iron Monopoly
Three Houses, 23, 24, 138, 147 (n. 4); as
advisors to Shogun, 26, 27; opposition
to Tanuma, 39, 50, 132, 139
Three Lords, 23, 136, 138, 147 (n. 4, 5),
152 (n. 42); opposed to Tanuma, 132
Thrice Beneficial Law. *See* Shogunal loans
Thunberg, Karl, 91, 94
Titsingh, Isaac, 53, 97–100, 166 (n. 39);
admirer of the Tanuma, 97, 158 (n. 8);
evaluation of information of, 98–99;
Japanese associates of, 91, 93–95; pub-
lications on Japan, 94–95
Tōkaidō, 150 (n. 17), 153 (n. 60)
Tokonoma, 109; defined, 167 (n. 9)
Tokugawa bureaucracy, 21–33, 146–147
(n. 1); alternation of office holders, 33;
corruption in, 117–119; gift-giving
practice of, 54–55, 156 (n. 113); income as a qualification for official appointment, 32; life of officials, 108;
stagnation of, 32; multiple office-hold-

Date Due

MAY 1 '64			
	PRINTED	IN U. S. A.	